rable detachment and respect, avoiding both Freudian hero-worshippers and polemical critics, Giora's sharp, critical eye offers a fascinating and original new concept of the unconscious and its relation to dreams, psychoneuroses, and psychotherapy. This book will be welcomed by students and professionals in the fields of psychology, psychiatry, and social work.

Psychoanalytic Crosscurrents

Born in Hungary, **Zvi Giora** is currently a clinical psychologist and Professor of Psychology at Tel-Aviv University. He is the author of *Psychopathology: A Cognitive View* and many articles.

The Unconscious and the Theory of Psychoneuroses

PSYCHOANALYTIC CROSSCURRENTS
General Editor: Leo Goldberger

THE DEATH OF DESIRE: A STUDY IN PSYCHOPATHOLOGY
by M. Guy Thompson

THE TALKING CURE: LITERARY REPRESENTATIONS OF PSYCHOANALYSIS
by Jeffrey Berman

NARCISSISM AND THE TEXT: STUDIES IN LITERATURE AND THE PSYCHOLOGY OF SELF
by Lynne Layton and Barbara Ann Schapiro, Editors

THE LANGUAGE OF PSYCHOSIS
by Bent Rosenbaum and Harly Sonne

SEXUALITY AND MIND: THE ROLE OF THE FATHER AND THE MOTHER IN THE PSYCHE
by Janine Chasseguet-Smirgel

ART AND LIFE: ASPECTS OF MICHELANGELO
by Nathan Leites

PATHOLOGIES OF THE MODERN SELF: POSTMODERN STUDIES ON NARCISSISM, SCHIZOPHRENIA, AND DEPRESSION
by David Michael Levin, Editor

FREUD'S THEORY OF PSYCHOANALYSIS
by Ole Andkjær Olsen and Simo Køppe

THE UNCONSCIOUS AND THE THEORY OF PSYCHONEUROSES
by Zvi Giora

THE UNCONSCIOUS AND THE THEORY OF PSYCHONEUROSES

Zvi Giora

NEW YORK UNIVERSITY PRESS
New York and London

Manufactured in the United States of America

LIBRARY OF CONGRESS
Library of Congress Cataloging-in-Publication Data

Giora, Zvi.
The unconscious and the theory of psychoneuroses / Zvi Gioria.
p. cm.—(Psychoanalytic crosscurrents)
Bibliography: p.
Includes indexes.
ISBN 0-8147-3021-3 (alk. paper)
1. Psychoanalysis. 2. Freud, Sigmund, 1856–1939.
3. Subconsciousness. 4. Personality disorders. I. Title.
II. Series.
RC506.G56 1989
150.19′5—dc19 88-25276
CIP

New York University Press books are printed on acid-free paper, and their binding materials are chosen for strength and durability.

CONTENTS

FOREWORD

The *Psychoanalytic Crosscurrents* series presents selected books and monographs that reveal the growing intellectual ferment within and across the boundaries of psychoanalysis.

Freud's theories and grand-scale speculative leaps have been found wanting, if not disturbing, from the very beginning and have led to a succession of derisive attacks, shifts in emphasis, revisions, modifications, and extensions. Despite the chronic and, at times, fierce debate that has characterized psychoanalysis, not only as a movement but also as a science, Freud's genius and transformational impact on the twentieth century have never been seriously questioned. Recent psychoanalytic thought has been subjected to dramatic reassessments under the sway of contemporary currents in the history of ideas, philosophy of science, epistemology, structuralism, critical theory, semantics, and semiology as well as in sociobiology, ethology, and neurocognitive science. Not only is Freud's place in intellectual history being meticulously scrutinized, his texts, too, are being carefully read, explicated, and debated within a variety of conceptual frameworks and sociopolitical contexts.

The legacy of Freud is perhaps most notably evident within the narrow confines of psychoanalysis itself, the "impossible profession" that has served as the central platform for the promulgation of official orthodoxy. But Freud's contributions—his original radical thrust—reach far beyond the parochial concerns of the clinician psychoanalyst as clinician. His writings touch on a wealth of issues, crossing traditional boundaries—be they situated in the biological, social, or humanistic spheres—that have profoundly altered our conception of the individual and society.

A rich and flowering literature, falling under the rubric of "applied psychoanalysis," came into being, reached its zenith many decades ago, and then almost vanished. Early contributors to this literature, in addition to Freud himself, came from a wide range of backgrounds both within and outside the medical/psychiatric field, many later becoming psychoanalysts themselves. These early efforts were characteristically reductionistic in their attempt to extrapolate from psychoanalytic theory (often the purely clinical theory) to explanations of phenomena lying at some distance from the clinical. Over the years, academic psychologists, educators, anthropologists, sociologists, political scientists, philosophers, jurists, literary critics, art historians, artists, and writers, among others (with or without formal psychoanalytic training) have joined in the proliferation of this literature.

The intent of the *Psychoanalytic Crosscurrents* series is to apply psychoanalytic ideas to topics that may lie beyond the narrowly clinical, but its essential conception and scope are quite different. The present series eschews the reductionistic tendency to be found in much traditional "applied psychoanalysis." It acknowledges not only the complexity of psychological phenomena but also the way in whcih they are embedded in social and scientific contexts that are constantly changing. It calls for a dialectical relationship to earlier theoretical views and conceptions rather than a mechanical repetition of Freud's dated thoughts. The series affirms the fact that contributions to and about psychoanalysis have come from many directions. It is designed as a forum for the multidisciplinary studies that interesect with psychoanalytic thought but without the requirement that psychoanalysis necessarily be the starting point or, indeed, the center focus. The criteria for inclusion in the series are that the work be significantly informed by psychoanalytic thought or that it be aimed at furthering our understanding of psychoanalysis in its broadest meaning as theory, practice, and sociocultural phenomenon; that it be of current topical interest and that it provide the critical reader with contemporary insights; and, above all, that it be high-quality scholarship, free of obsolete dogma, banalization, and empty jargon. The author's professional identity and particular theoretical orientation matters only to the extent that such facts may serve to frame the work for the reader, alerting him or her to inevitable biases of the author.

The *Psychoanalytic Crosscurrents* series presents an array of works from the multidisciplinary domain in an attempt to capture the ferment of scholarly activities at the core as well as at the boundaries of psychoanalysis. The books and monographs are from a variety of sources: authors will be psychoanalysts—traditional, eno- and post-Freudian, existential, object-relational, Kohutian, Lacanian, etc.—social scientists with quantitative or qualitative orientations to psychoanalytic data, and scholars from the vast diversity of approaches and interests that make up the humanities. The series entertains works on critical comparisons of psychoanalytic theories and concepts as well as philosophical examinations of fundamental assumptions and epistemic claims that furnish the base for psychoanalytic hypotheses. It includes studies of psychoanalysis as literature (discourse and narrative theory) as well as the application of psychoanalytic concepts to literary criticism. It will serve as an outlet for psychoanalytic studies of creativity and the arts. Works in the cognitive and the neurosciences will be included to the extent that they address some fundamental psychoanalytic tenet, such as the role of dreaming and other forms of unconscious mental processes.

It should be obvious that an exhaustive enumeration of the types of works that might fit into the *Psychoanalytic Crosscurrents* series is pointless. The studies comprise a lively and growing literature as a unique domain; books of this sort are frequently difficult to classify or catalog. Suffice it to say that the overriding aim of the editor of this series is to serve as a conduit for the identification of the outstanding yield of that emergent literature and to foster its further unhampered growth.

Leo Goldberger
Professor of Psychology
New York University

ACKNOWLEDGMENTS

Grateful acknowledgments are given to the following publishers who kindly permitted me to quote from their copyrighted material as follows:

Jason Aronson, Inc., from L. Salzman (1980), *Treatment of the Obsessive Personality,* and M. Horowitz (ed.) (1977), *Hysterical Personality.*

Basic Books Inc., Publishers, from S. Arieti and J. Bemporad (1978), *Severe and Mild Depressions,* and D. Shapiro (1967), *Neurotic Styles.*

Lawrence Erlbaum Associates, Inc., from J. D. Lichtenberg and S. Kaplan (eds.) (1983), *Reflections on Self Psychology.*

The editor of *Psychoanalysis and Contemporary Thought,* from M. Klein (1981), "On Mahler's Autistic and Symbiotic Phases: An exposition and evaluation," and from B. B. Barratt (1976), "Freud's Psychology as Interpretation."

The Sigmund Freud Copyrights Ltd., The Institute of Psycho-Analysis and the Hogarth Press, from the Standard Edition (1960–1974) of *The Complete Psychological Works of Sigmund Freud.*

Tavistock Publications Ltd., from J. Stone, H. T. Smith, and L. Murphy (eds.) (1973), *The Competent Infant.*

Miss Carol White skillfully turned my English into its present readable form, and Miss Ruth Bry typed the many versions of the manuscript patiently and with lively participation. To both of them many thanks for their help.

Tel-Aviv University supported me with the expenses for preparing the manuscript. My sincere gratitude to the Deans of the Humanities, Prof. Gavriel Cohen and Professor Moshe Gil.

The Unconscious and the Theory of Psychoneuroses

INTRODUCTION

"The psychodynamic concept of the unconscious," Shevrin and Dickman (1980) suggest, "can be defined in terms of three characteristics: it is psychological, it is active, and it can be different in character from conscious psychological processes" (p.422). More than 200 years earlier, Leibniz (1765) felt compelled to emphasize that "it is a great source of error to believe that there is no perception in the soul besides those of which it is conscious. There are also numberless perceptions, little noticed, which are not sufficiently distinguished to be perceived or remembered but which become known through certain consequences" (p. 117). Shevrin and Dickman's term, *active,* refers to the same feature which Leibniz defined as becoming known through certain consequences and their term, *psychological,* refers to what Leibniz called the soul.

Leibniz, Freud and, as we shall see in the next section, many other authors have agreed that no understanding of behavior is possible without assuming the existence of an active unconscious mental life. Freud elaborated this construction by adding a third feature, namely, that the unconscious is a mental system defined by modes of functioning different from those of self-consciousness. It was this particular feature of Freud's understanding of the unconscious which his biographer, Jones (1953–1957) considered to be the most valuable of Freud's many ideas:

> Freud's revolutionary contribution to psychology was not so much his demonstrating the existence of an unconscious, and perhaps not even his exploration of its content, as his proposition that there are two fundamentally different kinds of mental processes, which he termed primary and secondary respectively, together with his description of them. The laws applicable to the two groups are so widely different that any description of the earlier one must call up a picture of the more bizarre type of insanity. (Vol. 1, p. 397)

It is therefore not the division of mental life into conscious and unconscious realms or the assumption of an ongoing interaction between them itself that is original, "but"—to quote Jones once more—"Freud's detailed exploration and description of the two sets of processes, something that had never before been even attempted" (p. 398).

Seeming to agree fully with Jones, Matte-Blanco (1975) states:

> Freud's fundamental discovery is not that of the Unconscious, not even in the dynamic sense (however important this may be) but that of a world—which he unfortunately called the Unconscious—ruled by entirely different laws from those governing conscious thinking. He was not the first to speak of the Unconscious, and much about it was known before him, but he was the first to make the fundamental discovery of this strange 'Realm of the Illogical', submitted, in spite of its being illogical, to precise laws which he found, in an extraordinary stroke of genius. (P. 93)

In fact, Matte-Blanco thinks, "the names 'the Unconscious', 'primary process' and 'id' are all inappropriate to describe . . . [Freud's] greatest discovery, that of a mode of being, which nobody before him had ever described as he did" (p. 69).

Both Jones and Matte-Blanco made it clear that it would be a mistake to view Freud's conception of the unconscious as if it consists only of repressed impulses. Some readers and students of Freud, though, understand the unconscious in precisely this way. "But the fact is that this is the result of neglecting the essential theme of psycho-analysis. . . . psycho-analysis has wandered away from itself. . . . Psycho-analysis has neglected . . . its initial purpose of exploring . . . that mysterious world where everything is so different from what we see in conscious life" (Matte-Blanco, p. 9).

How can we understand such a curious neglect? Could it be that this most valued thesis of Freud is in danger of oblivion due to the carelessness of pupils who are known for their devotion to Freud's legacy and their scholarly pursuit of it? Or rather, shall we say that Matte-Blanco's reprimands of his colleagues: "recent analytic researchers are, on the whole, sadly uninterested in this fundamental topic," though justifiable, indicate his unwillingness to diagnose the reasons for this lack of interest?

As we have seen, Freud did not need to invent or discover the unconscious, and accepting this construct does not necessarily identify one as a follower of Freud. If one explicates the allusions of Jones and Matte-Blanco, a Freudian is one who subscribes to Freud's contention that we are bestowed with two differently working mental organizations, one of them adaptive and problem-solving and the other one deaf and blind to these imperatives of survival. The admonitions of Jones and Matte-Blanco may cause us to wonder whether all the pupils of Freud indeed are ready to follow this call. Matte-Blanco's writing leads us to believe that they are drifting away from this anchor hold and moving toward a position long held by many psychologists.

The following passage from Bleuler's (1911) *Dementia Praecox or the Group of Schizophrenias* may be taken as exemplifying this position: "We have reason to assume that a conscious psychic function differs from an unconscious one only in that the conscious function is associatively linked with conscious personality. We cannot understand schizophrenic symptoms, any more than other complicated psychic manifestations without taking into consideration the fact that there are unconscious processes which aside from the absence of qualities of consciousness are identical with conscious psychic processes" (p. 360). Bleuler was acquainted with Freud and interested in his ideas. Very soon, however, he severed his ties with psychoanalysis. We may see this difference of views about the unconscious as one of the factors turning Bleuler from an interested partner to a reserved observer.

Is human behavior ruled by two completely different sets of laws, and do these sets of laws subserve contradictory motives? Is any behavior the result of an incessantly ongoing conflict between two mental systems, which are controlled by different rules and pursue incompatible aims? The answer of the post-Freudian psychoanalytic literature to these questions was equivocal. It was the opinion of Hartmann (1939) that "not every adaptation to the environment, or every learning and maturation process is a conflict" (p. 8) and he proposed to adapt the provisional term *conflict-free ego sphere* for this ensemble of functions. This provisional term became so well established that, as Foulkes (1978) noted, the "intrapsychoanalytic" battle over the relative roles of the id and ego has largely ended, with a public victory, at least, for the forces of an autonomous ego. In contrast to the concept of conflict, ego psychologists did not even consider questioning Freud's understanding of the unconscious. For example, having stated that the crucial determinants of behaviors are unconscious Rapaport (1959) observes: "*Per se,* this thesis is not alien to *any* psychology. . . . The psychoanalytic thesis of unconscious determination, however, differs from these [in asserting] that the rules governing the *noticed* are different from those governing the *unnoticed*, and that unnoticed can be inferred by considering the deviations of the noticed from its usual patterns" (p. 88).

In contradistinction to any other approach, then, the psychoanalytic thesis of Freud, and of Hartmann (1939) and Rapaport (1959) as well, contends that conscious and unconscious mental functioning are different. Due to their many bewildering features, deviations from the usual patterns of thinking, dreams, and neurotic symptoms are the most important evidence of the peculiar rules prevailing in the unconscious. It is thus surprising to be informed that "not only do those who cultivate the so-called ego psychology seem to feel much more at home in 'the higher strata,' but also [those] who deal with 'deep material', such as the early relationship of the child to his mother, usually treat this material as though it were ruled by the laws of the preconscious, even though at times some passing reference is made to the contrary" (Matte-Blanco, p. 9). We may feel assured that these knowledgeable experts do not deal casually with the cornerstone of Freud's theory of behavior. Rather, their behavior, seemingly contradictory to the theory they apply, alerts us to consider whether or not dreams and neurotic symptoms prove what they are expected to prove.

One wonders, to say it differently, whether dreams and symptoms indeed are bewildering and alien to the usual ways of preconscious mentation. Freud's theory of dreams and psychoneuroses was built on this assumption. Nonetheless, as Matte-Blanco pointed out, most psychoanalysts behave as if mental life, conscious and unconscious, is governed by one set of rules only, thereby agreeing—but not stating so—with Bleuler's understanding of the unconscious. If one thinks that the quality of consciousness alone differentiates between a conscious and unconscious mental process, one has agreed, in effect, that the theory of psychoneuroses must seek a foundation different from that proposed by Freud. It seems, then, that we must ask ourselves: Is there an alogical unconscious as envisaged by Freud and, consequently, a foundation on which to rest his theories of dreams and psychoneuroses, or, rather, do the facts oblige us to conceive some alternative solutions? This question and a possible answer to it are the subject of this book.

1. THE COMMONEST OF ALL PSYCHOLOGICAL WONDERS

In his once very influential *Psychologie als Wissenschaft* (Psychology as a Science), Herbart (1824) saw the bifurcation of the human mind into conscious and unconscious realms as fundamental to our understanding of mental life. Inspired, perhaps exaltingly, by what he discerned, he reputed it to be "das allgemeinste aller psychologischen Wunder": "#47 . . . the commonest of all psychological wonders. We all have observed in ourselves that from all we know, think, desire, in any given moment only an incomparable small mass will keep us busy. That knowledge, absent yet not extinguished but rather, held and retained in our possession, in what condition does it exist in us?" (p. 174). This knowledge, Herbart reasoned, is kept under the threshold of consciousness, "I call the border, which a representation has to trespass in order to proceed from the state of complete suppression to that of actualized presentation, the *threshold of consciousness*" (p. 175, my translation). In order to become conscious, a thought, a desire must overcome an obstacle, which Herbart conceptualized as a threshold. Mental life is divided by this imaginary border into experiences above the threshold of consciousness and those below it. What determines which idea is conscious and which one is subliminal? Herbart's answer was a psychodynamic one: an idea which collides with other, contradictory ones, may be expelled from consciousness.

And now a warning. By sinking below the the threshold, the representation will undergo a metamorphosis: "#11. What will the indicated resistance now result in? . . . The representation must yield without being annihilated. *That is to say, the real representation will be transformed into an aspiration*" (Herbart 1816, p. 102, my translation).

It does not seem exaggerated to credit Herbart with opening the gate for the modern era to study the full scope of mental life, conscious and unconscious. Herbart's conception of the unconscious was truly innovative compared with that of his celebrated predecessor, Leibniz. Leibniz' contribution was the concept of *petites perceptions* or mental events which, too weak to be consciously perceived, are unconsciously registered. According to Leibniz, differences in intensity account for the fact that some stimuli are experienced consciously, while others are experienced unconsciously. One sees immediately the difference between Leibniz and Herbart. While Leibniz took into consideration only the strength of stimuli, Herbart introduced the ideas of intrapsychic conflicts and the bifurcation of mental life, separated by a "threshold" into subliminal and supraliminal realms.

While not the very first to draw attention to unconscious mental processes, Herbart was both more articulate in dealing with the notion of them than many of his predecessors and more acute than some authors writing after him. Under the influence of the French alienists, the second half of the nineteenth century witnesses a kind of reincarnation of the concept of unconscious. This new concept, however, was not quite identical to the former one. It was the opinion of Charcot and Janet that split-off fragments of the personality can follow an invisible development of their own, uncontrolled by consciousness, and manifest themselves through disturbances of behavior. Janet, Binet, and for a while, Freud thought that such a split of consciousness was not common to all people, but characteristic of certain disturbed persons only.

Janet distinguished between the *subconscious* and the *secondary consciousness*. The term *subconscious* is applied by him more often to those mental states that form the margin of consciousness of the normal mind, the penumbra of consciousness as he called it, than to the mental states of the hysteric. The phenomena of hysteria require, he thought, not only a subconscious in the sense of mental states existing outside the margin of consciousness, as they do in the case of the normal, but another consciousness analogous to the primary consciousness.

How does a secondary consciousness come into existence? Secondary consciousness is the result of dissociation: a part of consciousness becomes split off from the primary stream of conscious life, becomes independent, and functions as a sort of separate personality, leaving the field of primary consciousness greatly narrowed. "I maintain to this day," wrote Janet (1907), "that, if hysteria is a mental malady, it is not a mental malady like any other, impairing the social sentiments or destroying the constitution of ideas. It is a malady of the personal synthesis . . . hysteria is . . . characterized by the retraction of the field of personal consciousness and a tendency to the dissociation and emancipation of the systems of ideas and functions that constitute personality" (p. 332).

To Janet, this process of dissociation is the common characteristic of all the symptoms of hysteria. Healthy people may have a subconscious, but not a secondary consciousness. Those who become hysterics may have been born with a predisposition to acquire a secondary consciousness, but no one is actually born a hysteric. By good luck, one may end one's life without ever evolving a secondary consciousness.

Interestingly, in their joint work on hysteria, Breuer and Freud (1895) concurred with Janet's view. Having complimented Janet, "to whom the theory of hysteria owes so much," (p. 230) they agreed that what lies at the center of hysteria is a splitting off of a portion of psychical activity. They disagreed only regarding the assumed cause or causes of such a pathological dissociation. In the opinion of Janet, the splitting of consciousness observable in hysteria is due to an innate psychological inadequacy *(insuffisance psychologique)*. He considered normal mental activity to presuppose a certain capacity for synthesis, the ability to unite several ideas into a complex. In hysterical patients, however, he found this ability to be far below normal. He viewed the field of consciousness of hysterical patients as "restricted"; hysteria is a *maladie par faiblesse* (disease due to weakness).

Breuer and Freud could not agree that such a mental weakness was the essence of the disposition to hysteria for, *"Freud's observations and analyses show that the splitting of the mind can also be caused by 'defence', by the deliberate deflection of consciousness from distressing ideas: only however, in some people, to whom we must therefore ascribe a mental idiosyncracy.* In normal people, such ideas are either successfully suppressed in which case they vanish completely, or they are not, in which case they keep on emerging in consciousness. *I cannot tell what the nature of this idiosyncracy is"* (p. 235, emphasis added).

Thus, in the opinion of Breuer and Freud, a constitutional weakness of mental synthesis, the cause suggested by Janet, can be one reason, but not the sole reason for developing a hysteric mental disease. A conflict between opposing motives may be another cause. This disagreement notwithstanding, Breuer and Freud agreed that dissociation, the splitting off of experiences from the consciousness, be it due to "psychological weakness" or "defence," is an idiosyncracy which may occur in some, but not in all, and certainly not in normal people. In his paper on the defense-neuropsychoses, Freud (1894) further explicated this view by saying that, while a split of consciousness caused by the motive for forgetting is a sign of pathologic disposition, it should not necessarily be identified with personal or hereditary "degeneration."

Myers (1892), a founding father of the British Society for Psychical Research, in postulating the existence of a subliminal or ultramarginal consciousness in addition to the supramarginal, relied heavily on the evidence and arguments of Janet. In contrast to Janet, Breuer, and the early Freud, however, Myers found in the subliminal self a well of wisdom rather than a sign of degeneration. William James (1902), though, was careful enough to point out that, here too, only some of us are endowed with such a subliminal self. Praising the achievement of Myers, William James wrote:

> I cannot but think that the most important step forward that has occurred in psychology since I have been a student of that science is the discovery, first made in 1886, that *in certain subjects at least,* there is not only the consciousness of the ordinary field with its usual center and margin but in addition thereto in the shape of a set of memories, thoughts, and feelings which are extramarginal and outside of the primary consciousness altogether, but yet must be classed as conscious facts of some sort able to reveal their presence by unmistakable signs. (P. 188, emphasis added)

Likewise, in a rather cautious sentence, Binet (1890) stated that his experiments seemed to demonstrate that many normal subjects, if not all, are apt to have their consciousness split. Yet, as an indication of his hesitation, he did not pursue the possible consequences of his statement on the conception that an unconscious mental life is synonymous with mental disorder.

The furthest these students of hysteria went in postulating an unconscious mental life in healthy people, I have found in a fleeting comment of Dessoir (1890). In his enthusiastic report to the German reader of the findings of Janet and his colleagues, as if overcome by his emotions, Dessoir observed that, if one would allow oneself a daredevilish idea, one could say that everybody has an unconscious mental life. Althought Dessoir may have liked this idea, he was not daredevil enough to be responsible for it. He seems to have been unaware that Myers, and long before him Herbart and his followers, had already crossed this Rubicon. Years before Dessoir published his "daredevilish" idea, a leading authority of British psychiatry, Maudsley (1867) in *The Physiology and Pathology of Mind,* wrote these forceful sentences:

> *It is a truth which cannot be too distinctly borne in mind, that consciousness is not co-extensive with mind .... The preconscious action of the mind, as certain metaphysical psychologists in Germany have called it, and the unconscious action of the mind, which is now established beyond all rational doubt, are assuredly facts of which the most ardent psychologist must admit that self-consciousness can give us no account.*
>
> Consciousness is not able to give any account of the manner in which [memory] is perpetuated, and how it exists latent in the mind; but a fever, a poison in the blood, or a dream, may at any moment recall ideas, feelings, and activities which seemed for ever vanished. The lunatic sometimes reverts, in his ravings, to scenes and events of which, when in his sound senses, he has no memory. (P. 15, emphasis added)

In his important book on the discovery of the Unconscious, Ellenberger (1970) observed that the concept of Unconscious is a relatively new construction in psychology. It was hypnosis which, in his opinion, made it inevitable to "invent it." We have seen that hypnosis, indeed, could have led to a momentous deepening of our knowledge of the nature of mental life, but it did not. It led, rather, to an assumption according to which unconscious mental life is a sign of mental illness. Neither the masters of hypnosis nor the students of psychopathology opened the gate for a fuller understanding of human behavior. Rather it was the theoretical psychology of Herbart which did it; Maudsley is to be credited if not for "inventing" then for keeping alive the construction of a human mind divided into conscious and unconscious realms.

But Maudsley did not need to spend many days in splendid isolation, for Freud suddenly parted company with Janet and joined him. Soon after writing the previously quoted papers, in which he still agreed with Janet that a split—dissociation of consciousness is a mental idiosyncracy, Freud (1900) published *The Interpretation of Dreams*. Here, in a dramatic change of position, he suggested that everybody has a conscious mental life as well as an unconscious one.

To begin with, he believed that reflex processes are the model of mental functioning. Accordingly, he conceived a "psychical apparatus" with a sensory and a motor unit. At the sensory end there is a mental system for receiving information and, at the motor end another one for controlling motor activity. Further, he accepted the prevailing view at the time that sensory stimuli which impinge upon the organism leave a memory trace in the mental apparatus. A memory trace was understood to be a structural change in the system responsible for remembering. Such changes, however, would prevent the passive, unbiased, reception of stimuli which was thought to occur; therefore, Freud hypothesized the existence of a specialized system for perception, and another one for maintaining the "mnemic residues."

In light of these considerations, Freud constructed a diagram (figure 1) of the mental (reflex) apparatus:

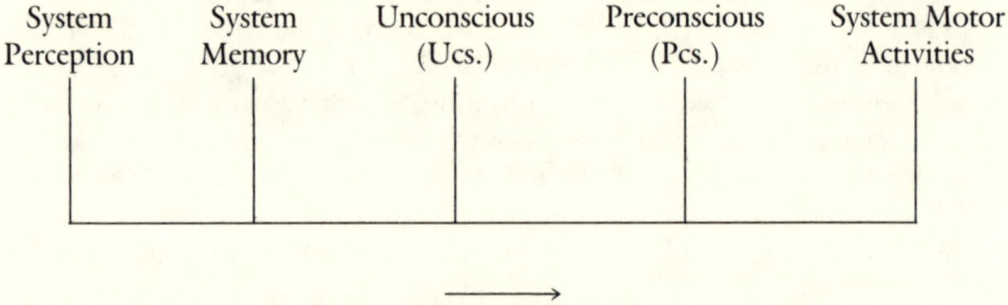

FIGURE 1. The Direction of Events in the Mental Apparatus

This diagram was meant to depict the *temporal* order of events in the wakeful central nervous system without any commitment to anatomical localization: the temporal order or direction of mental events is from the sensory to the motor end of the mental apparatus, from stimulus to reaction. In between, as one can see, there is a system unconscious. Here, the unconscious is an integral part of the "psychic apparatus"; everyone, not just the idiosyncratic and less fortunate, has an unconscious as well as conscious mental life.

It is interesting that, with all the information we have on Freud, we know nothing of the process of this singularly important turnover in his thinking and, of the possible influences which helped him to change his mind. One possible influence, though, was indicated by Jones (1955, vol. 2.) According to Jones, Freud read in 1898 a book of Lipps, "a man whose writings Freud greatly admired," and underlined the following passage: "We maintain not merely the existence of unconscious mental processes besides the conscious ones. We postulate further that unconscious mental processes are the basis of conscious ones and accompanying them, conscious processes rise out of the unconscious when conditions are favorable, and then sink back again into the unconscious" (p. 149).

Be that as it may, in his *Interpretation of Dreams* (1900), Freud began his journey of exploring the commonest of all psychological wonders. By so doing, Freud may seem to have followed the footsteps of Herbart. In fact, however, unlike all the other authors before him, Freud suggested an Unconscious whose nature is different from consciousness to such an extent that, in the words of Jones, it must call up a picture of the more bizarre type of insanity. Is this innovation of Freud verifiable and the theory of personality based on it acceptable? This is the issue we shall now examine.

2. THE UNCONSCIOUS: SIMPLE OR TRIVALENT?

It was Freud's opinion that system unconscious or id is characterized by a mode of functioning particular to this system only. Its reasoning is not controlled by a need for consistency, and logical contradictions do not matter. In consequence of this statement he conjectured the absence of both negation and the categories of time and causality in this mental system. In addition to being "the realm of a-logic" (1940), according to Freud (1915b), system unconscious is incapable of experiencing emotions for: "It is surely the essence of an emotion that we should feel it, i.e., that it enters consciousness. So for emotions, feelings and affects to be unconscious would be quite out of the question" (p. 177). The only motive recognizable here is a pressure to get rid of nervous excitation, irrespective of logic and reality testing.

There is yet another defining characteristic which regrettably did not receive attention commensurate with its importance. As early as his paper on "The Unconscious" (1915b) and later, in his essay *The Ego and the Id* (1923), Freud suggested that conscious representation consists of the joint representation of an object with the proper word, while unconscious representations are not supported by words. Freud (1915b) specified what happens when an idea is repressed: "What it [repression] denies to presentation is translation into words" (p. 202). The representation which now lacks verbal expression will become unconscious. In his *Outline of Psychoanalysis* (1940), Freud explained again that the easy access to consciousness and the interweaving with words are among the characterizing features of preconscious processes; in order to become preconscious or conscious, an impulse or idea must be attached to a verbal code.

In contradistinction to system unconscious, reality testing, logical thinking, the use of verbal codes, and experiences of emotions define the mode of functioning in the preconscious. These are far-reaching and profound differences indeed. One feels that Jones and Matte-Blanco were not exaggerating when they pointed to the thesis of two completely different sets of laws governing mental life as the most Freudian among the many ideas of Freud. This thesis is also so well organized and sharply delineated that even a person who thinks that this picture of mental functioning requires evidence, cannot help appreciating the boldness of imagination demonstrated here.

In spite of the boldness and elegance of Freud's position, he felt unsure of it and, though hesitatingly, reformulated his theory of mental apparatus. In his essay, *The Ego and the Id* (1923), he suggested a new view of the unconscious:

> We recognize that the Unconscious does not coincide with the repressed; it is still true that all that is repressed is Unconscious, but not all that is Unconscious is repressed. A part of the ego, too—and Heaven knows how important a part—may be Unconscious, undoubtedly is Unconscious. And this Unconscious belonging to the ego is not latent like the Preconscious; for if it were, it could not be activated without becoming conscious; and the process of making it conscious would not encounter such great difficulties. (P. 18)

What a change of outlook, condensed in a few sentences. The most important of the changes proposed here is this: Freud thinks that the ego has unconscious parts, too. What differentiates the preconscious and unconscious elements belonging to the ego? It is the resistance or difficulty one experiences in attempting to make conscious (activating) that which at a given moment is pre- or unconscious. Unlike the unconscious elements of the ego, the activation of preconscious elements proceeds without difficulty; it is not resisted by any intrapsychic counterforce. In other words, the unconscious elements of the ego are not repressed but resisted or prevented from becoming conscious. This is why one should not identify unconscious with repressed, but rather should distinguish between repressed unconscious elements belonging to the id and unrepressed, dynamic, unconscious elements belonging to the ego. The word "dynamic" refers to the resistance with which unconscious elements of the ego are confronted on their way to becoming conscious.

Except for resistance there are no differences between the preconscious and (dynamic) unconscious elements of the ego, as one may see from the following remark of Freud in his *New Introductory Lectures* (1933): "You can see, incidentally, that we are in a position to attribute to the id characteristics other than that of its being unconscious, and you can recognize the possibility of portions of the ego and super-ego being unconscious without possessing the same primitive and irrational characteristics" (p. 75). The repressed unconscious but not the dynamic unconscious, functions in accord with the laws of the irrational primary process. In the ego, on the other hand, whether preconscious or unconscious, reality testing and Aristotelian logic do prevail.

While it was for good reasons that Freud tried to restructure his vision of the mental apparatus, in fact, by doing so, he created new problems and even confusion. For as Matte-Blanco pointed out, if the unrepressed, dynamic, unconscious requires great efforts to be made conscious, "the question arises: what is the actual difference between repressed and dynamic unrepressed unconscious? . . . after all, repression is known—or better, its existence is postulated—from the difficulties encountered in bringing something into full consciousness. We are left in ignorance on this point" (p. 74).

The ambiguity now surrounding the concept of resistance, and whether or not it indicates repression, was later made even more acute. In his *Outline of Psychoanalysis* (1940), Freud speaks of the strong resistances which must be overcome for unconscious material to become conscious. Referring to psychotic states, where, as it seems, there are no such resistances, he states "that the maintenance of certain internal resistances is a sine qua non of normality" (p. 161). Matte-Blanco comments on that point by asking whether Freud is referring to the repressed, the unrepressed, or both types of consciousness. We can be certain only that Freud's statement does not apply to the preconscious. Unfortunately, this piece of information may not help us to dissipate the fog, which from now on will surround the concept of resistance.

As if to make matters worse, in his *Ego and the Id* (1923) Freud wrote that, "the ego is not sharply separated from the id; its lower portion merges into it. But the repressed merges into the id as well, as it is merely a part of it" (p. 24). Now, if the repressed merges into the id as well, and, in any case, the ego is not sharply separated from the id, one must conclude that the repressed dwells, simultaneously, in the ego and the id. Are we now led to believe in the existence of two differently working mental systems and, in consequence of such a decision to accept the distinction between the repressed and dynamic unconscious or shall we believe that both the ego and the id are governed by the selfsame rules?

There seems to be no easy way or no way at all to integrate these disparate views into one coherent picture, and all that can be done, if one has decided to follow Freud, is to work with his first or second (the topographic or structural) theory only. This, indeed, is the conclusion of Arlow and Brenner (1964), who would refuse any further attempt to combine the mutually incompatible concepts of the topographic and the structural theories because, "It is clear that those who follow this line of reasoning . . . will tend to equate id with the system Unconscious, and ego with the system Preconscious with all the attendant disadvantages we have so frequently stressed" (p. 122). They therefore urge the reader to discard forthrightly the topographic model and work exclusively with the second theory of mental apparatus, the structural.

The author who failed by equating id with system unconscious and who provoked these words of disapproval from Arlow and Brenner was none other than Freud. In his *Outline of Psychoanalysis* (1940), Freud, indeed, wrote: "we have found that processes in the unconscious or in id obey different laws from those in the preconscious ego. We name these laws in their totality the *primary process,* in contrast to the *secondary process* which governs the course of events in the preconscious, in the ego" (p. 164). Unconscious and id appear here as synonyms; such a usage of terms or indeed such an understanding of the unconscious is closer to the topographic than to the structural theory of mental apparatus. Freud seems here to have had some second thoughts in regard to his own suggestions put forth in *The Ego and the Id.* It was for this reason that earlier I called this essay a hesitating reformulation of his first, topographic, theory.

Arlow and Brenner, on the other hand, were outspoken in their criticism of this hesitation: "It must be noted that this is a step backward from the position which Freud took in his published work from 1923 onward. It also reverts to the topographic theory's idea that the primary and secondary processes are qualitatively distinct from each other and that each characterizes the operations of a separate division of the mental apparatus" (p. 111).

As one may recall, it was precisely this "step backward," the assumption that primary and secondary processes are qualitatively distinct from each other and that each characterizes the mode of functioning of a separate system of the mental apparatus, which was hailed by Jones and Matte-Blanco as the greatest contribution of Freud. While explaining Freud's ideas, Jones (1953) did his best to clarify the topographic theory of mind;

the structural theory, on the other hand, was dealt with briefly and sketchily. Matte-Blanco, who was more explicit in his complaints about the difficulties created by the structural theory than Jones, was also more explicit in suggesting the remedy. More than once, he indicated that he would prefer to reinstate the understanding of the unconscious prevailing before the structural revision. In a sense, this may seem to have been Freud's approach too.

The remedy suggested by Arlow and Brenner (1964) was the reverse; to abolish the distinction between the preconscious and the unconscious: "The term unconscious . . . should be used to indicate that something is not conscious, whether or not it can readily become conscious" (p. 113); and also to forget about the idea of two mental systems defined by idiosyncratic modes of functioning. In their opinion, "The activities of the ego and superego as well as those of the id may be characterized by the primary process. . . . The difference between primary and secondary processes is actually a quantitative one" (p. 91).

The dichotomy of two mutually exclusive sets of laws governing mental functioning, "Freud's revolutionary contribution to psychology," is here transformed into a difference of less or more. Any distinction between the ego and id is thus made questionable. It seems important to point out that Arlow and Brenner were not the only ones who thought they could improve the concept of primary and secondary process by turning it from a dichotomy of two completely different modes of thinking into a continuum of grades.

Such a revision was already proposed by Rapaport (1951) in his comments on the works of Schilder and Bleuler. Schilder (1920) reported that a patient suffering from optic agnosia reacted to the picture of a mouse by saying: "it isn't a cat"; to the picture of a bell: "I know that one, it isn't a bottle." Schilder interpreted this observation as follows: "Here we see in the field of perception that first only the sphere, the general conceptual realm, comes to consciousness; then recognition progresses within this sphere" (p. 502). Commenting on this statement of Schilder, Rapaport wrote: "The referent of the concept of 'sphere' is in many respects the same as that of Freud's concept 'primary process.' The difference appears to lie in that Schilder observed mechanisms attributed to the primary process operating not only on material of the unconscious but also on material on the fringe of consciousness. . . . The mechanisms of the primary process may not be as exclusive to the unconscious as has been thought" (p. 502).

Renowned as he was for his loyalty to Freud, but also known for his scholarship, Rapaport found himself at a crossroads. He saw only too well that the sharp dichotomy of primary/secondary processes does not fit the facts as revealed by organic disturbances and schizophrenia—topics he dealt with in his comments—and he respected the facts. He agreed that the facts are not favorable to Freud's theory of mental apparatus and that the mode of functioning called "primary" is also observable in the consciousness, as he put it. Incidentally, by using the term *"the" unconscious,* that is, by making no distinction between repressed and unrepressed unconscious, Rapaport indicated that he worked with the topographic theory of mind, which, as one may recall, assumes an incompatibility of aims and rules between the two mental systems.

Yet Rapaport admits that the mode of functioning called "primary" is also observable in the consciousness. One wonders what consequences would follow if one agreed that "primary process," the defining characteristic of one of the two clearly outlined mental systems, is observable in the second system as well. By acknowledging this, are we not abandoning grounds for assuming two mental systems which pursue different aims and are ruled by totally different laws? Further, should we not agree that Bleuler may have been correct in saying that aside from the quality of consciousness, unconscious processes are identical with conscious processes?

Freud (1923) seems to have foreseen this development. In the passage in which he introduced the concept of unrepressed unconscious, he reflected on the consequences of this decision by confessing that "the characteristic of being unconscious begins to lose significance for us. It becomes a quality which can have many meanings. A quality which we are unable to make, as we should have hoped to do, the basis of far-reaching and inevitable conclusions" (p. 18).

Maybe it was also because of his concern that the unconscious may lose its importance that Freud returned to his original view of mental apparatus. Conversely, Rapaport, Arlow and Brenner, and many more, who became aware of the weakness of this assumption were ready to renounce the sharp dichotomy of two differently working mental systems. Having discarded the distinction between two mental systems one feels that the next step should have been to ask whether we, indeed, have two modes of mental functioning.

Because of the importance of Rapaport's view, let us retrace the steps in his reasoning: his allowance for the discrediting of Freud's original theory of mental apparatus and his withdrawal back to it without, however, disproving the reasons which forced him to admit that "the primary" mode of functioning is also observable in the second mental system. As a part of his ambitious attempt to build a psychoanalytic theory of thinking, Rapaport (1951) collected, translated, and commented on an impressive list of European contributions to the psychology of thinking. As a measure of his encyclopaedic knowledge and open-mindedness, he included in his selections a paper of Schilder which appeared in 1920 in a German periodical for neurology and psychiatry, and which suggested a theory of thinking diametrically opposed to that of Freud.

The main thesis of Schilder's paper is formulated in a way which indicates a consensus among his contemporaries: "It is a recognized fact that images and thoughts pass through various (preparatory, transitory) stages before they appear in a clear (conscious) form. . . . Because this development often escapes observation, G. E. Muller considered it an open question whether or not all images undergo such development. I consider this doubt unjustified" (p. 497).

This is the essence of what Schilder had to say, but let us follow him step by step by recapitulating his paper. Schilder reports on the experiments of Nagel and Pieron. These authors, independently, found that when subjects were unable to find a syllable in the course of reproducing a series of syllables, they verbalized other syllables obtained by changing the vowels and consonants of a likely syllable until they felt they had found a correct one. Schilder concluded that this provides us with a glimpse of what goes on normally while we attempt to retrieve a word from our memory stores: it must be evolved slowly and with effort: "a presentation evolves through other presentations which are associated with it by similarity and contiguity, primarily by clang and external associations" (p. 499). Then he detailed some observations on patients afflicted with agnosia who would substitute conceptually related objects for each other. For example, they may call a pair of glasses a telescope. (It was at this point that Rapaport admitted that the mechanisms attributed to the primary process operate not only on material of the unconscious but also on material on the fringe of consciousness). Schilder explicated the meaning of these findings by outlining a general theory of thinking:

Images and thoughts have a development, a prehistory. What we know so far about this development process is:

1. Image and thought development progress from the indefinite to the definite;

2. This process of development passes through associatively related realms. Anything which is associated with the presentation by either objective relationship or subjective experience may come into play;
3. Incompletely evolved thoughts contain presentation-fragments from various phases of development;
4. Incompletely evolved thoughts are particularly amenable to affective transformation; and
5. they frequently have a symbol-like character (p. 507).

Then Schilder quoted a work of Stransky who asked his subjects to "relax their attention" and continue to verbalize all that went through their minds. In the utterings of his subjects Stransky found perseverations, contaminations (in the terminology of Freud: condensations of two words in one), and clang associations. Schilder commented on that, stating: "According to the analysis presented here, these formations are also preparatory steps, that is, developmental phases of normal thought" (p. 509).

Finally, in applying this idea to an understanding of schizophrenic thought disturbances, Schilder wrote: "I feel that my analysis of the formal characteristics of schizophrenic thinking warrants the thesis that in many schizophrenic cases such formations, which normally would be only transitory phases in thought-development, appear as the end results of thought processes. The point of view that these formations are abortive products of thought-development contributes considerably to this understanding" (p. 514).

Schilder ends his paper by elaborating some general reflections. He observes that, if the development of a thought progresses from schematic to individual forms, then in the phase of schematic representation in memory, the differentiation within its sphere is negligible. Thus, for example. the sphere: father—power—authority will not be differentiated, but will remain a single affectively anchored global concept the parts of which will be synonymous with the whole. The "sphere," then, should not be conceived of as something abstractly logical, but rather as a realm of similar and affectively equivalent experiences. Here he felt himself confronted with an intriguing problem: "what is really the relationship of meaning experience to the sphere, and how do feelings connect the actual experience that is in the foreground with the background-experience pertaining to the sphere" (p. 518).

On this Rapaport comments: "since Schilder does not differentiate between a primary and a secondary process, he has to attribute both drive- and reality syntonic functions to the sphere, and within it he has to *distinguish* reality and drive-orientation. Thus, the dichotomy of the primary and secondary process re-emerges *within* the sphere, that is, within the very concept that was to eliminate it." (p. 518).

In fact, Schilder has done nothing which can be interpreted as a revival of the dichotomy of the primary and secondary process. He has pointed out two questions here: (1) How is a new experience absorbed into one of the many spheres? This question was known to German psychology as the distinction between perception and apperception, apperception being the term for the assimilation of a meaningful experience to the "spheres" of memory store. (A further distinction was made between perception and sensation.) (2) How should one understand the interaction of meaning, experiences, and feelings? Clearly, Schilder distinguished between cognition and feeling, but not between two kinds of thinking.

Rapaport (1951) succeeded, though inadvertently, in disclosing some of the difficulties faced in defending the concept of primary and secondary processes. Here he states, as did Freud, that the "drive-and reality-syntonic" mental functions are dichotically different. He even tried to prove that Schilder, unknown to himself, was required to accept this fact. Earlier, however, he concurred with Bleuler and Schilder in denying such a dichotomy and suggested, instead, that "the mechanisms of the primary process may not be as exclusive to the unconscious as has been thought" (p. 502). Due to their unequivocal rejection of the topographic model of the mental apparatus, Arlow and Brenner's position is free of this self-contradiction. However, unlike Rapaport, they did not confront the challenge posed by Schilder, the possibility that there are not two but only one mode of thinking.

The theory expounded by Schilder *is* a challenge to those interested in the conceptual basis of psychoanalysis, and it demands serious consideration. Saying "telescope" instead of "glasses," condensing two words into one, or choosing a clang instead of a semantic association, and the many more products of reasoning which cannot be validated by reality testing and logic, Schilder suggests, are interim positions (revealed due to an obstruction of the normal process), in our procedure of retrieving from its global sphere a concept, a word, which eventually, will be validated by reality testing and logic. Thus, phenomena which were understood to be indices of a primary mode of thinking, in fact, are an integral part of the normal unfolding of a thought. This theory of thinking and the theory of primary and secondary process are totally incompatible. Which one sounds more plausible?

The direction pointed to by Schilder seems to be well taken and supported by evidence, as will be detailed here. Prior to this, however, we must complement this theory with an important element; if a sphere is activated, all its ingredients, the various individual bits of information, are activated. In other words, each of these individual bits of information is a likely candidate to be "retrieved." In addition to the general activation emphasized by Schilder, a need clearly exists for a process of selection which will enable us to reject all information activated except for what is relevant at a given moment. The agnosic patient, quoted above, who defined the picture of a mouse as "not a cat," may indicate the existence of such a regularly ongoing effort of selection or negation.

Any thought must be evolved from a global "sphere" and, since all the content of the sphere is simultaneously activated, we therefore incessantly must select one and reject the other members. If, however, due to tiredness or pathology, we are impeded in exerting the required effort, we may "retrieve" one of the not rejected members of the sphere. Normally, though, this member of the sphere will be rejected, and its activation will be no more than an interim position in the process of evolving specific information. This is the challenge posed to the theory of primary and secondary modes of thinking.

3.
MICROGENESIS VERSUS PRIMARY-SECONDARY PROCESSES

The crux of Schilder's suggestion was the assumption of global spheres which contain memory items organized into representational units in accord with semantic and affective equations. It was precisely this view which, as a result of recent developments in the psychology of remembering, became quite firmly established.

There is a striking discrepancy between the very limited number of pieces of information one can hold in immediate memory and the virtually limitless amount of information stored in long-term memory. G. A. Miller (1956) suggested that the only way we are able to store so much information is by "chunking" it into units. Each chunk of information is a recoded and shortened representation of the pieces of information stored in it. Johnson (1972) further elaborated on this conception by suggesting that chunks or sets of information are again recoded and stored in memory codes.

Memory codes, as Johnson puts it, are unitary. That is, they can be recovered from memory in an all-or-nothing manner. Once recovered, all the information they represent should be available for recall. This, as we may remember, was how Schilder understood the nature of spheres. The sphere or the code is activated in its entirety. Therefore, as I suggested, one must assume a parallel process: a mental effort of selecting one and rejecting all other pieces of information represented in one code.

One code may contain many chunks, and it is only a small step from here to assume a further hierarchical level in the organization of memory, that is "to suppose that a set of codes may be recoded into a higher-order code. Furthermore, at the highest level of the code hierarchy, the entire sequence may be represented in memory by a single code" (Johnson 1970, p. 172).

This extension of the concept of memory codes, though logical, may not be necessary if the holographic hypothesis of memory structure (Pribram, Nuwer, and Baron 1974; Pribram 1980) proves to be correct. One of the best established, yet puzzling, facts about the way memory works is that large lesions within a neural system do not seriously impair it. Lashley (1950) showed that 80% or more of the visual cortex of a rat could be damaged without loss of the ability to recognize patterns correctly learned prior to the damage. Later, other investigators have severed as much as 95% of the optic tracts of cats with similar results.

Thus, Galambos, Norton, and Frommer (1967) were unable to find any impairment in visual flux discrimination or pattern discrimination (e.g. 6 vs. 9), even when greater than 90%–95% of the entire optic tract was destroyed. How can such an extensive destruction of the optic system produce so little consequence? It was because of this puzzle that, in his influential paper on the search for the engram, Lashley (1950) despaired of comprehending the biological basis of memory organization. But a hologram has just the properties needed to solve this riddle: a hologram's store can be injured and an image can still be reconstructed from any of its pieces. Thus the name: hologram; every part contains sufficient information to establish the whole.

A hologram is a laser beam record that reproduces three-dimensional visual images. Both photographs and holograms consist of visual information on a photographic plate. But whereas in ordinary photographs the light from one point on the object is reflected at only a single point on the film, every point on the hologram records the entire picture. The hologram's information is stored in the form of an interference pattern; when a laser beam is shined through the plate, the original wave form is reconstructed and the stored information is again available. The angle of incidence of the laser beam and its wavelength determine which particular visual information is retrieved from the interference pattern.

Since the information contained in a hologram is distributed and reduplicated as an interference pattern over the whole photographic plate, any piece of the hologram will suffice to reconstruct the whole of the visual information. A process similar to that of the holographic interference may, then, explain Lashley's puzzling finding.

Pribram contends that there *is* a neural hologram, whereas Arbib (1972) would prefer to treat it as a metaphor borrowed from optics, where it properly belongs. Whatever the future of the hologram hypothesis will be, we may say that the view on the organization of memory and the process of recall suggested by Schilder has withstood the test of time; it is as modern and promising as it was 65 years ago.

Information contained in recoded form in a code must be decoded in order to be recalled. How does this process of decoding unfold? Thus far, we have had two sources from which to learn about the process of decoding: the "tip-of-the-tongue" phenomenon and the speech of aphasic patients.

In his *Principles of Psychology* (1890), William James beautifully and precisely described the tip-of-the-tongue phenomenon:

> Suppose we try to recall a forgotten name. The state of our consciousness is peculiar. There is a gap therein; but no mere gap. It is a gap that is intensely active. A sort of wraith of the name is in it, beckoning us in a given direction, making us at moments tingle with the sense of our closeness and then letting us sink back without the longed-for term. If wrong names are proposed to us, this singularly definite gap acts immediately so as to negate them. They do not fit into its mould. (Vol. 1, p. 251)

Recently, Brown and McNeill (1966), dissatisfied with the small number of naturally occurring tip-of-the-tongue (TOT) phenomena, decided to "prospect" for TOT states by letting their subjects read definitions of rare English words and asking them to supply the words. According to Brown and McNeill, the experience of knowing that one knows the answer and yet does not succeed in verbalizing it was unmistakable: "seized by a TOT state . . . he would appear to be in mild torment, something like the brink of a sneeze, and if he found the word his relief was considerable" (p. 325).

While searching for the target word, the subjects were required to tell all the words that came to their mind. Because of this procedure, we are now able to follow the normal process of evolving particular information from the comprehensive code. Seventy percent of the words that came to mind in a TOT state were similar in sound, but not in meaning, to the target; some of them were not real words. For example, when the target was *sampan,* words such as *Saipan, Siam, Cheyenne, sarong, sanching,* and *sympoon* were produced. Only 30% of these interim words were similar in meaning to the target. One may say that Schilder was correct in saying that clang associations and even neologisms are regular steps in the process of evolving a word from its code/sphere.

Approximately half of the interim words which are similar in sound had the same number of syllables as the target words, but only 20% of the words similar in meaning matched the number of syllables in the target words. Likewise, 49% of the initial letters of the words similar in sound matched the initial letters of the target words, as compared with only 8% matches for the words similar in meaning. All in all, Brown and McNeill argued, these findings and a few more related findings not detailed here, attest to a generic recall. "When complete recall of a word is not presently possible but is felt to be imminent, one can often correctly recall the general type of the word; *generic* recall may succeed when particular recall fails" (p. 325).

Actually, we should say that the generic recall, the activation of the code, is a prerequisite for recalling the word, but, of course, even after we have succeeded in activating the proper code, we may still fail to retrieve the information requested at the moment. This, precisely, is the meaning of the TOT phenomenon. Brown and McNeill, by making public what usually goes on quickly and unconsciously, gave us a glimpse of the process by which particular knowledge unfolds from its "generic" memory code.

Incidentally, we may now understand why it is easier to recognize an item of information than to recall it. In order to recognize something, it is enough to activate the proper code; the object or person before you saves you the laborious effort of negating all possible information, except for one item, represented in the code.

How do we then proceed from the general to the particular? Neither Brown and McNeill, nor Yarmey (1973), who confirmed their findings, fully reproduced protocols showing the stages of this process. I decided, therefore, to replicate, with some changes, the Brown and McNeill experiment. I asked volunteer subjects to read, in Hebrew, a list of rare words and their definitions. Following that, they were given the definitions only and asked to recall the proper words. This change in the procedure was meant to enhance the chances of creating a TOT experience. Here is an example of a relatively quick solution to the tension created by the feeling of knowledge and the failure to actualize this knowledge. In his search for the word KAMAI (ancient), one of the subjects reasoned as follows: not KADMON (a synonym of Kamai)—ARCHAI (another synonym)—it has to do with myths—it is like ARCHAI—EH—ACHAI—TEKES (ceremony)—D—it has to do with myths—D—N—EH—AH—like in ARCHAI—it begins with D or M—D—M—PARAS (Persia)—

MADAI (Paras and Madai were ruled by Achashverosh, husband of the biblical Queen Esther)—ASHMEDAI (king of the demons)—TALMAI—DANAI—KAMAI!!

We may see here the stepwise evolution of a word from its memory code. These steps begin with a demarcation of the area of the sought-after word, first by generating two synonyms, then by mentioning the topic of myths. This semantic demarcation was followed by an attempt to recapture the first syllable or letter of the word at the tip of the tongue. Eventually, the word was retrieved by means of a rhyme: MAD*AI,* ASHMED*AI,* TALM*AI,* DAN*AI,* KAM*AI*.

We see how interwoven the semantic and clang associations are and how unexpectedly the solution arrives. The subject was sure that the target word began with D or M, but it began with K. Also, if for some reason, the full unfolding had not been accomplished and the subject had stopped at one of the preparatory phases, we would have had before us a product which Freud might have interpreted as indicative of primary process thinking, but Schilder would have explained as a proof of the theory of microgenesis.

Let us turn now to aphasia. Rapaport, as we may recall, conceded that the speech of aphasic patients does not confirm, or rather refutes, the thesis of two clearly distinguished modes of thinking. As with TOT phenomena, one has difficulty finding in the literature on aphasia (in English) reproductions of ongoing conversations with a patient. In one such study Ross, Clarke, and Haddock (1964) reported a long conversation with an improving aphasic patient. I shall quote here part of this conversation, and hope to be able to illustrate through the peculiarities of the patient's speech the point of view represented here, i.e., that such disturbances of thought are the result of an interruption in the process of retrieving the sought-for information from its memory code.

(38) D: Is your speech back to normal yet?
P: Hear, Yes, definitely.
(39) D: Your speaking?
P: Speaking? Yes, yes.
(43) D: Good.
P: No, my lunging's perfect.
(44) D: Your what's perfect?
P: My lunging.
(45) D: Your lunging?
P: Longing, yes, my longing to you; to—to the story is perfect.

I understand, I—er—I get everything that I understand. I know.

(46) D: M'm, I see.

P: But whenever there is English between us—language, anything like that, I—I'm perfect. I can tell you that, definite.

(51) D: Yes.

P: I've got a very good luggage.

(52) D: M'm. Now that's not quite the right word, is it? not luggage.

P: Well—

(53) D: What's the word you were trying to think of?

P: Oh, good language, then.

(54) D: Ah, that's better.

P: Language. I—I'm saying now lot—roughly—I'm saying to you, luggage. I—I'm speaking language; I—I'm very good.

(55) D: M'm.

P: I've got a good language.

We have here an opportunity to follow the major steps of the microgenesis of the word "language." Fortunately, both participants in this conversation were interested in reaching the elusive word.

During the dialogue, the patient makes notable efforts to find the word; meanwhile, we can glance at the evolving of a word, something that normally cannot be observed. On the first occasion, not quoted above, he says: "I shall have lesson with the lungage of the hear itself." Later, "It'll underneath—underneath my luggage that's got my upper ha—er—the worst hand to me." In dialogue 43, "No, my lunging's perfect"; dialogue 45, "longing, yes, my longing to you; to—to the story is perfect." Then, suddenly (dialogue 46), "But whenever there is English between us—language, anything like that, I—I'm perfect. I can tell you that, definite." After this comes a retreat (the to-and-from oscillation); "I've got a very good luggage," which is followed by, in dialogue 53; "Oh, good language then"; repeating it with great affect in dialogue 54: "I—I'm saying now lot roughly—I'm saying to you, luggage. I—I'm speaking language; I—I'm very good."

The order of the spoken words was lungage—luggage—lunging—longing—language—luggage—language—luggage—language. It is possible that the patient had many more intermediate associations, but perhaps because of his intense goal-directedness, his awareness of being examined, and his self-consciousness ("I've had a good education. . . . I'm not admitting tale to you, sir, or any man your level. . . . I'll easy hold my own"), he may have withheld some words that came to his mind. In any case, the dialogue as it stands demonstrates the process of word evolving which normally goes on rapidly and unrecognized. We may understand why Rapaport felt compelled to conclude that the speech of aphasic patients cannot susbtantiate Freud's theory of thinking.

The disturbance called paralexia invites the same conclusion. For example, Marshall and Newcombe (1966) report a patient who at first suffered from a complete aphasia and right hemiplegia. He improved slowly in spontaneous speech and in the understanding of language, but not in reading and writing. The most salient feature of the patient's language impairment was his paralexic errors. The patient read *antique* as *vase, canary* as *parrot, liberty* as *freedom.* Any explanation of this paralexic disturbance must account for the fact that in another context the patient was able to produce the very word he failed to retrieve in reading. Thus, *thunder* was read as storm and *storm* read as thunder. Clearly, the patient was able to activate the proper memory code but failed in rejecting the associatively connected concepts. Because of this failure, his performance discloses what usually is covered up, the microgenesis of thoughts and precepts.

Warrington and Shallice's (1979) analysis of a related problem may underscore this conclusion. Their patient had great difficulty in reading or understanding the written word but was able to write words both spontaneously and in response to dictation. He succeeded in reading accurately not more than 30%–50% of the words with which he was presented. Yet, he demonstrated a striking capacity to categorize words which he failed to read.

Twenty-five words from each of five categories (animals, plants, parts of the body, foods, and objects) were typed individually in lower case on index cards. He was able to read thirty-four of the words and indicate the meaning of four. A two-choice categorization task was immediately given for the remaining eighty-seven words. For example, unable to read or identify *crocus* he was asked "Is it an animal or plant?" He correctly categorized sixty-eight of these eighty-seven words. Occasionally categorization led to word reading. The patient would study a word and comment that he did not "know" it. Subsequently, after had had been guided through the semantic choices, he might identify the word or even read it aloud.

Warrington and Shallice conclude that the category tasks appeared to facilitate the patient's capacity to gain access to the semantic connotation of the written word. Saying it differently, this patient suffered from "a difficulty in accessing the full semantic representation of the word" (p. 59). Warrington and Shallice's belief in the hypothesis that gaining access to the semantic representation of words does not have an "all-or-nothing" character, but is a complex process that can be partially disturbed, may seem counterintuitive. However, this patient's behavior makes it clear that there *is* an order in the access process. It seems distinctly possible, they add, that gaining access to word meaning in normal subjects follows a similar but more rapid course. It seems to me that the theory of microgenesis could very well account for the intriguing findings of Warrington and Shallice. In this light, their patient was able to activate, to gain access to the category or memory code of the visually presented words, but, for reasons inherent in aphasia, was unable to evolve the specific word contained in this code.

In view of the evidence presented here, it is possible to suggest that the microgenetic approach provides a unified theory of perception and thinking. Without hypothesizing two systems of thinking, it explains both reality-adapted and disturbed performances. Usually, we are aware of only the end product and the process of unfolding a percept or thought goes on unconsciously; yet this quality of "unconsciousness" and these steps of unfolding lend no support to Freud's conception of primary process.

Ever since Herbart impressed upon his followers the belief that the human mind is structured, and that an understanding of behavior is possible only by taking into account its supra and subliminal contents and dynamics, students of psychology have emphasized the similarity of the rules governing mental processes. For example, in his *L'imagination créatrice* (The creative imagination [1900]), reviewing the theory of "unconscious cerebration" Ribot summarized the psychological theories of his days as "the belief that if we descend from clear to obscure consciousness, and from this to the unconsciousness that manifests itself in motor reaction, the first state, thus successfully impoverished, still remains down to its lowest term identical in basis with consciousness" (p. 341).

As we have seen earlier, this was also the opinion of Bleuler. At the beginning of this century, except for Freud, this was the opinion of the students of psychopathology in general. The main sources of their knowledge of unconscious processes were hypnosis and the so-called double or, multiple personality, a phenomenon which according to Ellenberger (1970), "by 1880 . . . was among the most discussed [topics] by psychiatrists and philosophers" (p.126). Both these experimentally provoked and naturally occurring alterations of personality have convincingly shown, first, that self-consciousness may be segmentalized and, second, that the different segments, like the two personalities of a double personality, different as they may be in their values, and their outlook, in their mental functioning are, by any measure, governed by the same rules.

Dr. Jekyll and Mr. Hyde pursued different aims in life, but both spoke the same language. Their reasoning was shaped by the same rules, and their perceptions and relationship to reality was of the same quality. Mr. Hyde though was the unconscious aspect of Dr. Jekyll, yet when Mr. Hyde became manifest and observable, his reasoning, understanding of reality, or capacity for emotions were very much like those of Dr. Jekyll. What hypnosis and the pathology of double personality did show was only the existence of dissociated memory systems subserving the different states of mind. This easy segmentation of our memory storage does not prove, either logically or empirically, the necessity or the possibility of having two totally different modes of mental functioning.

Freud, however, had an important piece of evidence on which to rely —dreams. It was through his theory of dreams that he thought to prove his conception of the unconscious. Freud stated that the analysis of dreams should show that the laws which govern the unconscious mental life differ to a great extent from those of consciousness. Let us, therefore, now listen to the witness of dreams.

4.
THE ROYAL ROAD: WAS IT EVER PAVED?

THE RIDDLE OF DREAMS

"If our viscera made as many mistakes in sleep as the brain, we should all die of ingestion after our first nursing," Susanne Langer (1942) stated, not without astonishment. "It may be replied that the mistakes of dreams are harmless, since they have no motor terminals, though they enter into waking life as memories, and we have to learn to discount them. . . . Yet it is a natural organ which presumably does nothing that is not relevant to the total behavior, the response to nature that constitutes human life" (p. 30). Succinctly and sensitively, Langer succeeded in putting in a few sentences the reason for our continuing interest in dreams. Dreams seem to defy the confines of rational reasoning, and do not seem to "respond to nature," to reality. Philosophers and psychologists through the ages have been puzzled and, while they have not been unanimous in their explanations, again and again they have confirmed that dreams are indeed at variance with mental functioning in wakefulness.

In his *Interpretation of Dreams* (1900), Freud put together an impressive collection of these views prevailing among nineteenth-century authors and I shall quote here a few of them: Maury (1878), a respected and often quoted author, wrote: "There are no dreams that are *absolutely* reasonable and that do not contain *some* incoherence, anachronism, or absurdity" (p. 163). Fechner (1889), to whom Freud referred as the Great Fechner, stated: "It is as though psychological activity had been transported from the brain of a reasonable man into that of a fool" (vol. 2, p. 522). Let us finish this display of consensus by quoting Binz (1878): "The content of at least nine out of ten dreams is nonsensical. We bring together in them people and things that have no connection whatever with one another. Next moment there is a shift in the kaleidoscope and we are faced by a new grouping, more senseless and crazy, if possible, than the last" (p. 33).

Freud (1900) concurred in this description of dreams, if not in the explanation given by the earlier authors: "The renunciation of voluntary direction of the flow of ideas cannot be disputed . . . . We have not merely accepted the fact of the looseness of associative connections in dreams, but we have shown that it extends far further than had been suspected; we have found however, that these loose connections are merely obligatory substitutes for others which are valid and significant. It is quite true that we have described dreams as absurd; but examples have taught us how sensible a dream can be even when it appears to be absurd" (p. 591).

Incidentally Jung (1945), too, agreed that "dreams that form logically, morally, or aesthetically satisfying wholes are exceptional. Usually a dream is a strange and disconcerting product distinguished by many 'bad qualities', such as lack of logic, questionable morality, uncouth form, and apparent absurdity and nonsense" (p. 245). Both Freud and Jung, then, in agreement with earlier authors, described dreams as absurd and nonsensical, but they contended, this absurdity notwithstanding, that dreams have a meaning; though hidden from our eyes, they do respond to nature.

Meaningful though dreams may be, their appearance is absurd and meaningless. Why is that so? This is the riddle of dreams. How can a natural "organ" such as thinking not "respond" to nature, not be in the service of adaptation to reality and cooperate with it? Saying it differently, with Freud (1900): "dreams . . . are products of our mental activity. Nevertheless, the finished dream strikes us as something alien to us" (p. 48). How can we explain this impression?

The views of the authors quoted above and those who were influenced by them may be grouped into two main streams of reasoning. Some thought that these peculiarities of dreams are the result of a lowering of efficiency of psychic functions during sleep. Others, including Fechner (1889), who influenced Freud, thought that there is an essential difference between dreaming and waking life and, thus, that dreams indicate the existence of a hitherto unknown mode of mental functioning, the rules of which are completely different from those prevailing in wakefulness. For example, Delboeuf (1885) believed that in sleep, all mental faculties remain essentially intact, except for perception, intelligence, imagination, memory, will, and morality; they are merely applied to imaginary and unstable objects. In contrast, Fechner (1889) argued that neither the lowering of conscious and directed mental life "below the main threshold," nor the withdrawal of attention from the influence of the external world are enough to explain the characteristics of dreams. Rather, he suggested, since there is no continuity between the waking and sleeping ideational lives, the scene of action of dreams is different from that of waking ideational life. Freud (1900) agreed with him and, observing that no one else had pursued Fechner's suggestion, he (1900) stated: "This is the only hypothesis that makes the special peculiarities of dream-life intelligible" (p. 536), by applying it to a mental apparatus built up of a number of agencies arranged in a series, one behind the other, whose ways of functioning are quite dissimilar.

If we assume, as Freud did, that mental life is controlled by two differently working "agencies," we may find ourselves obliged to choose between two possibilities: (1) all our mental activities are the result of an interaction, of a conflict, between the discordant agencies of the mental apparatus; or (2) at any given time, one of these agencies has the upper hand and our mental activities reflect this change of rules and quality of mental functioning, this change of scene, to use Fechner's term. Freud preferred, if one may say so, a third possibility. He agreed with Fechner that in sleeping there is a change of scene; the mental agency which now takes the lead is not the mental agency which is in control during wakefulness. Yet the temporarily subdued, "minor" agency, though weakened, does interfere and, thus, the conflict between the mental agencies is continuous. Accordingly, the peculiarities of the dream, which long puzzled researchers, will be explained by the mode of functioning of a mental agency which by daylight is unknown, as if it does not exist; these peculiarities will also be known as the outcome of the conflict which was ongoing while the dream was actualized.

This is how Freud (1940) formulated his suggestion: "What makes dreams so invaluable in giving insight is the circumstance that, when the unconscious material makes its way into the ego, it brings its own modes of working along with it. . . . It is only in this way that we learn the laws which govern the passage of events in the unconscious and the respects in which they differ from the rules that are familiar to us in waking thought" (p. 167). Forty years earlier, Freud (1900) expressed the same idea in a short sentence which was destined to become famous: "The interpretation of dreams is the royal road to a knowledge of the unconscious activities of the mind" (p. 608). Both of these formulations emphasize the responsibility of the unknown, unconscious, mental agency for the peculiarities of the dream. Soon we will consider the contribution of the incessantly ongoing conflict between the agencies of the mental apparatus to the creation of a dream. But for the moment, let us follow the path of the above statements and look again at these features of nonsense and absurdity; as we have seen, they may reveal to us the laws of functioning in the unconscious.

In *The Interpretation of Dreams* (1900) Freud described the absurdity of dreams as follows: "Dreams are disconnected, they accept the most violent contradictions without the least objection, they admit impossibilities, they disregard knowledge which carries great weight with us in daytime, they reveal us as ethical and moral imbeciles" (p. 54). There is nothing in this characterization of the dreams to brand them as colorful but empty bubbles. In fact, it was precisely because of these qualities that Freud held dreams in high estimation. The strangeness and absurdity of dreams, Freud suggested, may prove that their bearing mother was an alogical and irrationally working mental system.

Everything rests now upon the bizarreness of dreams; their psychosis-like appearance became the prerequisite of the thesis of two different modes of mental functioning. The first question then is this: are dreams, indeed, strange and different from our waking thought?

WHAT A DREAM IS

A closer study of Freud's writing on dreams shows him to hesitate between promoting the traditional view depicted above and introducing a quite different definition of the subject matter. Resuming his study Freud (1900) concluded that the dream, motivated by a wish, is a psychic act full of import: "the fact that it is unrecognizable as a wish, and its many peculiarities and absurdities are due to the influence of psychic censorship to which it has been subjected during its formation." (Here we meet the concept of conflict and its impact on dreams, but we shall postpone discussing it until a later section.) Then he continued: "Besides the necessity of evading the censorship, the following factors have played a part in its formation: first, a necessity for condensing the psychic material; second, regard for representability in sensory images; and third (though not constantly) regard for a rational and intelligible exterior of the dream structure" (pp. 485–86).

There is a contradiction between the first and second parts of this statement. It begins with an affirmation of the traditional views, that dreams are characterized by many peculiarities and absurdities, but it ends with the surprising announcement that some (not all) dreams have a rational and intelligible exterior. Dreams, then, are not by necessity nonsensical; some of them are rational and intelligible. It goes without saying that intelligible dreams do not invoke or justify constructs such as primary process or mental censorship. Freud's theory of behavior, which was based precisely on the assumption that the appearance of dreams (but not their covered up, latent thought), is nonsensical, is thus jeopardized—by Freud himself.

There are many more instances of this inconsistency, each of which casts doubt on the theory of Freud. Propounding his thesis that not all wishes are of equal importance and power in dreams, Freud (1900) concedes that children's dreams prove that a wish that has not been dealt with during the day can act as a dream instigator. "But it must not be forgotten that it is a *child's* wish. . . . I think it is highly doubtful whether in the case of an adult a wish that has not been fulfilled during the day would be strong enough to produce a dream" (p. 552). Children's dreams are undistorted fulfillments of wishes carried over from their frustrated wills and intents in wakefulness. The wishes of adults' dreams stem from more distant periods of life and they are disguised and made unrecognizable. Then, as an afterthought, he added: "It is possible that there are individual differences in this respect, and that some people retain an infantile type of mental process longer than others" (p. 552).

In other words, Freud acknowledged here that some dreams are undistorted, rational, and intelligible expressions of wishes, which presumably reflect the dreamer's preoccupations while awake. In contrast to the dreams of infantile persons, in adults "the dream would not materialize if the preconscious wish did not succeed in finding reinforcement from elsewhere, from the unconscious, in fact" (p. 553). Again, Freud suggested that dreams are heterogeneous. Some of them originate in the repressed unconscious and they are peculiar and absurd, but other dreams actualize undistorted and well-thought-out preconscious wishes. Freud left unanswered how his theory accounts for this diversity of dreams. One wonders whether a theory which was meant to explain why all dreams are bizarre can be maintained if only some dreams are bizarre, while others are logical.

Not only in the dreams of the "infantile type," but also in the so-called punishment-dreams as well, the motivating wish was relegated to the ego. The discussion of punishment-dreams in *The Interpretation of Dreams* is essentially an analysis of a recurring dream of Rosegger, a famous Austrian writer who came from very humble, peasant beginnings. In one of his stories, entitled "Alienated," Rosegger describes how he was unable for many years to free himself from the shadow of his earlier life. In his dreams he was always a journeyman tailor, working without pay in a shop. Now and then, when something went awry, he had to put up with a scolding, though there was never any talk of wages.

These dreams persisted for years with uncanny regularity. Then, in one of these dreams, another journeyman was taken on, but there was no more room for another seat. The master said to Rosegger, "You've no gift for tailoring, you can go! You are alienated." Rosegger awoke feeling an overpowering fright, but from that night on he enjoyed peace. He dreamed no more of the tailoring days; he was alienated. While, usually, alienation is not regarded as being a great blessing, Rosegger was satisfied. What he was told in his dream was no more than confirmation of the facts which pleased him greatly in his awake life.

Freud agreed that this class of dreams "offers a hard test to the theory of wish-fulfillment." These are punishment-dreams of a parvenu, he suggested. They remind the dreamer, who is inclined to boast, of his humble origins. "The essential characteristic of punishment-dreams would thus be that in their case the dream-constructing wish is not an unconscious wish derived from the repressed . . . but a punitive one reacting against it and belonging to the ego. . . . Thus punishment-dreams indicate the possibility that the ego may have a greater share than was supposed in the construction of dreams" (p. 558).

Interestingly, Freud seemed not to realize that, if punishment-dreams do not originate in repressed wishes, there are no reasons for disguising them. Moreover, if they come from the super-ego, one can hardly conceive of any other intrapsychic power which would censor them. We may thus expect punishment-dreams to be like any other product of system ego, rational and intelligible, and not peculiar and absurd. Although Freud's understanding of punishment-dreams is not clearly stated, such dreams are a further exemption from the supposition that a dream, by definition, is nonsensical. Rather, punishment-dreams bear testimony to the diversity of dreams.

But we must not dwell on conjectures. In some writings, Freud explicitly conceded that some dreams are rational and well-constructed. Describing the process of transforming latent thoughts into the manifest content of a dream, Freud (1900) remembered a dream which was so particularly well-constructed, flawless, and clear that, while he was still half-dazed with sleep, he thought of introducing "a new category of dreams which were not subject to the mechanisms of condensation and displacement but were to be described as 'phantasies during sleep'. Closer examination showed that this rarity among dreams showed the same gaps and flaws in its structure as any other, and for that reason I dropped the category of 'dream-phantasies' " (p. 331).

Thirty years later, Freud added a footnote: "Whether rightly I am now uncertain." As these few words indicate, Freud was on the verge of acknowledging the existence of the category of sensible and well-constructed dreams. Allowing for two categories of dreams, Freud might have felt obliged to reconsider his theory. Instead, while admitting his doubts, he continued as if nothing had happened. In the same footnote, his editor, Strachey, added a remark of his own, reminding the reader that Freud (1922) did argue in favour of such a category in some remarks at the end of the discussion of his first example in his paper "Dreams and Telepathy." It is apparent that Freud was well aware of the existence of categories of dreams and, we may presume, that, more than anyone else, he understood the implications of this fact on his own theory. This theory, to say it simply, was not made to account for the heterogeneity of dreams. Freud's undecidedness is thus understandable. And yet, one cannot help feeling disappointed that Freud did not direct the limelight on his dilemma, but rather preferred to leave it ambiguously lit.

The most perplexing of all his writings dealing with the question of logical dreams is his essay "On Dreams" (1901). Without much preamble, Freud suggested a complete taxonomy of dreams, dividing them into three categories: (1) "dreams which make *sense* and are . . . *intelligible,* which that is to say, can be inserted without further difficulty into the context of our mental life. We have numbers of such dreams"; (2) dreams which, although they "have a clear sense, nevertheless have a *bewildering* effect because we cannot see how to fit that sense into our mental life"; and (3) "dreams which are without either sense or intelligibility, which seem *disconnected, confused* and *meaningless*" (pp. 642–43).

Here Freud suggested a continuum ranging from sensible and intelligible, through sensible but bewildering, to disconnected and meaningless dreams. One wonders whether it was the same Freud who a year or so earlier described the transformation of dream-thoughts into the content of "the" dream as "completely different from (waking thought) and for that reason not immediately comparable with it" (Freud 1900, p. 507). Similarly, in his *Outline of Psychoanalysis* (1940), Freud stated: "A dream then is a psychosis, with all the absurdities, delusions and illusions of a psychosis" (p. 172). By "a dream," Freud implied all dreams, and not one of the many categories of dreams.

Whom should we believe; the Freud of 1901 or the Freud of 1900 and 1940? Who was right, Freud (1900) who rejected the possibility of "phantasies during sleep," (another name for rational and intelligible dreams), or Freud (1922) who had no doubts that they exist, or Freud, in 1930, who could not make up his mind? One thing, at any rate, seems to be certain. All the theories of behavior, including Freud's, which are based on the assumption that dreams by definition, are bizarre and different from our waking thoughts, paid too much respect to the traditional view or the stereotyped notion of dreams; their feelings of respect were strong enough to let the theorists disregard what their ears and eyes taught them.

Consider, for example, the following dream: "I was in a wood; it was threaded with watercourses, and in the darkest place I saw a circular pool, surrounded by dense undergrowth. Half immersed in the water lay the strangest and most wonderful creature: a round animal, shimmering in opalescent hues, and consisting of innumerable little cells, or of organs shaped like tentacles. It was a giant radiolarian, measuring about three feet across. It seemed to me indescribably wonderful that this magnificent creature should be lying there undisturbed, in the hidden place, in the clear, deep water. It aroused in me an intense desire for knowledge, so that I awoke with a beating heart" (p. 105). This was a dream of Jung (1961) in his student days, recalled in his *Memories, Dreams, Reflections*. Jung (1945), as we have seen, was of the opinion that, "usually a dream is a disconcerting product distinguished by . . . lack of logic, questionable morality, uncouth form, and apparent absurdity and nonsense" (p. 245).

Jung (1961) had other dreams, too, such as the following one: "I saw coming from the door (of my mother) a faintly luminous, indefinite figure whose head detached itself from the neck and floated along in front of it, in the air, like a little moon. Immediately another head was produced and again detached itself. This process was repeated six or seven times" (p. 33).

If Jung and Freud had been uninfluenced by what I label the stereotyped notion of dreams, and were led by their own experience alone, I dare to surmise that both of them would have agreed to reject the conception of "a" dream. Their own dreams would have been enough to convince them that dreams are heterogeneous, and that there are categories of dreams, bizarre and logical. Furthermore, in any sample of dreams, more rational and intelligible dreams will be found than absurd and nonsensical ones.

Almost one hundred years ago, Calkins (1893), complaining "that the phenomenon of dreaming has rarely been discussed or investigated in a thorough and experimental manner" (p. 331), resolved to do just that. She and her male coworker recorded each night for eight weeks, immediately after waking from a dream, every remembered feature of it. At the end of this period she had recorded 205 dreams in 55 nights and her coworker had recorded 170 dreams in 46 nights. She grouped these dreams under the headings: rather improbable; very improbable; impossible. Under the head "impossible" were included only natural impossibilities, such as an elephant having a conversation with the dreamer, and a skull transferred by a surgical operation to the head of a living subject, but not such dreams as those of meeting with people who had died.

Here is a dream reported by Calkins as a "very improbable dream":

> (I am at first the reader of a story; then the servant and then the sister of the hero; finally I assume my own character). A hero goes through great distresses, runs up and down long stair-cases, has false information given him (here, the scene is partly in Italy, looking off to the Mediterranean); finally after eluding pursuers, the hero plunges through a sort of tunnel in the snow, which, a guide-post warns us, is very dangerous. I, his servant, follow; we are unharmed; we realize that the guide-post was treacherous. We reach, up many stairs, the home of the hero's beloved. He and I, now his sister, enter the room; she is not there. Then we enter the dining-room. He demands her. The family shudder, and one says: *"Du hast sie"* (You have her). I realize that she has died, and cry out to him: *"Ich felicitire dich* (My congratulations). She is yours now. Here, *eine untreue Familie* (an unfaithful family) has kept her from you." It now appears that all the hero's ribs are broken. I advise him to die and join his beloved, but for some reason he refuses. Suddenly, the hero turns into my father, whose ribs are broken, and who is questioning whether he would not better die, while I (in my own character) refuse to let him. (P. 336)

The "rather improbable" dreams, as one may understand, are rational dreams which leave some doubt about whether to define them as improbable. Table 1 gives the number of "impossible" and "improbable" dreams in the records of both experimenters:

TABLE 1. The Distribution of Categories of Dreams in Calkins' Study

	Rather improbable	*Very improbable*	*Impossible*	*Total of "absurd"*
♀	42	35	3	80 (39%)
♂	29	28	5	62 (36%)

Note that "impossible dreams" comprise a negligible quantity. More important, however, is the fact that almost two-thirds of the dreams were logical.

In Calkins' precise statement: "The most important feature of the present investigation is really the very prosaic and ordinary nature of most of the dreams recorded" (p. 320). Lately, Snyder (1970) collected 635 dream reports from fifty-eight subjects, males and females, wakened from their REM sleep. Calkins would have been pleased by his report: "By far the largest portion of (dream) reports were entirely credible as descriptions of waking events. . . . There were many reports which did display these very dreamlike features of bizarreness and incredibleness, but the really surprising thing to us was just how uncommon these were" (p. 146).

While not explicitly stating so, both Calkins and Snyder found that during a night's sleep one generates two kinds of dreams, rational and bizarre ones, with the rational predominating. Somewhat before Snyder's study, Foulkes (1962) established that dreaming occurs continuously throughout the sleeping hours; subjects who wakened from NREM sleep, as well as REM sleep, reported having dreams. This finding contrasts with the view prevailing at the time. An equally important finding was that there are important differences between dreams generated during REM and NREM. The dreams reported form REM sleep were "dreamy." They could be described as hallucinatory, varying in vividness, bizarreness, and the amount of participation of the dreamer. Foulkes labeled them "dreams." Dreams reported from NREM were not hallucinatory, but consisted more of thoughts, usually somewhat drifting and undirected. Foulkes labeled them "thoughts."

While the allocation of "dreams" to REM and "thoughts" to NREM periods of sleep has become less certain than it was at the time of Foulkes' study (Broughton 1975), the distinction between two types of mental activity during sleep seems quite well founded. We must then conclude that dreams do not live up to their reputation: they are not "dreamy." The majority of our dreams are like our waking thoughts. "The question facing the dream psychologist," Palombo (1978) stated, "remains what it has always been: why, if dreams are meaningful, are the formal properties of dreams so unlike those of waking thought? . . . why the strangeness of the dream language?" (p.3). In truth, however, dreams pose us with a different problem: during a night's sleep we generate two kinds of dreams; why is this so, and what relevance may it have for a general theory of mind?

Even before we are in a position to answer these questions satisfactorily, we may state that Freud's theory of dreams was, in fact, an attempt to solve a nonexisting riddle. "Why, if dreams are meaningful, are the formal properties of dreams so unlike those of waking thought, why the strangeness of the dream language?" It was this apparent contradiction that Freud addressed in his theory of dreams. Is it really a contradiction, though; is the dream indeed strange? We are reading nothing into the facts, but rather letting them speak for themselves when we state that the majority of dreams are like our waking thoughts while a minority of dreams are bizarre and improbable and a few of them are sheer nonsense. It is amazing that this fact, daily observable and repeatedly confirmed, lives an underground existence, while the ungrounded stereotyped notion of dreams enjoys a scientific status.

What better evidence for the hypnotizing power of this stereotype than the terms suggested by Foulkes: "dreams" and "thoughts." Cassell's *New English Dictionary* defines dream as "thoughts and images that pass through the mind of a sleeping person." Thoughts generated during sleep are dreams as much as imagery is. Incidentally, this was also Freud's (1900) understanding. He knew "that not every dream exhibits this transformation of thoughts from idea into sensory image. There are dreams which consist only of thoughts but which cannot on that account be denied the essential nature of dreams" (p. 535). Thus, the "thoughts" of Foulkes are, in fact, dreams; rational and intelligible dreams. In spite of the fact that he proved, experimentally, that there are two categories of dreams, Foulkes allowed the stereotype of dreams, i.e., bizarre imagery, to continue usurping the title of "the" dream.

Words are power, though their influence is difficult to weigh or measure, and labeling is never without a consequence. Labeling one category of dreams, the heir of the stereotyped notion, as "dream" necessitates using a complex language in order to distinguish between dreams and "dreams." Eventually, people may yield to the force of the stereotype and return to thinking that dreams, by definition, are "dreamy." Indeed, Foulkes' study and its far-reaching implications notwithstanding, the laboratory research of dreams continues to concentrate on REM sleep; there are still experts who write on "dreaming sleep" and worry about the dangers of eliminating dreaming by suppressing REM sleep. Antrobus (1978) tells us that "some physicians in an elite training hospital avoid very early morning surgery and the administration of REM-suppressing tranquilizers in order to minimize risk of psychotic behavior in their patients!" (p. 485); Writing on sleep disorders, Ablon and Mack (1979) stated that "it is commonly supposed that sleepwalking is the acting out of a dream. This is not readily reconcilable with the discovery that sleepwalking occurs during NREM sleep" (p. 653). Both the experts of the training hospital and Ablon and Mack seemed to suggest that NREM mentation is not really a dream. A dream is a "dream."

The charm of REM sleep in dream research was established by the mistaken conclusion—corrected by Foulkes—that we dream only during REM periods. This mistake, though, has been eliminated, but the temptation to equate dreams with "dreams" has not. Snyder's (1970) study, quoted above, dealt with dream reports from REM sleep; yet it concluded with the statement that the dreamlike features of bizarreness and incredibleness were quite uncommon. Snyder saw in this finding "the really surprising thing" in his research. Indeed where, if not in REM sleep, may we meet dreams fitting their stereotype? But, surprisingly, even the dreams of REM sleep are, to a great extent, "thought"-like.

The heterogeneity, and not the untenable stereotyped notion, of dreams is the basic fact with which the psychology of dreams must deal. During a night's sleep we generate two kinds of dreams. The fact that the majority of them are rational and intelligible contradicts the contention that the origin of any dream must be in an alogical mental system. There is nothing new or surprising in this statement. One hundred years ago, Calkins (1893) put it as follows: "This tendency of consciousness, both sleeping and waking, to coerce experience into some reasonable shape is one of the most interesting aspects of the study of dreams" (p. 341).

While the heterogeneity of dreams does necessitate a revision of Freud's position that any dream originates in the repressed unconscious, it is possible that at least bizarre dreams are produced by this unconscious. Their bizarreness, then, would indicate the laws governing the events in this unconscious. Alas, Freud expressly prevented such a possibility. It was Freud's (1900) opinion that dreaming and sleeping are incongruous, for sleeping should mean a cessation of conscious mental activity: "Bearing in mind the expediency which is everywhere else the rule, we may ask why a dream, that is an unconscious wish, is given the power to interfere with sleep, that is with the fulfillment of the preconscious wish" (p. 577).

Clearly, to Freud's understanding, a dream—any dream—begins as a (repressed) unconscious wish. Thus, to continue this line of reasoning, a dream is bound to be different from our waking thought. But it is not.

Actually, even if all dreams and not just a minority of them violate logic and reality, Freud's theory would face an insoluble dilemma. As one may recall, Freud (1940) explained the presumed absurdity of "the" dream by the peculiar modes of functioning of the repressed unconscious. "It is only (through the dreams) that we learn the laws which govern the passage of events in the unconscious and the respects in which they differ from the rules that are familiar to us in waking thought" (p. 167). Freud suggested here that dreams bear the imprint of the peculiarities of unconscious mental functioning. Through the characteristics of dreams we may learn about the nature of the unconscious; this, in fact, is the reason for our interest in dreams.

However, Freud (1900) also suggested a quite different explanation of the presumed absurdity of dreams. In *The Interpretation of Dreams,* Freud repeatedly stated that "the dream-thoughts are immediately comprehensible, as soon as we have learnt them" (p. 277). He also said he was "driven to conclude that two fundamentally different kinds of psychical processes are concerned in the formation of dreams. One of these produces perfectly rational dream-thoughts, of no less validity than normal thinking; while the other treats these thoughts in a manner which is in the highest degree bewildering and irrational. We have already . . . segregated this second psychical process as being the dream-work proper" (p. 597). Freud seemed to be quite certain of his position here. His formulation is not qualified by doubts or second thoughts. He might have had some, though, for as we have seen, he also thought that the latent thoughts responsible for generating the dream are irrational and different from our waking thoughts. Here, however, the "irrationality" of the manifest dream was stated to be due to the dream-work, which is a function of the ego. Are the latent dream-thoughts rational or absurd and nonsensical?

If all the absurdities and peculiarities of dreams are effected by the psychical censorship, that is, by system ego, what lessons do dreams teach us? Do they disclose some remarkable features of our conscious cognizing, or rather, of the laws governing unconscious processes? If it is system ego which surprises itself by producing such peculiar pieces of mental work, how can dreams be understood to display the laws of an illogically working unconscious mental system?

"At bottom," Freud summarized his view, "dreams are nothing other than a particular *form* of thinking. . . . It is the *dream-work* which creates that form, and it alone is the essence of dreaming—the explanation of its peculiar nature" (p. 506n–7n). This statement, too, lets us conclude that the latent-dream thoughts *are* rational, and it is only because of the struggle with an inner psychic force, which opposes the realization of these thoughts, that their conscious expression becomes so peculiar. But, in this case, one must ask again: are dreams indeed capable of proving Freud's suggestion with regard to the primary process?

If the indispensable motive power of any dream, the latent dream-thoughts, were strange and incomprehensible, then dreams could teach us the laws of unconscious processes. Since, however, in the opinion of Freud "the dream-thoughts are immediately comprehensible, as soon as we have learnt them" (p. 277), and the strangeness of a dream is due to a manipulation by system ego, we must conclude that, the thoughts which have infiltrated from the unconscious are logical and comprehensible. Thus, we have arrived where we were not supposed to arrive, at the conclusion that unconscious processes are not different from the conscious ones. One cannot say that rational dream-thoughts, arising from the unconscious, were made irrational by a mental censorship which is an ego-function, and at the same time conclude that it was proven that dreams invariably originate in an irrationally working system.

Freud's contradictory views on the nature of what he thought to be the indispensable motive power of any dream may affect his whole theory of behavior. If the latent dream-thoughts were originally logical and communicative and became distorted only later on, during dreaming, what evidence had Freud for supporting his concept of primary process and two differently working psychic systems in general? If, however, the dream-thoughts, originating in the peculiarly working unconscious, are nonsensical due to the characteristics of their place of origin, then why further distort them? The concepts of mental censorship, dream-work, and, in fact, repression may have meaning only if we assume that all these constructs relate to rational and intelligible thoughts. But, if the motivating force of dreams is meaningless utterings, which, in any case, are "distorted" enough so as not to be comprehensible, why further distort them? Freud did not solve this problem; in fact, he did not tackle it at all. Therefore, we are left with no alternative but to point out this impasse: if the dream-thoughts are rational, then the presence of well-thought-out ideas in the id counters the assumption of two mental systems characterized by different modes of reasoning: on the other hand, irrational utterings as the basis of dreams make superfluous the conception of "repression" and the whole metastructure built upon this concept.

Although Freud maintained that there *is* a mental system governed by the rules of primary process, he also let us believe that dream-thoughts and repressed wishes underlying neurotic symptoms are perfectly rational. One wonders how such rational and well-articulated thoughts can prove the existence of an alogically working mental system.

A THEORY OF DREAMS

From Calkins through Freud to Foulkes and Snyder, to mention only the few whose findings we have quoted above, researchers have shown that we generate two kinds of dreams: probable and improbable ones, dreams and "phantasies" in sleep, "dreams" and "thoughts." And yet, as if we had not perceived what lay before our eyes, we did what the stereotype of dreams demanded of us to do. We learned and taught that dreams are different from our waking thoughts, and we thought of this difference as the key, the "open sesame," to the mysteries of mental life. One may hope that we will eventually abandon the stereotype, and consider the consequences of the heterogeneity of dreams on our understanding of behavior.

During a night's sleep, we generate both logical and bizarre dreams. Why is that so? In these days of burgeoning interest in the differences in functioning of the cerebral hemispheres, it is quite natural to investigate whether the heterogeneity of dreams produced during a night's sleep is contingent on a shift in dominance between the two hemispheres. Such a contingency, indeed, has been found. Goldstein, Stolzfuss, and Gardocki (1972) found a shift of increased left to right ratio of integrated EEG, indicating a relative desynchronization or greater activity of the right hemisphere during REM sleep. Bakan (1977) summarized many findings and added some interesting speculations in favour of the thesis that cerebral dominance shifts during sleep from right hemisphere dominance during REM to left hemisphere dominance during NREM sleep.

Such a shift in the dominance of cerebral hemispheres may, indeed, explain what seemed to Freud to be a mystery: the hallucinatory quality of our dreams. However, the other distinguishing aspect, the bizarreness, is still unexplained. Nowhere in the literature dealing with the psychological effect of separating the two cerebral hemispheres by cutting through the corpus callosum has it ever been shown or argued that the reasoning controlled by the right hemisphere is bizarre, and impervious to logic and reality testing. Quite on the contrary, mute as it is, the right hemisphere has proved to be as useful and "intelligent" as the left one.

And yet, a study of Ehrlichman and Wiener (1980) indicates that the shift in dominance from left to right hemisphere and back to the left may explain why dreams generated during REM, but not during NREM periods of sleep, are often bizarre. REM sleep, as one may recall, was also called paradoxical sleep, because of the contradiction between mental activation and deep body relaxation. REMs, which were then regarded as the only dreaming periods of sleep, are characterized by a motor relaxation. On the other hand, sleeptalking, sleepwalking, and, in general, body activities which would demand a rise in muscle tone, occur during NREM sleep. To be attentive or alert demands a similar rise in muscle tone.

Ehrlichman and Wiener's (1980) study suggests a similar fluctuation in the levels of mental effort as a function of the prevalence of the left or the right hemisphere. They wrote, though, of grades of concentration and not of levels of mental effort. Ehrlichman and Wiener requested their subjects to engage in covert, self-generated types of mental activity, while they lay quietly on a cot with their eyes closed. The tasks were like this: please compose a letter, subvocally, about some topic of interest to you. Concentrate on the composition of the letter subvocally. Or: is there any orchestral (nonvocal) melody which you are familiar with, that you can mentally reproduce? For the next two minutes please concentrate on hearing this melody in your mind. Do not hum it, but rather hear it.

Ehrlichman and Wiener define concentration as one's ability to engage in the task as requested without being distracted or having one's attention wander. Their subjects rated themselves on a seven-point scale, which ranged from inability to concentrate to complete involvement. They found, as expected, that higher verbal ratings were associated with relatively greater left hemisphere activation, and higher imagery with relatively greater right hemisphere activation.

Unexpectedly, they also found a correlation between better concentration and greater left hemisphere activation. Nothing in the hemispheric literature, as they put it, led them to anticipate a substantive relationship between concentration ratings and EEG asymmetry. An exclusive emphasis on verbal and visuospatial processes as correlated with the left and right hemisphere, respectively, may be shortsighted, they think. Many other functions, such as concentration, are controlled asymmetrically by the two hemispheres.

One may say, then, that REM sleep, controlled by the right hemisphere, lacks the conditions for an effortful concentrated mental activity; mental activity, however, to be efficient, does demand effort.

One is reminded of one of the favorite authors of William James, Bergson, whose concept of mental effort was a contribution cognitive psychologists may still find useful today. This is how Bergson (1901) formulated his thesis of mental effort:

> You imagine that in order to hear a dog barking, and to know that it is a dog that barks, you have nothing to do. That is a great mistake. You accomplish, without suspecting it, a considerable effort. You take your entire memory, all of your accumulated experience, and you bring this formidable mass of memories to converge upon a single point, in such a way as to insert exactly in the sources you heard that one of your memories which is the most capable of being adapted to it. You exert, then, continuously, every moment of the day, an enormous effort. (P. 22)

According to Bergson, our waking life is a period of uninterrupted mental effort, even when one thinks that one is doing nothing—for, at every minute, one has to choose and exclude. "That is what it is to be aware . . . it is to will." In sleep, however, one no longer wills, one lets oneself go. This is why he thought it easy to explain the incoherence of the dream. "As it is characteristic of the dream not to demand a complete adjustment between the memory image and the sensation, but on the contrary, to allow some play between them, very different memories can suit the same sensation" (p. 24).

The same sensation—one can immediately grasp here the essence of Bergson's theory of dreams. It was intended to explain the differences between perception, realistic and subserving adaptation, in wakefulness, and the inaccurate and strange elaborations of the same stimuli, during sleep. He did not consider the possibility that dreaming, like daydreaming, while not impervious to external stimuli, is essentially independent of perception and unfolds in parallel to it.

On the other hand, his concept of mental effort is of value today as it was in his time. Perception, that is, the process of giving meaning to external stimuli, is indeed an active process. But so is any attempt to retrieve memory. Without the mental effort of judging, selecting, and eliminating all the ingredients of a memory code except for the one relevant at that moment, our waking mentation would not differ from that which produces the most bizarre, confused, and disconnected dreams.

The concept of mental effort, as one may recall, was the "missing link" in the theory of microgenesis of Schilder. Applying this concept to the questions of dreaming, we may assume (Giora 1981) that during sleep there are fluctuations in the level of mental effort the dreamer is capable of mobilizing and that, as a result, dreams generated during a period of high mental effort will be different from dreams generated during a period of low mental effort. With exceptions, as we have seen earlier, the two phases of sleep may be distinguished by their capacity to mobilize mental effort, to push the microgenesis of dream-thoughts to their final stage. During NREM sleep we are capable of a quite normal evolving of the process of microgenesis and the dreams generated here will be "thoughtlike." REM sleep is the phase of lower mental effort, of the incompletely unfolding microgenesis. The dreams generated here may contain interim positions of words and thoughts, instead of final positions (e.g., the use of *luggage* for *language*), and inevitably they will be judged as incomprehensible or bizarre.

These fluctuations during sleep in the level of mental effort necessary for completing the microgenesis of thoughts are the reason for generating both logical and bizarre dreams.

I would like to report briefly here an experiment designed to test the assertion that during NREM sleep the processes of microgenesis are accomplished and, at any rate, are accomplished more completely than during REM sleep. The procedure applied in this experiment was influenced by an important finding of Fiss, Klein, and Bokert (1966). These authors awakened their subjects from periods of REM sleep and immediately handed them a Thematic Apperception Test (TAT) card asking the subject to make up a story about it. It was found that stories produced after interrupted REM sleep were longer, more visually complex, emotional, and bizarre than stories told during control waking periods. That is to say, the features of cognition prevailing during REM sleep were "carried over" into the waking state close to this particular sleep stage. This finding of Fiss et al. led me to assume that by interrupting REM and

NREM stages of sleep and asking our subjects immediately to perform some task, we might capture the "carried-over" characteristics of the cognition prevailing during REM and NREM, respectively.

Six volunteer subjects (three males and three females, in their twenties) participated in this experiment. Before preparing themselves for sleep, they learned for five minutes a list of thirty-two rare words together with their definitions. The sleep of each subject was interrupted twice: once in REM and once in NREM sleep. Three subjects were awakened first from REM and three subjects first from NREM sleep. The experimenter read to the awakened subjects nine randomly chosen definitions from the list of thirty-two and asked the subjects to name the appropriate words.

It was immediately apparent that subjects awakened from NREM sleep were quicker and more successful in retrieving their learning than when awakened from REM sleep ($t=2.5512, p<0.01$). The possible meaning of this finding is underscored by the fact that more subjects were in a "tip-of-the-tongue" situation when awakened from REM than from NREM sleep. This difference, though, did not reach statistical significance ($t=1.5932, p>0.05$).

These two findings seem to be two sides of a coin: the process of microgenesis necessary for finding a word is, by and large, accomplished during NREM sleep, but not during REM sleep. During REM sleep, it often gets stuck somewhere between the preparatory stages of the words to be evolved. The subject knows that he knows the word and yet he is not able to retrieve it. Instead, he produces words which, as an interim position, may be excused, but taken by themselves are peculiar or nonsensical.

These differences in cognition during REM and NREM sleep were found at a time when the subject was requested to reproduce a single word. Let us now imagine that someone is on his way to develop an idea or many interlocking ideas. Obviously, the differences in the level of cognition will become more evident and more salient. This, in fact, is what Foulkes has found: the dreams generated during NREM sleep are usually short and make sense, while the dreams of REM sleep are vivid, emotional, complex, and bizarre. The findings of Foulkes and of our experiment are complementary and support each other. The differences in the quality of dreams generated during REM and NREM sleep, found by Foulkes, may be explained by a shift in dominance of the cerebral hemispheres and by the differences in mental effort the sleeping person is able to mobilize during the different stages of sleep.

This suggestion, that the differences in the ability to mobilize mental effort are the reason for the heterogeneity of dreams, calls up a possibility dealt with earlier, that the pecularities of dreams are the result of the lowering of efficiency of psychic functions during sleep. Freud did not disprove or even attempt to refute the possibility that the peculiarities of dreams may be explained by a lowering in the efficiency of mental functions during sleep. Instead, he argued by means of a quote from Fechner (1889), that "If the scene of action of psychophysical activity were the same in sleeping and waking, dreams could, in my view, only be a prolongation at a lower degree of intensity of waking ideational life and, moreover, would necessarily be of the same material and form. But the facts are quite otherwise" (Freud 1900, pp. 520–21).

However, the characteristics of dreams may fit both of the competing explanations. Disconnected dreams which accept the most violent contradictions, very much like the similar phenomena of the hypnotic trance, may be explained by a suspension of the critical faculties as well as by the assumption of two modes of thinking. In fact, the first suggestion seems more plausible and in need of less evidence than the second one. For example, Straus (1956) remarked that the dream does not condense, as Freud assumed, many "elements" into one. Rather, the dreamer is incapable of stabilizing discrimination. While relating to a particular issue, Straus actually hints at the broader one, that the characteristics of dreams may be equally well explained and in a simpler and more elegant way by the conception of a lowered mental efficiency in sleeping as by Freud's suggestion of two mental systems which pursue incompatible aims and are characterized by totally different modes of functioning.

Recalling the results of our analysis here and especially Freud's contradictory explanations of the assumed bizarreness of dreams, the suggestion of lowered efficiency of psychic functions during sleep seems not only equally possible but preferable to the theory of primary and secondary processes. Let us, however, emphasize, that in contrast to earlier authors who accepted the stereotyped notion of dreams and thought of sleep as a unity, we pointed to a rise and fall in the level of mental effort. During the ebb of mental alertness, we intend to think and communicate as clearly and intelligibly as we do during the tide, but we fail. This is why during a night's sleep we generate both rational and bizarre dreams.

THE FUNCTION OF DREAMS

This understanding of the characteristics of dreams enables us to have second thoughts on the question of the function of dreams. In Freud's (1900) opinion, dreaming and sleeping are incongruous, for a dream, by definition, interrupts sleep. The reason given by Freud for this interruption of the wish to sleep was as follows:

> allowing the dream to take its course and expending a certain amount of more or less detached attention on it is an economy of energy compared with holding the unconscious as tightly under control at night as in the daytime. . . . Experience shows us that dreaming is compatible with sleeping, even if it interrupts sleep several times during the night. One wakes up for an instant and then falls asleep again at once. It is like brushing away a fly in one's sleep: a case of *ad hoc* awakening. (P. 577)

In order to agree with this explanation, we must agree that we are programmed to phasically sever our contact, for many hours daily, with the world around us. The preconscious mind, in Freud's terms, which communicates with the environment and is in charge of adaptation and survival, is allowed periodically to reject information coming from the environment. If this were true, it would be impossible to wake us, whether by calling our name, making indistinct noise, or by silence. The anecdotal miller, though, woke up because his machines for grinding corn turned silent; this anecdote is a generalizable experience of people over the ages. At the other extreme, Ullman's (1966) controlled experiments on the telepathic reception of messages in sleeping and their incorporation into dreams may indicate that while sleeping we continuously receive external and internal stimuli and elaborate their meaning. The mind is only metaphorically vacant, though, and in truth, it works incessantly. The silence of mind is death and not sleep.

The fully awake person is integrated with his environment, ready to learn about it and cope with it adaptively; while indulging in daydreams, one never seeks outer stimuli, one is momentarily "introverted," and assimilates into the ongoing mentation the messages one receives. A fatigued or drowsy man struggles to maintain contact with his surroundings, but he is able to do so only intermittently. While sleeping, one will recede from all activity in one's relationship with the environment. This passivity is the main behavioral characteristic of sleep. But cognition does not cease even in the midst of passivity; it is only that its level of organization will shift. In other words, we may say that there are many states of mind, each characterized by different interaction with the environment and by a specific cognitive organization, but there is no state of mind without any interaction with the environment and cognition.

Cognition has many levels, as has consciousness. In fact, the level of cognition is one of the distinctive features of the level of consciousness. They are different aspects of a common essence, namely, living. Living means interacting with the environment, not haphazardly or suicidally, but adaptively and intelligently. Yet, this responding to nature, as Susanne Langer put it, is not steady; there are rises and falls in its quality. The reasons for these fluctuations were quite convincingly clarified by Oswald (1962): "If the degree of excitement of the intact reticular formation were to fluctuate, either by reason of inherent properties or by reason of the oscillations which are inevitable in a system governed by the homeostatic devices, one would expect to see these fluctuations of bodily functions which are characteristic of sleep and wakefulness" (p. 22).

Such momentary fluctuations, as well as the circadian rhythms, are the causes of the different levels of responsiveness and the concomitant cognitive organization. Fluctuating, though, in its adaptiveness to reality and in its value in preparing our responses to nature, the living brain never ceases to process information. One cannot, therefore, assign a special function to the information processing in certain states of mind, such as dreaming, while taking it for granted at other times. This is, however, what Freud (1900) did. Assuming that sleep and dreaming are incompatible, he went on to explain how, then, dreaming is possible. Elaborating on Aristotle's "accurate but bald definition," according to which a dream is a thinking under the conditions of sleep, he stated: "Since, then, our daytime thinking produces psychical acts of such various sorts—judgements, inferences, denials, expectations, intentions and so on—why should it be obliged during the night to restrict itself to the production of wishes alone?" (p. 550).

In fact, Freud suggested that not wishes in general but repressed unconscious wishes took advantage of the sleeping, i.e., inactive, nonresponding (preconscious) mind. In opposition to this view, the logic of the condition of living and the results of experiments agree that the mind, conscious and unconscious, never stops absorbing information and responding to it. The function of this cognizing, but not its efficiency, is the selfsame throughout all levels of existence: knowing the world around us and ourselves. Dreaming fulfills the same function or, to say it pointedly, it has no special function.

STYLES OF DREAMS

The basic question facing the dream psychologist, as suggested above, is this: why do we generate two types of dreams? My answer combines the theories of mental effort and microgenesis. In this view, thoughts are seen to evolve gradually out of the codes in which our memories are stored. This rather laborious process consists of many steps and demands certain mental effort. Under conditions of low mental effort, the microgenesis of thoughts stops at an interim position, and the product generated may indeed be bizarre or incomprehensible. During the hours of sleep, our level of mental effort fluctuates, which causes some of our dreams to differ from our waking thoughts. These bizarre dreams occur, usually, but not exclusively, during REM sleep when we are able to mobilize less mental effort than during NREM sleep.

This fluctuation of mental effort during sleep quite regularly varies in relation to the shifts from NREM to REM sleep and back again. Yet, in accord with what we know of mental functioning in general, we may expect the fluctuation in mental effort to be subject to individual variations. While most people have two main levels of mental effort, it is logical to assume that there are also dreamers whose dreams are "thought-like" only or bizarre with a hallucinatory quality only. We must assume the existence of personal styles of dreaming: a mixed style, of people who generate both types of dreams, and pure styles, of people who generate bizarre or logical dreams only.

Before elaborating on the question of styles of dreaming, it is necessary to make consistent the terminology used here concerning the two types of dreams. Foulkes designated the two types as "dreams" and "thought-like" mentations. Freud (1901) distinguished between dreams which make sense and are intelligible; dreams which although they have a clear sense, nevertheless have a bewildering effect because we cannot see that sense in our mental life; and dreams which are either without sense or intelligibility. I suggest the term "bizarre dreams" for the category of dreams Freud described as being either without sense or intelligibility, dreams which seem disconnected and meaningless. For Freud's two other categories, i.e., dreams which make sense and are intelligible and dreams which have a clear sense but are bewildering because we cannot fit them into our waking life, I suggest the term "logical dreams."

This distinction between logical and bizarre dreams comes quite close to the concept and criteria applied by Snyder (1970). "Sometimes things are extremely unlikely from the standpoint of waking reality; yet, they are conceivable, so we would not necessarily judge these as bizarre." Conceivable but unlikely from the standpoint of the dreamer's waking reality—this seems to be a reformulation of Freud's second category. Snyder too seems then to argue that Freud's first two categories may be unified in one concept. "On the other hand, episodes which were plausible might contain just one single inconceivable element: for example, a cat suddenly turning into a rabbit. This would be sufficient to rate that report as at least moderately bizarre" (p. 146).

Aside from the quality of conceivability or inconceivability, Freud also evaluated the general composition of the dream-story, as connected or disconnected. We will do justice to all these considerations by defining a dream logical if its story is conceivable and shows an orderly sequence of events. Bizarre dreams are to be defined by one or more of the following criteria: inconceivable stories, fairy-tale happenings, and sudden shifts in setting.

According to these criteria, my students and I categorized hundreds of dreams with quite stable results: the majority of subjects, indeed, recall both logical and bizarre dreams. At the extremes was a minority of pure types (with a tendency toward having only bizarre dreams among the American students and a tendency toward having only logical dreams among the Israeli students). Thus, we may characterize any given dreamer as of a mixed style, a pure bizarre style, or a pure logical style of dreaming.

Is this style of dreaming a stable feature of one's personality or just a reflection of one's momentary mood? In order to answer this question, Miriam Rass (1983) asked forty-eight volunteer subjects in their twenties to keep a dream-log and for two weeks to write down every morning, as fully as possible, any dream they recalled. A month later, they were again requested to keep a dream-log for a week.

Some reported more than five dreams and a few reported less than that. The dream-logs containing fewer than five dreams were excluded from this study; consequently, in the first set forty-four (out of forty-eight) subjects participated, and in the second set twenty (out of twenty-two who had agreed to the additional effort requested). In order to determine the subjects' style of dreaming, three judges, independently and in accord with the criteria summarized above, categorized the first five dreams of every diary. The correlations between the evaluations of the judges were convincing: 0.89 ($p<0.01$).

In the evaluation of Judge A, three of the four subjects who in the first set dreamed logical dreams only, reported logical dreams only in the second set, and one subject reported dreams of mixed style. From five subjects whose dreams were originally of bizarre style, four reported bizarre dreams only in the second set and one reported dreams of mixed style. Finally, from the original eleven subjects who dreamed in mixed style, nine reported dreams of mixed style in the second set, one reported bizarre dreams only and one logical dreams only ($x^2=19.074$, $p<0.0008$). Judge B evaluated the consistency between the two sets of dreams to be of the level $p<0.019$; the third judge found it to be of the level $p<0.0001$. Combined, these results reveal that one's style of dreaming is remarkably stable ($p<0.01$).

There are then people who, unlike the majority, dream one type of dream only. These pure styles of dreaming, quite evidently, cannot be explained by the fluctuation in the level of mental effort during sleep. On the contrary, it looks as if these dreamers do not experience any fluctuation during sleep at all, or at least, not to any considerable degree. Broughton (1975) indeed indicated that sometimes "dreamlike" reports can follow awakening from either REM or NREM sleep, and we may assume that those dreamers are of pure bizarre style. Regarding the dreamers of pure logical style, one is reminded of a study of McDonald, Shallenberger, and Carpenter (1968). They found that individuals who are more alert during wakefulness have stronger spontaneous (GSR) discharges during sleep than those who are less alert while awake. That is to say, there are individual differences in mental alertness, as measured by GSR, and these differences also prevail during sleep. It seems likely that the more alert subjects of McDonald et al. are the people who dream logical dreams only.

Shall we then assume a similar continuity of the habitual level of mental effort in individuals whose style of dreaming is pure bizarre? If that should mean breakdown of reality testing and Aristotelian logic, then the answer must be no. Instead, considering the fact that the pure styles of dreaming constitute the two extreme positions in the continuum of styles,

I suggest that we draw a parallel between the extremes of heightened attention to logic versus casual disregard for violations of logic, and logical versus bizarre dream styles.

The fact that one is able to apply the rules of Aristotelian logic does not guarantee that one will be ready to make use of this ability. In fact, as Ross and Nisbett (1982) observed, "beliefs—from relatively narrow personal impressions to broader social theories—are remarkably resilient in the face of empirical challenges that seem logically devastating" (p. 144). Lord, Ross, and Lepper (1979) described one of the more simple and convenient ways to withstand the "assault" of facts not favorable to one's own belief or theory. They first selected subjects who either supported capital punishment and believed it to be an effective deterrent or opposed capital punishment and believed it not to be a deterrent. Then the subjects were presented with two purportedly authentic empirical studies. One provided empirical support for their position, the other opposed it. After reading these two studies, the two groups, proponents and opponents of capital punishment, rated their evaluations of the two studies and their own changes in attitude. The authors found that ratings dramatically revealed the capacity of theory holders to interpret new evidence in a manner that not only sustains but also strengthens their theories. Both proponents and opponents of capital punishment consistently rated the study that supported their beliefs as "more convincing" and "better conducted" than the study that opposed them.

Interestingly enough, Polanyi (1963) thought that this is the way things should be. "There must be at all times a predominantly accepted scientific view of the nature of things, in the light of which research is jointly conducted by members of the community of scientists; a strong presumption that any contradictory evidence has to be disregarded, even if it cannot be accounted for, in the hope it will eventually turn out to be false or irrelevant" (p. 1012). He acknowledged, though, the dangers of suppressing or disregarding evidence that runs counter to orthodox views; nevertheless, he urged scientific opinion to consider and decide "at its ultimate risk," how far it could allow dissent from its orthodoxy.

Lord and his associates and Polanyi seem to represent two extremes in relating to evidence which contradicts our belief; while Lord and his associates regarded it a shortcoming to persevere in one's belief in the face of empirical challenge, Polanyi supported such an orthodoxy because "scientific method is, and must be disciplined by an orthodoxy, which can permit only a limited degree of dissent." There is nothing wrong with disregarding some self-contradictions, Polanyi seems to suggest.

The inclination to "live" with self-contradiction while fully awake may become even more salient under the conditions of low mental effort prevailing during sleep and, thus, may generate bizarre dreams. He who is alert to pointing out differences and inconsistencies while awake will not agree with their existence even while sleeping and thus, may generate logical dreams. And there are, of course, the majority, who are neither overly scrupulous nor blithely unconcerned, but somewhere in between. Because of the fluctuation in their level of mental effort while asleep, their styles of dreaming may be mixed.

To see whether this construction is not only conceivable but also factual, Miriam Rass (1983) asked her subjects who kept dream-logs to participate in a sequential guessing game, based on Shouksmith's (1965) test. Her purpose here was to examine whether the dream style is indeed bizarre in those individuals who, as revealed by this test, are ready to "live" with inconsistencies.

In this sequential game, the subject was presented with white and red disks, one at a time, and had to guess whether or not the experimenter would present a red disk next. The subject's guesses obviously implied some hypothesis about the order of presentation of the disks. Four separate conditions were used. Under condition A, the red disk was presented on every alternate trial, beginning with the second one. Ten trials were given; thus the sequence was repeated five times. Under condition B, the red disk was shown on every third trial, beginning with the third. Fifteen trials were given; thus the sequence was repeated five times. Under condition C, the red disk was presented on trials 2, 8, and 16; since thirty-three trials were given, the sequence was repeated twice. Under condition D, the red disk was presented on trials 4, 6, and 9, with the sequence recurring three times.

Subjects were informed that there would be four different sequences. Under conditions A and B, it was rather easy to learn the pattern and predict the red disk's appearance. These two conditions may be likened to a preparatory phase, in which the subject developed certain expectations about the structure of events. Conditions C and D introduced the element of capriciousness into what seemed to be a comprehensible and predictable environment.

It was to be expected that persons who were alert to inconsistencies would be quicker in recognizing the need to abandon learned expectations than would those who tended to stick to their initial hypotheses despite contradictions. Yet even those who were tolerant of self-contradictions and were ready to "live" with them would eventually acknowledge the facts. What differentiated the two groups was the speed with which they came to terms with the reality. Thus, while alert individuals already felt the need to generate a new hypothesis under condition C, individuals tolerant of self-contradictions may have begun to adjust their expectations only later, under condition D.

As the results of planned comparison tests showed, the average of correct guesses of the subjects who dreamt logical dreams only was 3.000, those of mixed style of dreams 1.6786, and the average of the dreamers of bizarre dreams only 0.8000. A one-tailed analysis of variance showed a high-level correlation ($p < 0.0001$) between success in eliminating hypotheses contradicted by new evidence and styles of dreaming (DF: 2, sum of squares: 20.7292, mean squares: 10:3646, F: 14.700, $p < 0.0001$).

As expected, individuals whose style of dreaming is logical are the most vigilant in detecting inconsistencies and are immediately active in doing justice to all the known facts: individuals whose style of dreaming is bizarre are the most relaxed in their relation to facts which contradict their beliefs. In between these two extremes, we find the majority composed of individuals whose dreams are of mixed style. They display both a measure of vigilance and a measure of relaxation if confronted by self-contradiction. In the sleep state, the variance between the two extremes of this continuum becomes more salient. Those who are ready to "live" with contradictions are likely to be satisfied with the mental products generated during a period of low mental effort; their dreams will be bizarre. At the other extreme are persons who are alert to inconsistencies and quick to notice contradictory evidence. These persons will not become nonchalant even during sleep; their dreams will be logical. The majority of people are not as consistent; their mental products (both awake and asleep) will reflect the periodic rise and fall of their level of mental effort.

We see here a continuity between performance in wakefulness and in dreaming, and we may thus speak of one's cognitive style rather than of styles in dreaming. The style of dreaming is a particular instance of the broader category of cognitive style. Rather than a difference in thinking in wakefulness and in sleep, we see the same individually characteristic style prevailing in both states of consciousness. Dreams, then, cannot indicate, let alone prove, the existence of two kinds of thinking. If dreams indeed are the closest possible reflection of the unconscious mental process, then they reveal the homogeneity rather than heterogeneity of mental life.

A DREAM-QUESTIONNAIRE

Let us assume that during a night someone dreamed one hundred dreams, ninety logical and ten bizarre. If he were able, later on, to recall all of these dreams, we would define him as of pure logical style. If at least one-third of his dreams were bizarre and the rest logical, we would define him as a man of mixed style of dreaming. If, however, the dreamer whose style is logical is not able to recall all of his dreams, the probability is 0.0001% that the first five of his recalled dreams will be bizarre. If his dreams are mixed, two-thirds logical and one-third bizarre, the probability for recalling at first five logical or bizarre dreams is 0.5%. In other words, having a report of the first five dreams, we may be confident that in 99% of the cases these five dreams correctly identified his style of dreaming.

If the same dreamer (90% logical and 10% bizarre dreams) were to recall only three dreams, the probability that these dreams will be bizarre is 0.1%. If two-thirds of his dreams are logical and one-third bizarre, then the probability that these first three dreams will be bizarre is 4.3%. Thus, we may be confident that in 95% of the cases our identification of the *pure styles* of dreaming was correct.

This conclusion may have some practical consequences. Not everyone is prepared to keep a dream-log. Many more might be ready to spend fifteen to twenty minutes in answering the request: Please, write here three dreams of yours as fully as possible. Applying this questionnaire (Giora 1981), I asked fifty-six high school students (thirty-two girls and twenty-four boys, mean age fifteen years) to report three dreams. Nine students (five girls and four boys) whose dreams were all logical and nine students (seven girls and two boys) whose dreams were all bizarre were asked to participate in the sequential guessing game, described earlier. This test, as one may recall, reveals the differences in behavior if one is confronted by a self-contradiction (see table 2). We measured here only the difference between the correct guesses under conditions C and D. The smaller the difference, the sooner the subject took into account the conflicting evidence.

TABLE 2. Dream Styles and Differences in Eliminating Impaired Hypothesis

Styles of dreaming	*N*	$\bar{x}$	*SD*
logical	9	0.33	2.56
bizarre	9	4.77	3.27
	$t = 3.09$	$p < 0.01$	

The two groups did indeed differ in dealing with self-contradictions in the waking state. While awake, logical dreamers appeared to be sensitive in perceiving the incongruities, while bizarre dreamers were not. These results replicated the finding reported above of the subjects who kept a dream-log for two weeks. Both methods of collecting dreams (diary and questionnaire) allow us to establish the same correlations between styles of dreaming and styles of thinking in general.

Of course, the differences in relating to a challenge of one's belief are only one aspect of a more comprehensive issue and they alone may not define styles of thinking, such as the analytic versus holistic. A finding of Bruner, Goodnow, and Austin (1956) relevant to our discussion is that holistic individuals are less disconcerted by contradictory evidence than individuals whose strategy of knowledge attainment is analytic. Holistic individuals stick to their initial hypothesis, in spite of its being contradicted by some facts. In contrast, analytic individuals are more alert in recognizing incongruities and more ready to change their views accordingly. Individuals whose dreams are only logical may thus be regarded as having an analytic style of thinking, and individuals with bizarre dreams only as having a holistic style.

A further attribute of these styles of thinking is the speed of decision characteristic of each of them. While analytic individuals extensively scan their field, holistic individuals make up their mind without hesitating much, in a way which might almost be called impulsive. One may assume then that individuals who dream logical dreams only are slower in their decision than are their counterparts with bizarre dreams only.

In an experiment designed to elucidate the microgenesis of some optic illusions, Reynolds (1978) found some individual differences which may be interpreted as differences in the speed of decision making. He found that the illusory perception occurred only after 150 ms of processing time. Prior to the onset of the illusion, the parts of the figure are first processed independently, followed by the interaction of those parts. The optic illusion is an outcome of this interaction. But not everyone behaves in this way. With respect to the rod and frame test, Reynolds was able to show that for field-dependent subjects the tilt of the frame affects the perceived orientation of the rod after 100 ms of processing time. As compared with field-independents, field-dependent people make up their minds quickly or even impulsively: their strategy of knowledge attainment is likely to be holistic and their dreams bizarre.

The Necker cube seems to be an easy-to-handle and convenient way to test these individual differences in decision-making speed. If one fixates the Necker cube, its position in depth will change. Usually, at first, the perceived orientation of the cube is with the lower face as the side in front. After a while, however, this lower face will be seen to slant upwards as the bottom of the cube. As one continues to fixate, the perceived position fluctuates between the two views.

While the reasons for these shifts in position remain unclear, we can postulate that the rate of shifts indicates the speed of making a decision. Thus, we would expect individuals whose dreams are of bizarre style and who make up their minds without much fuss to show a relatively high rate of reversal with the Necker cube. Conversely, individuals whose dreams are logical and who sample a great deal of information before making up their minds are expected to experience a relatively low rate of reversal. Forty-four freshmen volunteers were asked to write down three dreams as fully as possible; eight subjects had only logical and eight subjects only bizarre dreams. They were asked to fixate on the Necker cube (see figure 2) for one minute.

As can be seen from table 3, the subjects with logical dreams perceived significantly fewer fluctuations than did the subjects with bizarre dreams; one's style of dreaming indeed reflects one's style of thinking in wakefulness. Subjects who dream bizarre dreams only have a holistic strategy of knowledge attainment. In spite of contradictory evidence, they may stick to their initial hypothesis and, in general, behave in accord with the orthodoxy demanded by Polanyi. Conversely, subjects with logical dream style have an analytic strategy of knowledge-attainment, make up their minds only after extensively scanning their mental and visual field, and agree with Lord et al. that beliefs and facts must support each other.

Weaving these threads into one fabric, we may conclude that one's style

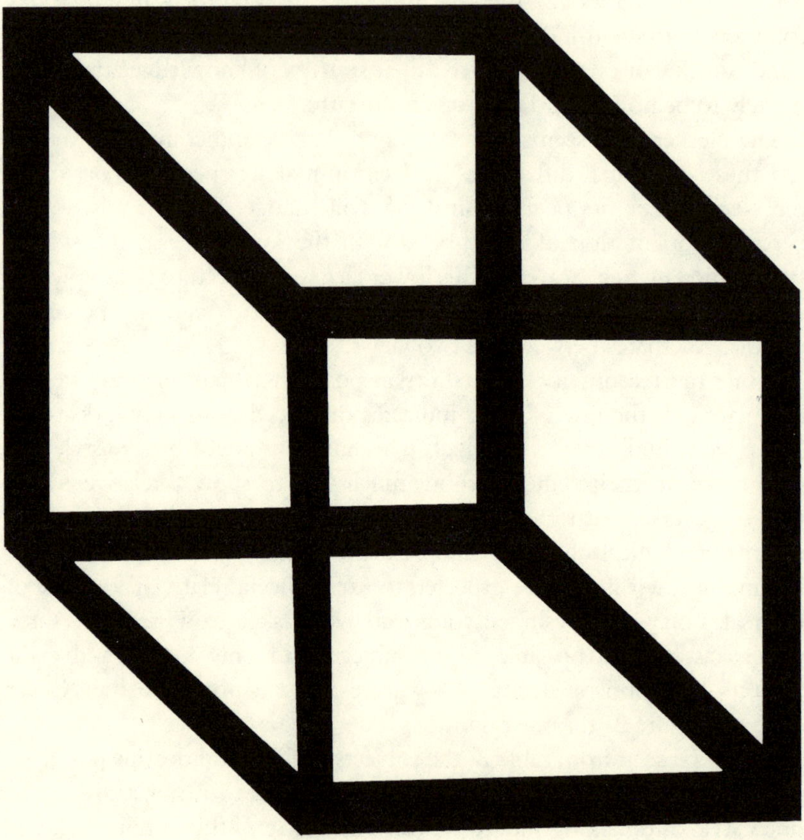

FIGURE 2. Necker Cube

TABLE 3. Dream Styles and Rates of Reversal

Styles of dreams	*N*	$\bar{x}$	*SD*
logical	8	4.12	2.17
bizarre	8	9.38	4.31
	$t = 3.08$	$p < 0.01$	

of dreaming—mixed, purely bizarre, purely logical—may be explained by one's style of thinking prevailing through all the states of mind, i.e., whether one is analytic, broadly scanning one's field and alert to recognize any violation of logic; or holistic, impulsive, and nonchalant if confronted by self-contradiction; or whether one's style of thinking and, particularly, one's approach to a violation of logic is contingent on the level of mental effort available from time to time.

DREAM STYLES, AESTHETICS, AND PERSONALITY

Art, Kris (1948) suggested, is a process of communication and recreation in which ambiguity plays a central role. Ambiguity, not unlike health and intelligence, may turn out to be a continuum of gradations rather than a single point in our mental cosmos. We may assume that different people, characterized by their styles of dreaming and thinking, create and enjoy works of differing degrees of ambiguity. Following this reasoning, Miriam Rass has shown our forty-four subjects, who had kept a dream-log for two weeks, six reproductions of Escher's (1974) graphic work *(Waterfall, Castrovala, Belvedere, Ascending and Descending, Tower of Babel, Palm)*, three of which Escher defined as impossible and contradicting reality. The subjects were requested to select their preferred pictures.

The direction of correlation found between styles of dreams and preferred pictures ($x^2 = 5.84249$, $p < 0.539$) was as expected: individuals whose dreams were of bizarre style preferred the pictures depicting impossible events; individuals whose dreams were of logical style preferred the pictures which did not affront reality testing. Individuals who had a mixed style of dreaming, though inclined to prefer pictures which contradicted reality, were divided between these two directions of preference.

It is apparent that one's style of dreaming indicates, with some precision, one's aesthetic preferences. He who is nonchalant in his relation to self-contradiction feels at home amidst creations which reflect his own mental makeup. He who is alert and watchful of self-contradictions prefers the orderly and harmonious. These findings appear to be connected with an interesting analysis by Barron (1952) of what he defines as personality style and perceptual choice.

Investigating preferences for paintings, Barron established two types. One of these holds a preference for what is stable, regular, balanced, predictable, clear-cut, traditional, and follows some general abstract principle, which in human affairs is personified as authority. The other type prefers the unstable, asymmetrical, unbalanced, whimsical, rebellious against tradition, and at times, seemingly irrational, disordered, and chaotic. These differences in "perceptual choice" were correlated with differences in self-descriptions, as revealed by the Gough Adjective Checklist. The individuals who preferred the regular and predictable turned out to be contented, gentle, conservative, unaffected, patient, stable, timid, and thrifty. Individuals who preferred the complex and irregular turned out to be gloomy, loud, unstable, bitter, cool, dissatisfied, pessimistic, emotional, irritable, and pleasure-seeking.

In the interpretation of Barron, under the best of circumstances the decision in favor of order makes for personal stability and balance, a sort of easy-going optimism combined with religious faith, a friendliness toward tradition and respect for authority without subservience to it. At its worst, the decision in favor of order makes for categorical rejection of all that threatens disorder, a fear of anything which might bring disequilibrium. The thinking of these people is stereotyped and the morality rigid and conservative. They hate instinctual, aggressive, and erotic forces which might upset their precariously maintained equilibrium. In contrast, the decision in favor of complexity, at its best, makes for originality and tolerance of unusual ideas. For such a person, as Barron eloquently notes, "optimism is impossible, but pessimism is lifted from the personal to the tragic level, resulting not in apathy but in participation in the business of life" (p. 400). At its worst, such an attitude leads to a surrender to chaos, nihilism, despair, and disintegration.

We have found a correlation between one's style of thinking and one's aesthetic preference, and Barron was able to show a similar correlation between one's aesthetic preference and one's personality makeup. It is tempting to connect the results of both of these studies and suggest that individuals who have logical dreams and who prefer realistic art, behave along the lines of Barron's first type, while those whose style of dreaming is bizarre behave along the lines of Barron's second type.

Another approach for exploring the possible correlations between dream styles and personality is suggested by the method of content analysis elaborated by Hall and his associates (1966, 1968, 1970). Their system of content analysis is focused upon some important aspects of a dream story. Its potential use as an instrument for diagnosing personality was demonstrated by means of their analysis of the dreams of Freud, Jung, and Kafka. The lives of Freud, Jung, and Kafka are so well known to so many people that a comparison between the facts of their respective biographies and the results of the analysis of Hall and his associates may indicate whether there is a continuity in behavior across the states of mind, and whether an analysis of the manifest dream is the proper method for studying this continuum.

Here is the essence of Hall and Domhoff's (1968) study on the dreams of Freud and Jung. Twenty-eight dreams of Freud, reported in *The Interpretation of Dreams* (1900) and thirty-one dreams of Jung, recollected in his *Memories, Dreams, Reflections* (1961), were the topic of this study. While Freud might have selected dreams to illustrate some aspects of his dream theory and Jung's purpose, perhaps, was to indicate, by means of those dreams, his inner life and development, Hall and Domhoff felt that nevertheless, their method of dream analysis would reveal differences between the two men which are congruous with the differences in their biographies.

According to the norms established by Hall and Van de Castle (1966), men dream more about men than about women, but women dream equally of the two sexes. How can this intriguing difference between the sexes be explained? While one may consider many possible reasons for dreaming more of men than of women, Hall and his associates seem to have been disinclined to enter speculations. Instead, their question was whether or not the dreams of a particular dreamer are in accord with the norms of his sex. Regarding the sex of the characters there were no differences between Jung and Freud. The ratio of men to women in Freud's dreams is 2.56 to 1, and in Jung's dreams it is 2.5 to 1. However, they differed in the quality of their relationship with men and women.

Hall and Domhoff note that a man typically has more hostile interactions with men than with women, and more friendly interactions with women than with men. Jung's encounters, in his dreams, with men and women are, by and large, as expected. He has a hostile interaction with about one of every four male characters in his dreams, and none at all with females. As for friendly interactions, Jung has about an equal number with men and women. In Freud's dreams, the typical pattern is reversed. He has a hostile interaction with one of every four female characters, and almost none with males. On the other hand, he has many more friendly encounters with men than with women.

Hall and Domhoff interpreted these results as indicating that Jung was more positively oriented toward women and Freud toward men. Freud had an "inverted oedipus complex," as they put it. In support of this contention, they quoted some data from Freud's life and the following statement from his biography by Jones: "The more passionate side of married life subsided with [Freud] earlier than it does with many men" (vol. 2, p. 386). Hall and Domhoff may or may not be correct in their understanding of Jones' intention, but even without this particular fact (or fiction) their view seems to be supported by some well-known data and their conclusions are quite acceptable. Behavior in dreams and while awake, indeed, proves to be continuous.

Other dimensions of a dream-story elaborated by Hall and his associates are success/failure and good fortune/misfortune. According to the norms of Hall and Van de Castle (1966), most men have an equal amount of success and failure in their dreams. Again, Jung behaves like a typical man, but Freud dreamed of more success than failure. To be more precise, Freud succeeded six times and failed only once. Freud was ambitious, Hall and Domhoff suggest, and much more so than Jung. Not only was Freud more ambitious, but he did not seem to be afraid or uncomfortable in carrying out his impulse to compete and seek victory.

Good fortune is defined as something favorable that happens to a character in a dream without any effort on his part and without a friendly intent of another character. In the succinct statement of Hall and Domhoff, good fortune in dreams is rare, misfortune is commonplace. In his dreams, Freud had no good fortune at all. Conversely, Jung had more good fortune than is to be expected. Taking together the lack of good fortune and the large amount of success relative to failure, Freud's dreams indicate that he thought success to be a result of his own effort and not of luck. Jung appears here to be more fatalistic than Freud was. Jung felt that his life was ruled by forces over which he had no control. Unlike him, Freud felt that by exercising reason and effort, one could master the world.

We may stop here and refer the reader interested in further details to the study of Hall and Domhoff (1968). One reason for quoting some of their analysis was to demonstrate that dreams, indeed, reflect the dreamer's waking personality. The contents of a dream, the manifest dream, may become a key to the unraveling of the dreamer's personality makeup. Or rather it could become a key; until now, the method of content analysis, as we have seen, was used mainly to identify and interpret the deviations of an individual dreamer from the norms of his or her sex. It is precisely here that our knowledge of the styles of dreams may contribute to a better understanding of a dreamer's personality.

It goes without saying that one's behavior is to a great extent determined by one's sex. But, speaking of dreams, we must also be aware of the differences in behavior due to the variety of dream styles. A man or a woman whose style of dreams is bizarre may experience his or her world differently from a man or a woman who habitually dreams logical dreams. Adapting the norms of men and women established by Hall and Van de Castle (1966) to the complexities of dream styles may enrich the potentialities inherent in this approach to studying personality.

We turned once more, therefore, to the dream-diaries of our subjects with which we had already become acquainted and, by applying Hall and Van de Castle's scoring method, analyzed the dreams of the female students. Four of them had only bizarre dreams, seven only logical dreams, and twenty were of mixed style. While such a sample size will not allow us to draw definitive conclusions, it may be suggestive of the correlation between dream styles and personality.

Women, as one may recall, dream equally of the two sexes. We found that women of a mixed dream style, indeed, dream equally of male and female characters. Women whose style of dreams is bizarre dream slightly more of male characters (1.18 male to 1 female character). However, women whose style of dreams is logical dream almost twice as much of men as of women (1.74 male to 1 female characters). Here the behavior of women who habitually dream logical dreams is closer to that of men. Again, one may feel intrigued: why do some people dream more of men than of women? As the example of Freud and Jung indicates, this preference of men is independent of an inclination to have friendly or hostile interactions with men. Whether a man is or is not homosexually inclined, his mental world is mainly populated by men. Love and family, important as they are, are only second in importance. It looks as if ambition, competition or, to put it differently, the achievement motive has a greater impact on a man's life than on a woman's life. Let us not forget, however, that the priorities of some women, characterized by their logical dream style, are similar to those of men.

According to Hall and Van de Castle (1966), most men have an equal amount of success and failure in their dreams, but women dream more of failure than success. In point of fact, some women dream much more of failure, but some, here too, feel as men do. The ratio of failure to success is 4:1 for women who dream bizarre dreams, 3.15:1 for women whose style is mixed, but only 1.3 failure to 1 success for women whose dreams are logical.

Earlier, I have quoted Hall and Domhoff as saying that good fortune in dreams is rare, misfortune is commonplace. Dreamers of logical dreams had no good fortune at all. Women whose dreams are of mixed style had some instances of good luck, but the group characterized by bizarre dreams had the most of all. On the other hand, all of these groups dreamed of misfortune. For the women whose dream style is bizarre or mixed, a large percentage of these events affect the dreamer herself, but for the dreamers of logical dreams, the dreamers experienced only a small part of these calamities (29% misfortune to the dreamer and 71% to the other characters; 56%:44% for the bizarre, and 78%:22% for the mixed dream style).

That is to say, women whose dream style is bizarre or mixed do not believe in their powers to control their life; often they feel weak and inadequate and rest their hopes on the benevolence of external agencies. They are prone to experience anxiety and depression. Conversely, women whose style of dreams is logical are ambitious; they strive for mastery and believe in their ability to steer their lives. They are not fatalistic, as a rule, nor are they pessimistic.

One is reminded here of the characterization by Barron (1952) of people who prefer what is stable, regular, and balanced, and of people whose predilection is toward the unstable, the whimsical, and the disordered. By now, we feel not only tempted, but also assured that the character types described by Barron and the results of our analysis here complement and reinforce each other. One's style of dreams, indeed, indicates one's aesthetic preferences. More broadly, it indicates many important aspects of the personality, aesthetic preferences included.

DREAMS AND THE UNCONSCIOUS

It may have occurred to the reader that the concept of the unconscious, which loomed large at the beginning of this essay, has vanished completely. This disappearance of the concept of the unconscious—and especially in a chapter dealing with dreams—cannot go unnoticed. Let us, then, say explicitly what was thus far indicated only implicitly: (1) there is no need to look for special reasons—we dream because we are unable not to; aware or asleep the mind does not stop working; (2) dreams are not different, by definition, from our waking thinking; and (3) manifest dreams allow us to draw conclusions about the dreamer's personality. We do not find substantiation for Freud's claim that the dream is the royal road to the understanding of a peculiarly working unconscious.

Many psychoanalysts seem to have reached a similar conclusion, with the result that they have lost any interest in the theory of dreams and its clinical application. Thus, in a monograph entitled *The Place of the Dream in Clinical Psychoanalysis* (Joseph 1967), the members of the Kris Study Group stated that: (1) the dream is a communication in the course of analysis similar to all others; (2) it does not provide access to material otherwise unavailable; (3) it is not particularly useful for the recovery of repressed childhood memories; and, especially relevant to our discussion here, (4) Freud's theory that the dream-work is governed by an interplay between the primary and secondary process is not compatible with the structural theory and ought to be discarded.

As the reader may recall, this was also the understanding of Arlow and Brenner (1964). They, too, proposed to dismiss Freud's topographic theory of mental apparatus, the assumption of two distinct mental systems whose motives and rules of working are incompatible. Instead, Arlow and Brenner, like the Kris Study Group, preferred to work only with Freud's structural theory of mind.

If the structural theory of mental apparatus has rendered the earlier assumption of two tightly organized mental systems useless, how will the structural theory convince us to believe in what has been the heart of the topographic theory, namely, the existence of two sets of mental functioning? For, interestingly enough, Rapaport as well as Arlow and Brenner seem to be sure that, as suggested by Freud, we indeed are endowed with two different strategies of thinking. Is it possible to discard Freud's proof of an alogically working unconscious, i.e., the peculiarity of dreams and their origination in the unconscious, and yet to maintain that nonetheless there are two different modes of thinking: a logical and an alogical one, one which is sensitive to the demands of adaptation and survival and the other impervious to them?

One may argue, though, that the proponents of the structural theory of mental apparatus proposed viewing the primary and secondary process as a developmental issue. We begin our life by behaving in accord with the rules of the primary process and only later on yield to the necessity of reality testing. Of course, earlier stages of development are not eradicated but only superseded by the later ones; under certain circumstances, a mature person, too, will disregard reality and reason alogically, showing signs of primary process.

Indeed, it used to be customary to regard the infant as a bundle of reflexes, as functionally decorticated. It was, then, conceivable to extend this view by saying that an infant's mental functioning at the beginning of its life may be characterized by the features of primary process. However, very few today would subscribe to this description of the first months of life. As a rapidly growing literature shows, the infant is far from being functionally decorticated. The infant, as Stone, Smith, and Murphy (1973) put it, is "competent." Explaining the title of their book *The Competent Infant,* Stone et al. (1973) wrote:

> We have ample reason now to think that [the neonatal experience] is neither a buzzing nor a confusion. . . . So much does the evidence of recent research belie the earlier contention, so much does it underscore the competence of the young infant, that we have chosen the title of this book to crystallize the single overriding trend of the findings. . . . from his earliest days, every infant is an active, perceiving, learning, and information-organizing individual. (P. 4)

In order to indicate the amazing abilities of an infant and, thus, the impossibility of an early, qualitatively different, mode of mental functioning, it will suffice here to mention just one study. The issue will be discussed more fully in chapter 13. Aronson and Rosenbloom (1971) allowed infants to observe their mothers talking through the window, while they listened to her voice over loudspeakers. The speakers were arranged so that the mother's voice seemed to come first from in front of the infant—from the same location as her face—and then from a source 90° to one side. Infants as young as one month were reported to show signs of distress when the face and the voice appeared to come from different places. Clearly, the infant seems to have a concept of an object defined by some attributes, for example that it must be seen and heard from the same point in space. It is only one step from here, though a highly important step, to assume that the infant differentiates between the objects "out there" and itself. Significantly, some psychoanalytic authors propose to consider seriously such a possibility.

Brazelton, Koslowski, and Main (1974) observed that infants as young as four weeks of age react in a markedly different fashion to their mothers than to a toy animal. Brief episodes of these differential reactions were seen as early as two weeks; by four weeks, as these authors put it, the difference "was striking." Commenting on this finding, Klein (1981) observed: "Concepts such as drive-reduction, undifferentiation, objectlessness, and narcissim (whether absolute or conditional) can no longer theoretically support the weight of findings from infancy research. The infant is highly differentiated and begins to differentiate objects from day one. We need only to postulate a separate self that does so" (p. 102). Clearly, the contention, which saw in the infant largely a reflex organism, belongs to the history of ideas. But then, the corollary of this contention, namely, that such a reflexlike primary mode of mental functioning is lurking, forever, as a well-prepared former position to regress to, is left without any base.

If, nevertheless, one would like to argue that children and adults think differently, be reminded that Piaget (1964) felt compelled to clarify this popular misunderstanding which, as it seems, was supported by his writings: "I maintained in my earlier books that the child began by being 'prelogical,' not in the sense of a fundamental heterogeneity between the child and the adult, but in the sense of the necessity for a progressive construction of the logical structures" (p. 78). Maybe it was also to avoid any misunderstanding that he substituted the concept of preoperational for prelogical: "An operation is an internalized action which becomes reversible and is coordinated with other operations into an integrated operational grouping. However, since operations materialize only toward seven or eight years of age, there is a long 'preoperational' period of development which corresponds to what I used to call the 'prelogical' period" (p. 78).

This attempt, though, to set right what seemed to go astray may come as a surprise to some of the experts. For example, Bryant (1977) argued against Piaget's contention that before the age of seven or eight children are unable to make inferences from problems such as: John is bigger than Mary. Bob is smaller than Mary. Who is bigger, John or Bob? He stated that Piaget's evidence on this point "turns out to be rather flimsy," and touches on the very base of such considerations as follows: "What do we mean by logical development? It really has two possible senses. The first and weaker sense is that children will get better at solving logical problems as they grow older" (p. 54). This meaning of the term, however, did not seem to be important. "The second and much stronger sense of the term logical development . . . is that young children initially lack and only rather gradually acquire the logical mechanisms which are needed to solve even the simplest logical problems. This in fact is the sense which has been adopted in all the theories of logical development of which I know" (p. 54).

Bryant thinks that all of the theories of logical development and, of course, Piaget as well, believed in such a dichotomy between the early and later mental functioning. One could not find two more disparate approaches to children, two more divergent traditions, than Piaget's and the S-R behaviorist tradition. They disagree on practically every point. "And yet when it comes to deductive inferences they speak with one voice" (p. 55). In fact, however, Bryant argues, none of the researchers before him checked whether those young children did, indeed, remember the information which they must put together. Once he ensured that they remembered the necessary information well, he found that even four-year-old children do possess the ability to make an inference.

If Bryant is correct in his understanding, then Piaget made a complete reversal; if, however, Piaget knew his own ideas and intentions better, then he merely substituted a precise term, preoperational, for a misleading one, prelogical. In both cases one must conclude that Piaget, at least later, defined mental development in the "weak" sense. That is to say, we live and think along the rules of one logic and one mode of mental functioning alone, which becomes more successful, more flexible, and more competent, as we grow older.

Incidentally, Freud and Piaget were not the only authors attempting to establish a distinction between logical and prelogical thinking. At the beginning of this century, Lévy-Bruhl (1910) won great popularity by a similar suggestion proposed in his *How Natives Think*. "The institutions, customs, and beliefs of primitives," he argued,

> imply a mentality which is prelogical and mystic, with a different orientation from our own; they take but little account of the law of contradiction. We must then reject beforehand any idea of reducing mental operations to a single type. . . . It would be idle to institute any comparison between the

> discursive processes of prelogical mentality and those of our thought or, to look for any correspondence between the two. . . . prelogical mentality has its own laws, to which its discursive operations must necessarily submit. (P. 105).

According to Lévy-Bruhl (1910), prelogical mentality is not antilogical; it is not alogical either. "It is wholly indifferent to contradictions, and that makes it so hard to follow" (p. 78). This clarification, or rather qualification, of the prelogical mentality may indicate the ambiguities and the ultimate fate of this concept. Lévy-Bruhl rejected in advance any comparison between the two mentalities, only to admit later on that the "prelogical" mentality is not really lacking the logic we are acquainted to, but rather does not take pains to adhere to it.

With the passing years, Lévy-Bruhl became more sensitive to opposing voices and more ready to listen to them. At the end of his life, he wrote in his diary (1949) the following remarkable sentences: "The step which I have just taken, and hope is decisive, consists, in a word, in abandoning a badly posed problem, which resulted in some inextricable difficulties. . . . Until now, I had not entirely renounced the assumption fixed in my mind at the time of writing *Les fonctions mentales* and which dominated its composition. . . . let us expressly rectify what I believed correct in 1910: there is not a primitive mentality distinguished from the others by two characteristics (mystical and prelogical), which are peculiar to it" (p. 60–70).

Lévy-Bruhl, like Piaget, had to admit that there are no two different modes of thinking and that the term "prelogical," handy and well known, is, in fact, slippery. Instead of trying to redefine its meaning, we must take it out of circulation. As for the services supposedly rendered by the concepts of prelogical and primary process, they may be better accomplished by the theories of decentration of Piaget, "The most universal manner in which the initial logic of the child differs from our own is undoubtedly its *irreversibility* due to the initial absence of decentration, hence its lack of conservations" (p. 79), and of microgenesis.

We may, thus, come back to our question: why insist on the distinction between primary and secondary processes? This question is especially acute if, like the proponents of the structural theory of mental apparatus, one has already concurred that, actually, these modes of thinking are only degrees of the same mental functioning rather than two separate modes of existence.

It is possible that the reason for the unwillingness of the adherents of the structural theory of mental apparatus to give up Freud's assumption of two modes of thinking is their awareness that the psychoanalytic theory of psychoneuroses stands or falls with the conception of an unconscious that is alogical and alien to reality, and whose functions are governed by the rules of the primary process. The proponents of the structural theory are here caught on the horns of a real dilemma. If they assign to the unconscious the functions and processes envisaged by Freud, then they cannot discard Freud's theory of dreams and, eventually, may feel compelled to reestablish the topographic model. If, on the other hand, they reject, without any reservation, the topographic model, (the assumption of primary-secondary process included), then they must acknowledge that they have also discarded Freud's conception of the unconscious.

By suggesting that "the term unconscious . . . should be used to indicate that something is not conscious, whether or not it can readily become conscious" (p. 113), Arlow and Brenner (1964) made a decisive step in the latter direction. At a closer look it is apparent that, in fact, we were well advised to speak of the unconscious in the manner of cognitive psychologists before and after Freud. Arlow and Brenner, perhaps unintentionally, led us to conclude that the concept of an alogical unconscious, the foundation and soul of Freud's theory of dreams and psychoneuroses, is an indefensible position, and that Bleuler (1911) was correct in stating that "aside from the absence of qualities of consciousness [unconscious processes] are identical with conscious psychic process" (p. 360).

Having arrived at this conclusion, we must now turn to Freud's theory of psychoneuroses. To Freud's understanding neurotic behavior disturbances are the outcome of a conflict over instinctual motives kept in the repressed unconscious. These motives and the concepts of repression and a repressed unconscious are so tightly integrated that one cannot remove one of them and yet hope that the remaining concepts may succeed in supporting the edifice built upon them. The assumption of a repressed unconscious which, due to its formal properties should be different from our controlled thinking in wakefulness, seems now be disproved. Having had to reject Freud's conception of the unconscious and his theory of dreams, can we maintain his theory of psychoneuroses? In the next chapters, we shall attempt an answer to this question.

5.
HYSTERIA: A DEFINITION

Psychology, literally translated, is the study of the soul, but psychologists define it as the study of behavior. While the meaning of the word *behavior* seems to be well understood, many psychologists have found it worthwhile to define explicitly the nature and boundaries of their subject matter. What then is behavior? In his essay, "On the Nature of the Psyche," Jung (1946) put it succinctly: "the psychic is an emancipation of function from its instinctual form and so from compulsiveness" (p. 182). That is to say, instinctual behavior is fixed and impervious to individual experiences. In contradistinction to instinct, psychic behavior is characterized by flexibility and by the impact learning and reasoning may exert on it.

While both instinctual and psychic behavior are motivated and subserve adaptation and survival, they are essentially different. Unlike instinctual behavior, which is a prefixed action pattern, psychic behavior is the result of an ability to choose, of self-determination. Further, while instinctual behavior does not imply reasoning and its effectiveness is not dependent on an ability to contemplate and foresee the consequences of an act, psychic behavior does imply reasoning. In the precise words of Jung: "Driesch rightly emphasizes: There is no willing without knowing! Volition presupposes a choosing subject who envisages different possibilities" (p. 184).

Incidentally, this was also the opinion of W. James (1890): "The first fact for us as psychologists," he wrote, is "that thinking of some sort goes on" (p. 1). The domain of psychology, to say it as briefly as he did, consists of life phenomena that are indicative of thinking.

Freud (1915b) seems to have agreed with this definition of the psychic for, in his essay on "The Unconscious" he stated that, "An instinct can never become an object of consciousness—only the idea that represents the instinct. Even in the unconscious, moreover, an instinct cannot be represented otherwise than by an idea" (p. 177). It is apparent that Freud, too, seems to have thought that psychic behavior, be it conscious or unconscious, implies reasoning.

Actually, Freud's understanding is already indicated in the central position he assigned to the meaning of any behavior, attempted or actualized, and to the disclosure of this meaning to the naive subject. Clearly, by such an interpretation he did not pretend to influence any of the prefixed action patterns, but only the changeable psychic behavior. It was in accord with this view of Freud that Fenichel (1945) defined neurosis as "something . . . that is outside the realm of conscious will . . . the common denominator of all neurotic phenomena is an insufficiency of the normal control apparatus" (p. 18). Freud and Jung, then, seem to concur that the ability to knowingly choose is the hallmark of psychic behavior; it is this ability which grants a behavior its psychic quality. It is also the most comprehensive definition of mental health.

If a human being or an animal has lost its ability for self-determination and, instead, behaves in an unalterable, stereotypic manner, the very base of its psychic life has been flawed and its behavior is prototypic of disturbed behavior. "The essence of normality," Kubie (1954) suggested, "is flexibility, in contrast to the freezing of behavior into patterns of unalterability that characterizes every manifestation of the neurotic process. No moment of behavior can be looked upon as neurotic unless the processes that have set it in motion predetermine its automatic repetition irrespective of the situation, the utility, or the consequence of the act" (p. 183).

How does one lose one's ability for self-determination? An answer to this question is, in substance, a theory of psychoneuroses. While, in fact, there are many categories of psychoneuroses, the theories available were formulated with the model-phenomenon chosen only in mind (hysteria by Freud, phobias by behaviorists), in the hope that the respective principles would suit the other forms of neurotic behavior disturbances as well.

The prelude to any discussion of Freud's theory of psychoneurosis is an attempt to define hysteria. We will see immediately that this commitment is by no means a negligible or pseudoproblem. It was for good reasons that Sydenham (1624–1689), whose work became a landmark in the history of this concept, called hysteria "that Proteus that cannot be laid hold of." Centuries later, Kris (in Laplanche 1974) still warns us: Hysteria is "an ever amorphous entity." Chodoff and Lyons (1958) found it even necessary to speak of "hysteria," in quotation marks. In their opinion, "because it has been used to describe quite different and poorly delimited varieties of behavior, 'hysteria' has taken on some of the attributes of both a fossil and a chameleon, so that . . . there is often a total failure of agreement as to just what is meant when something is referred to as 'hysteria' or hysterical" (p. 734).

The concept of hysteria was born—what a fitting word—to designate the "suffocation of womb," a disease of the hysteron. The experts of the ancient world believed that the uterus was able to change its position in the body if it was deficient in fulfilling its natural function: bearing children. The possible consequences of such a commotion are succinctly summarized in Plato's "Timaeus":

> and the same is the case with the womb or matrix of woman; The animal within them is desirous of procreating children, and when remaining unfruitful long beyond its proper time, gets disconnected and angry, and wandering in every direction through the body, closes up the passages of the breath, and, by obstructing respiration, drives them to extremity, causing all varieties of disease. (P. 272)

This theory of hysteria, which attributes some somatic malfunctions to a migration of the uterus, was challenged by Galen whose fame, according to Veith (1965), was second only to that of Hippocrates and whose influence on the subsequent ages was greater than that of any other Graeco-Roman medical writer. In Galen's opinion it was not a wandering uterus, but the lack of sexual relations that were responsible for the many disturbances subsumed under the label of hysteria. But then, he concluded, a similar cause should lead to analogous disorders in men. Through the centuries to come, this view of Galen was endorsed by many important authors, but it will suffice here to quote Charcot's (1877) clear statement: "Keep it well in mind and this should not require a great effort, that the word 'hysteria' means nothing, and little by little you will acquire the habit of speaking of hysteria in man without thinking in any way of the uterus" (p. 37). Although Plato would have rejected this suggestion as wrong, at least he and Charcot could not have complained of difficulties in understanding. Plato, Galen, Charcot, Sydenham (1676), and Briquet (1859), Veith (1965), Abse (1959), and who knows how many others, all agreed that the term hysteria means somatic dysfunctions which are not really organically conditioned. Hysteria, to use the term so well known in our days, means the "conversion" of mental problems into somatic disorder. This long-standing tradition notwithstanding, the concept of (conversion) hysteria seems to be shaky. Much evidence cautions us: it is more than difficult to prove that a somatic dysfunction is, in fact, a hysteric conversion of mental problems into somatic disorder.

Globus hystericus is a case in point. This phenomenon, a sensation of a lump in the throat for which no organic cause can be established, enjoys a sort of notoriety and, in a sense, became the trademark of conversion hysteria. In individuals complaining of globus, the throat feels tight, sometimes amounting to a choking sensation. Frequent swallowing in vain attempts to dislodge the lump only intensifies the sensation. Is this globus, indeed hystericus? Applying clinical and radiological examinations, Malcolmson (1966) found that only 20% (47) of his 231 globus patients were free of any demonstrable organic etiology. The point to be stressed here is this: of the 184 patients with positive findings, the main lesion was in close anatomical relationship to the site of the complaint in only 68 patients (37% of this group). In no fewer than 116 patients (63% of this group) was the principal lesion demonstrated distally.

The radiological findings in the group of 116 patients showed 66% with a hiatus hernia, 18% with duodenal ulceration, and 11% with gastric lesions. In all, the presenting symptom was a lump in the throat, and only on further inquiry was information confirming the radiological diagnosis forthcoming. Had he not applied the full range of clinical and radiological examination, Malcolmson observes, it could have been easily said that all had a nonexistent lump in the throat and could have been diagnosed as globus hystericus. But, in fact, if increased visceromotor tone affects the whole of the foregut when irritative lesions are present, a sensation of tightness or a lump is likely to occur in its most sensitive part.

This is a finding worthy of consideration. But, there are yet other considerations to be taken into account. Ziegler and Paul (1954) reminded us that hysteria should not be diagnosed, as is usually the case, in a static manner, disregarding the natural history of the disease. When followed up for a number of years, diagnoses of conversion hysteria, they found, often turned out to be wrong: what was thought to be a conversion symptom actually was an organic disease. These authors checked the records of all female patients who were given a final diagnosis of psychoneurosis hysteria when discharged from the Boston Psychopathic Hospital in the years 1927–1932. Over the five-year period, there were sixty-six such patients. (One-third of the original group were readmitted at least once to another mental hospital with a diagnosis of psychosis; seven patients in this group were defined as suffering from severe psychosis. We will consider this problem later in detail.)

Some of the conversion symptoms were, in fact, signs of organic diseases. In five patients with seizures, for example, subsequent developments made the diagnosis of epilepsy more or less certain. One patient with frequent one-sided clonic movements and speech difficulty subsequently developed complete right spastic hemiparesis with aphasia. "It is fair to presume," Ziegler and Paul concluded, "that this is only a fraction of organic disease which may have been present in this group" (p. 305). This, indeed, is possible. But then, the findings of Ziegler and Paul cause us to hesitate and wonder whether even the 20% of patients in the sample of Malcolmson who were found to be free of any organic etiology and might therefore be regarded as suffering from globus hystericus did, indeed, suffer from hysteria. Only with the passing years may we be sure enough of the nature of their complaint.

As if to add weight to these considerations, Slater (1965), in a similar retrospective inquiry, pointed to the seriousness of the later life history and the frequency of misdiagnoses as his most important and most surprising finding. We are well advised, then, to be skeptical about whether a hysteric conversion symptom is possible at all.

In his study, Slater (1965) followed up the medical history of eighty-five patients—thirty-two men and fifty-three women—who had been diagnosed, nine years earlier, as suffering from hysteria. At the time of their first diagnosis, these patients were mainly young or middle-aged, yet during the follow-up period twelve of them died. One was a man with weakness of the legs, thought to be hysterical because of a convincing history of psychogenesis, who was later rediagnosed as having an atypical myopathy. Another was a man with unsteadiness of gait, pain in his legs, urgency of micturition, and impotence. Both a neurologist and Slater agreed with a diagnosis of hysteria. The man, however, suffered from disseminated sclerosis. Another example was a woman who, because of her complaints of severe headaches and poor vision, was diagnosed as "conversion hysteria." She died two years later of an angioma of the brain stem. At least half of this subgroup of patients was misdiagnosed as suffering from conversion hysteria.

As in the sample of Ziegler and Paul, some patients whose blackouts, fits, or postictal symptoms were thought to be hysterical were later rediagnosed and treated as epileptics. Sometimes the diagnosis of hysteria was based on the disproportion between the degree of disability and the physical signs. Actually, in a number of these cases, organic personality changes of oncoming dementia contributed to this disproportion. In approximately 40% of the follow-up group (nine men and twenty-four women) Slater noted that no evidence for organic disease "had yet been found." He added, however; "But even here the concept of 'hysteria' fragments as we touch it. Among this group we find two schizophrenics . . . and seven patients with recurrent endogenous depressions" (p. 1399). As one may recall, Ziegler and Paul (1954), too, found that many patients who, in fact, suffered from schizophrenia were mistakenly diagnosed as hysterics. We shall postpone the discussion of this topic and note that, if sifting these patients out, we are left with twenty-four of the eighty-five patients followed up. Twenty-eight percent of the originally so diagnosed patients may, then be regarded as truly afflicted with conversion hysteria.

Malcolmson found that only 20% of his patients complaining of globus were, at the time of their medical examination, free of any organic etiology. Slater found that nine years later only 28% of the originally so diagnosed patients were, indeed, suffering from conversion hysteria. The results of a related study by Whitlock (1967) buttress these findings. His sample was composed of forty-four patients diagnosed as suffering from conversion or dissociative states. Fits, fugues, amnesias, Ganser and twilight states were defined as dissociative hysteria, while pareses, abnormalities of movement and posture, anaesthesias, and disturbances of speech, sight, and hearing were defined as conversion hysteria. In addition, a small number of patients with hysterical polydipsia, retention of urine, vomiting, and dysphagia was included. Justifying the diagnoses of hysteria, Whitlock states that all of these cases seemed to imply some disturbance of the voluntary control of the affected functions.

The purpose of this study was to see whether these hysteric disturbances coexisted with some organic disturbances of brain function or were preceded by brain injury. Infections, head injuries with concussion, chronic sequelae of such episodes, and all forms of central nervous system disease, whether metabolic or physical, were noted. An equal number of patients matched for age and sex, suffering from depression and/or anxiety states, formed the control group. The results were impressive: 63.5% of the patients diagnosed as hysterics showed evidence of accompanying or preceding organic brain disorder, compared with the incidence of similar disorders in 5.5% of the control group.

This is, then, evidence and a warning one cannot overlook or belittle. Combining the results of these three studies, one may say that, in any sample of patients diagnosed as conversion hysterics not more than 30% of the diagnoses, and probably less, have a chance of being correct. More than two-thirds of these patients may, in fact, suffer from organic disturbances misdiagnosed as functional ones. The least one may say is that Malcolmson, Ziegler and Paul, and Whitlock, among a few others not mentioned here, succeeded in casting a shadow of doubt on every diagnosis of conversion hysteria. Slater (1965) went as far as branding any diagnosis of conversion hysteria as a disguise for ignorance and a fertile source of clinical error. "It is in fact," Slater observed, "not only a delusion but also a snare" (p. 1399). The facts detailed here do not compel us to agree with such a radical stand. But, we should conclude that conversion hysteria is a phenomenon which occurs much less than the diagnoses of experts would lead us to believe.

As the term *somatic compliance* may indicate, Freud would have not been surprised by Whitlock's or Malcolmson's findings. Yet, his rather ambiguous formulations led many to believe that, by a "mysterious leap" from the mental to the somatic, masses of (conversion) hysterical symptoms are daily produced. Schilder (1939) seems to have taken an in-between position in this debate. Basing his conclusions on cases with Korsakoff's syndrome, he argued that the same symptom might be the end result of either an organic disease or a psychological disturbance. In fact, as we have seen, there is a greater chance that such disturbances will turn out to be organic than functional ones.

There is, then, no need to erase hysteria from our vocabulary. Nevertheless, the uncertainties and doubts created by the cumulative effect of the relevant research do impose a measure of cautiousness in applying the concept of conversion hysteria. Indeed, a few researchers opposed the formula hysteria = somatic disorders whose causes are provably nonorganic. In his Harvard lectures, Janet (1907) reflected on this topic as follows:

> If one admits that somnambulism, paralysis, vomiting are, all of them, hysterical phenomena, in spite of their enormous differences, there must be something common among them . . . that common character is the stigma. . . . Of course this stigma has varied very much, for it reflects the theories of each period on the diseases one considers. For about fifty years past, and you are aware that, especially under the influence of the school of Charcot, one symptom has become the preeminent stigma; namely, *anesthesia* . . .
>
> Anesthesia pleased the physicians, because this symptom is in some manner intermediate between physical and moral phenomena. *They could not make up their minds to make hysteria a purely mental malady.* They always declared that such was the case, but, in reality, they quickly forgot that declaration to consider by preference physical symptoms and measure them through physi-

cal methods. *Since hysteria has become a more distinctly mental malady, it is in the mind that we must seek for the stigmata.* (Emphasis added)

Seventy years later, led by a very different outlook Krohn (1978) complained that while Freud clearly believed the presence of conversion reactions was not a necessary or sufficient condition for defining patients as hysterical, "it is unfortunately the case that much of the psychoanalytic literature on this subject has fallen back on conversion reactions as definitional of the disorder" (p. 35).

Krohn based his criticism on the following statement of Freud (1905a): "I should without question consider a person hysterical in whom an occasion for sexual excitement elicited feelings which were preponderantly or exclusively unpleasurable; and I should do so whether or not the person was capable of producing somatic symptoms" (p. 28). Here, Krohn observes, Freud presented a new definition of hysteria. Instead of defining hysteria by the presence of conversion symptoms, Freud suggested the reliance on a feeling of displeasure in response to a potentially sexually stimulating experience.

Krohn seems to have stretched his point here for, as pointed out earlier, Freud shares responsibility for causing his staunchest followers such as Laplanche (1974) to think that "the hysterical symptom remains essentially a conversion symptom" (p. 468). Nonetheless, ambiguously and open to conflicting interpretations, Freud did suggest that conversion symptoms are not synonymous with hysteria.

It is the habit of medical doctors, to repeat Janet, to prefer phenomena with which they are acquainted, which may cause them to erroneously identify hysteria with conversion hysteria. Krohn might have added here that even psychoanalysts are not safe from this lapse. In truth, however, Krohn was emphatic that the definition of hysteria ("a purely mental malady," to quote Janet again) should be that: ". . . neurotic conflict, when it occurs, results primarily from fixation at the phallic-Oedipal level and regressive and defensive attempts to flee from such conflicts. The unconscious wishes that produce neurotic conflict involve . . . triangular, Oedipal rivalries" (p. 214).

In accord with this definition: (1) hysteria may or may not have conversion symptoms: and (2) the cause of the disorder is not seen but reconstructed, because it is unconscious. It is understood that the symptoms indicate the specific nature of the neurotic conflict and the rules of mental functioning prevailing in the unconscious, in general. It is this dual aspect of the Oedipal conflict to which we will now turn.

6.
OEDIPUS IN US

Krohn (1978) spoke not only for himself when he stated that "Freud illustrated the positive Oedipus-complex most clearly in the case of an infantile anxiety hysteria (phobia), 'Little Hans,' whose fear of horses involved the displacement of his fear of his father's retaliation for his phallic-sexual wishes" (p. 238). We have here, then, an opportunity to see how Freud (1909a) identified the existence of an unconscious Oedipal wish and also, how he recognized, by means of a neurotic symptom, the ways of mental functioning peculiar to the unconscious.

"Little Hans" was less than five years old when his parents asked for Freud's help because Hans suffered from the fear that a horse might bite him. Remaining at home would not grant him freedom from this fear because Hans feared that the horse might enter their home and bite him at night in his room. During the months of Hans' phobia, the father had lengthy conversations with him, the contents of which he reported to Freud. Freud gave his instructions on how to conduct further conversations; he himself had seen Hans only once.

The information we have on the early childhood of Hans is rather sparse. We know only of two salient events which may prove helpful for the understanding of some aspects of his phobia. The first piece of information is that Hans was an inveterate onanist: "When he was three-and-a-half his mother found him with his hand on his penis—she threatened him in these words: 'If you do that, I shall send for Dr. A. to cut off your widdler. And then what will you widdle with?'"

One year later, Hans had the following dialogue with his mother. Hans was given his usual daily bath by his mother and afterwards was dried and powdered. As his mother was powdering around his penis and taking care not to touch it, Hans said: "Why don't you put your fingers there?" Mother: "Because that would be piggish!" Hans: "What is that? Piggish?

Why?" Mother: "Because it is not proper!" Hans (laughing): "But it is great fun!" A few months later his mother asked him: "Do you put your hand to your widdler?" "Yes," he answered, "every evening, when I am in bed." The next day he was warned, before his afternoon sleep, not to put his hand to his widdler.

Hans' mother, then, had threatened him with what is usually, though not quite correctly, called castration. Although perturbed, as we may assume, Hans was, nevertheless, not ready or able to stop his forbidden practices. This is the first piece of information given about Hans' early childhood. The other is this: Hans' sister was born when he was three-and-a-half years old. He was not happy with her, found her ugly, and would not have been sorry if she disappeared.

On the very day when, after questioning by his mother, he confessed that he was still practicing onania, he suddenly refused to go out for a walk with her. Eventually, he went out with her, but was visibly frightened in the street. Later, he admitted that he was afraid that a horse might bite him, and while going to bed, he said with tears: "the horse will come to my room." Thus began his phobia, and his worried parents turned to Freud.

The first advice of Freud (1909a) to the father was, "that he should tell the boy that all his business about horses was a piece of nonsense and nothing more. The truth was, his father was to say, that he was very fond of his mother and wanted to be taken into her bed. The reason he was afraid of horses now was that he had taken too much interest in the widdlers. He himself had noticed that it was not right to be so very much preoccupied with widdlers, even with his own, and he was quite right in thinking this" (p. 30).

Freud endorsed, then, the campaign of the mother against the onania, but at the same time would not agree that this conflict might be connected with the fears of Hans: "That the child was getting pleasure for himself by masturbating does not by any means explain his anxiety; on the contrary, it makes it more problematical than ever. A state of anxiety is not produced by masturbation or by getting satisfaction in any shape." Freud's evaluation of the impact of this protracted conflict is the more remarkable since he also reports the following dialogue: "Father: 'Do you know what? This nonsense of yours [your phobia] will get better if you go for more walks. It is so bad now because you have not been able to go out as you were ill.' Hans: 'Oh no, it is so bad because I still put my hand to my widdler every night'" (p. 32).

As it seems, Hans was torn between his impulses and his mother's will, and he felt that this conflict was responsible for his fears. If one took Hans' explanation seriously, the conflict to be treated would be that between Hans and his mother and not between him and his father. Such a change in the understanding of the meaning of Hans' phobia may lead to a more than slight reorientation in our thinking. But, before attempting to suggest such a reorientation, I would like to emphasize that some authors have, indeed, recognized the necessity of paying attention to Hans' statement. While agreeing that what Hans was afraid of was, indeed, castration, Fromm and his associates (1968) commented that:

> This fear is not based on 'very slight allusions' as Freud states. On the contrary, they are clear, strong threats. But where do those threats come from? They are not made by the father but, rather, by the mother. We must consequently deduce that the dread of castration originates with Hans' mother, not with his father. His mother not only terrorizes him with castration, but also tells him that she will abandon him. . . . There can be no doubt but that Hans' true apprehensions are caused by the mother, not by the father. (P. 181)

Fromm and his associates conclude that Hans needed his father to protect him from the menacing mother, and that the success of the therapy was due not so much to the interpretations as to the protective role of the father.

But Freud, as we know, had a different view. To his understanding, "Hans really was a little Oedipus who wanted to have his father 'out of the way' to get rid of him, so that he might be alone with his beautiful mother and sleep with her" (p. 111). Freud found evidence for this Oedipal love in this conversation between Hans and his father:

> Hans: And I am most afraid of furniture vans too. Father: Why? Hans: Because once a horse in a bus fell down. . . . Father: You had your nonsense [phobia] already at that time? Hans: No, I only got it then. When the horse in the bus fell down, it gave me such a fright, really! That was when I got the nonsense. . . . Because the horse went like this with its feet. (He lay down on the ground and showed me how it kicked about). It gave me a fright *because it made a row with its feet*. . . . Father: When the horse fell down, did you think of your daddy? Hans: Perhaps, yes, it is possible. (Pp. 50–51)

Freud commented on this conversation as follows: "We have learned the immediate precipitating cause after which the phobia broke out. This was when the boy saw a big heavy horse fall down, and one at least of the interpretations of this impression seems to be that emphasized by his father, namely, that Hans at that moment perceived a wish that his father might fall down in the same way—and be dead" (pp. 51–52).

This was, then, the proof of Hans' Oedipus complex. Or was it? Because of a surprise Hans gave him, as he put it, Freud seems to have considered other possibilities of interpretation, too: "We can now recognise that all furniture vans and drays and buses were only stork-box carts, and were only of interest to Hans as being symbolic representations of pregnancy; and that *when a heavy or heavily loaded horse fell down he can have seen in it only one thing—a childbirth, a delivery. Thus the falling horse was not only his dying father but also his mother in childbirth*" (p. 128).

Hans witnessed the desperate struggle of a fallen horse to regain its equilibrium and felt fearful—this experience was interpreted as a symbolic expression of his wish that the father might also fall. Since Hans was thought to have death wishes against his father, who was symbolized by a horse, it was logical to assume that he expected retaliation from a biting horse. But now that the falling horse became the symbol of the delivering mother, the first question to be answered is this: which aspect of the mother is symbolized by the biting horse?

Freud may have pondered this question, but he did not answer it. He also did not answer another question made urgent by his suggestion that the falling horse symbolizes, *simultaneously,* both the dying father and the delivering mother. Are we now to proceed simultaneously in two different but equally important directions or rather, should we prefer one of them? Freud now had an excellent opportunity to follow up the different meanings of a symptom and to prove that the Oedipus complex is more important in causing behavior disturbances than is sibling rivalry. Alas, neither sibling rivalry nor onania as possibly connected with this conflict or the biting horse in connection with the delivering mother were dealt with. It is as if these problems did not exist.

"There are no grounds for fearing," Freud (1912/13) exclaimed once, "that psychoanalysis, which first discovered that psychical acts and structures are invariably overdetermined, will be tempted to trace the origin of anything so complicated as religion, to a single source. If psychoanalysis is compelled—and is, indeed, in duty bound—to lay all the emphasis upon one particular source, that does not mean it is claiming either that the source is the only one or that it occupies first place among the numerous contributory factors" (p. 110). Had Freud consistently applied his own principle of overdetermination of psychic acts, he could hardly have assigned the role to the Oedipus complex that he did. By making two contradictory assumptions: the exclusiveness of the Oedipus complex in causing behavior disturbances and the overdetermination of symptoms and dreams, Freud created a built-in and unsolvable self-contradiction in his theory. For reasons he did not disclose, Freud did not attempt to solve this self-contradiction. Instead, as the later chapters of the case of Little Hans may indicate, he behaved as if the facts reported by himself which necessitate the application of the principle of overdetermination, were not known.

In his study *Totem and Taboo* (1912/13), we read among others, the following passage:

> He expressed a fear that the horse would come into the room and bite him; and it turned out that this must be punishment for a wish that the horse might fall down (that is, die). After the boy's fears of his father had been removed by reassurances, it became evident that he was struggling against wishes which had as their subject the idea of his father being absent (going away on a journey, dying). He regarded his father (as he made all too clear) as a competitor for the favours of his mother, towards whom the obscure foreshadowings of his budding sexual wishes were aimed. Thus he was situated in the typical attitude of a male child toward his parents to which we have given the name of the "Oedipus complex" and which we regard in general as the nuclear complex of the neuroses. (Pp. 128–29)

In all fairness, it is difficult to understand reports such as this: "after the boy's fears of his father had been removed by reassurances." Nothing of the like appears in the original report. "Hans' analysis shows," to say it in Fromm's words, "that he was neither very afraid of, nor hated his father. Had he been, he would not have spoken so openly to him; nor would he have reacted as positively to the father's questions. If we study the relationship between Hans and his father, without the premise of the Oedipus complex, we can clearly see that it is a relationship based on friendship and confidence" (p. 168). One has only to add to this that, Hans' mother, on the other hand, fought relentlessly, castration threats included, against his onania, and this fact was not mentioned here.

More distracting than these inaccuracies is the fact that Hans' feelings regarding the pregnancy and delivery of his mother are ignored, as if they had never existed! Years later, in his *Inhibitions, Symptoms, and Anxiety* (1926), Freud reminded his readers, once more, of the study of Little Hans and, again, we find no mention of the surprise Hans caused Freud by his thoughts and feelings regarding his mother's pregnancy:

> The instinctive impulse which underwent repression in 'Little Hans' was a hostile one against his father. Proof of this was obtained in his analysis while

> the idea of the biting horse was being followed up. He had seen a horse fall down and he had also seen a playmate, with whom he was playing horses, fall down and hurt himself. Analysis justified the inference that he had a wishful impulse that his father should fall down and hurt himself as his playmate and the horse had done. Moreover, his attitude towards someone's departure on a certain occasion makes it probable that his wish for his father to be out of the way also found less hesitating expression. But a wish of this sort is tantamount to the murderous impulse of the Oedipus complex. (P. 102)

As in *Totem and Taboo,* it is as if we are asked to forget that the falling horse was also a symbol of the delivering mother and that, therefore, the meaning of the fear of the biting horse is yet to be explained in this context, too. But is it possible to agree with such an approach? The very facts reported by Freud would not allow such a partiality. In not dealing with—and solving—the incompatibility between the principle of over-determination and the exclusive position granted to the Oedipus complex, Freud turned the case of Little Hans into a dramatic demonstration of dogmatism rather than a convincing proof of the Oedipus complex.

This dogmatism was already demonstrated at the very beginning of Hans' treatment. At the first meeting, Freud instructed the father to inform Hans that, in fact, he was a little Oedipus. Hans' preoccupation with his mother's pregnancy came to Freud as a surprise. Soon, however, as the quotations above show, he reverted to his (one cannot call it otherwise) preconceived idea.

Freud (1913), though, found supporting evidence for his Oedipal thesis in the case-study of Ferenczi (1913) of a child of lesser fame, "Little Arpad." Ferenczi described the attitude of Little Arpad toward his "totem-animal" as "superlatively ambivalent": he showed both hatred and love to an unusual degree. "The slaughtering of poultry was a regular festival for him. He would dance around the animals' bodies for hours at a time in a state of intense excitement" (p. 246). Afterward he would caress and stroke the very animals he had mistreated. Freud (1913) believed that Arpad's behavior toward his "totem-animal" justified Freud in "substituting the father for the totem animal" (p. 131).

In fact, however, Ferenczi also reported that Arpad "ran to the bed of a grown-up girl and called out: 'I'll cut your head off, lay it on your belly, and eat it up.' Once he said quite suddenly: 'I should like to eat a potted mother (by analogy of potted fowl), my mother must be put in a pot and cooked . . . (He grunted and danced the while)" (pp. 248–49). In his interesting study on *Freud and Anthropology,* Wallace (1983), indeed, agrees that, "reading Ferenczi's case provides us with further evidence of just how dominated by his thesis Freud was at this point. Because of the a priori nature of Freud's reasoning, he ignored data which could have supported an alternative or at least supplementary explanation" (p. 111, note 24).

Because of the weight of these statements, it seems proper to insert here a similar observation by Sherwood (1969). According to Jones (vol. 2, 1955), Freud's habit was to burn all drafts of preliminary writings once finished material was published. For some unknown reason, his notes regarding the treatment of the patient code-named as "Rat-man" (Freud 1909b) remained among his papers and were discovered after his death. These notes, often written immediately after each session, are the sole extant record of Freud's analytic methods. Regrettably, the editors of the Standard Edition decided to publish only part of this material. "It might be expected," Sherwood complains, "that the potential for an analyst's influence would be the greatest in the very first sessions with the patient in which the general themes and areas for eventual exploration are mapped out. Interestingly, it is precisely these notes, for the first seven sessions . . . which are omitted by the editors" (p. 262).

Comparing the published notes with the account given in Freud's (1909b) "Notes Upon a Case of Obsessional Neurosis," Sherwood points to the virtual absence of any exploration of the patient's relationship to his mother. One could, though, counter that Freud only followed the lead of the material that did in fact emerge. However, comparing the case study with the privately kept notes, Sherwood observes, "we can see that this answer will not do," for in the very first session we find this twenty-nine-year-old lawyer confessing that he must ask his mother whether to begin a course of medical treatment. "And this peculiar piece of behavior is *not* explained, but made more *incongruous* when we learn that this consultation with his mother is necessitated by the fact that she controlled all the patient's finances. . . . It is evident . . . that a very different analysis might quickly emerge if the analyst's interest were different" (p. 265).

Freud, indeed, was interested mainly in the relationship of the patient with his father. In fact, one may say that he was only interested in this relationship and, as Sherwood put it, "When some material about other relationships does emerge, it tends to be disregarded, omitted, even when Freud has the material in front of him as he must have done when he wrote up the case. We could hardly find a better example of differential recollection and emphasis, presumably dependent upon the analyst's theoretical presuppositions and interests" (p. 265). Sherwood's conclusions fit equally well the case of Little Hans. The original form of this case, and especially the subsequent versions in Freud's later writings, are not less a good example of such a differential recollection and emphasis.

Freud was aware of the possibility of such a criticism, but he did not seem to have thought much about it. "It must be borne in mind," Freud (1912a) wrote in his recommendations to physicians practicing psychoanalysis, "the exact reports of analytic case histories are of less value than might be expected . . . . Experience invariably shows that if readers are willing to believe an analyst they will have confidence in any slight revision to which he has submitted this material; if, on the other hand, they are unwilling to take analysis and the analyst seriously, they will pay no attention to accurate verbatim records of the treatment either" (p. 114). Stoller (1971) wryly commented on this statement of Freud: "'Any slight revision'—that's the worm in the apple" (p. xii). Well, then, shall we follow Freud in disregarding what Hans insisted upon in regard to his onania and the pregnancy of his mother and agree that an Oedipal wish and rivalry alone were the hidden causes of his phobia?

In addition, let us not forget that the main justification for assuming an Oedipal rivalry between Hans and his father was Hans' hesitating "Perhaps, yes, it is possible" answer to his father's heavily loaded, leading question. No expert would approve a question of this sort in a survey of opinions. But even if this inference were not as dubious as it is, conclusions obtained by such methods should not be taken for hard facts which they are not. Incidentally, this seemed to have been Freud's understanding as well, for he admitted that "*the existence of an [unconscious] origin and the meaning attributed to the act cannot be conclusively established.* We must content ourselves with recording the fact that such a meaning fits in quite extraordinarily well with the situation as a whole" (1905a, p. 77, emphasis added).

Furthermore, Freud agreed that the source of his inferences, the psychoanalytic treatment, was tainted by his expectations. Because of its importance, I shall quote this statement at length: It is true, Freud (1909a) admitted, that during the analysis Hans had to be told many things that he could not say himself:

> that he had to be presented with thoughts which he had so far shown no signs of possessing, and that his attention had to be turned in the direction from which his father was expecting something to come. This detracts from the authentical value of the analysis; but the procedure is the same in every

> case. *For psychoanalysis is not an impartial scientific investigation, but a therapeutic measure. Its essence is not to prove anything, but merely to alter something.* (P. 104, emphasis added)

The therapist is not a dispassionate observer. He listens to the patient's talk with the intent of guiding and eventually helping; this is why he cannot avoid giving suggestions to the patient. However, due to these suggestions, there is a likelihood that the themes a patient now dreams or speaks about in the analytic sessions are influenced by the expectations of the therapist. It is, then, questionable, to say the least, whether phenomena observed in analytic sessions may be used for proving the validity of the very expectations suggested to the patient.

In his "Constructions in Analysis," though, Freud (1937b) noted that, quite often, the analyst's expectations notwithstanding, "we do not succeed in bringing the patient to recollect what has been repressed. Instead of that, if the analysis is carried out correctly, we produce in him an assured conviction of the truth of the construction which achieves the same therapeutic result as a recaptured memory" (pp. 265–66). Are we allowed to promote such "assured convictions" to the status of valid proofs? Rather, they may evidence the power of the analyst to influence his patient and, it is precisely because of this influence that the analytic process cannot be used for validating concepts such as the Oedipus complex.

The limitations acknowledged by Freud entail, though implicitly, a further weakness: such inferences are highly individual and subjective. This is how Krohn (1978) clearly and sharply formulated it: "the higher-order processes and conflicts, such as repression and Oedipal conflict, are ascertained according to each clinician's skill, theoretical bias, and personal understanding of these concepts. Second, owing to . . . the difficulty of describing the process of clinical inference, the method of inferring these dynamics has never been made explicit enough for research purposes" (p. 51).

Can, then, clinical case studies such as that of Little Hans prove the existence of an unconscious Oedipus conflict? While the facts detailed here may indicate a possible answer, in order to bring these considerations into a sharper relief let us have a quick glance at Freud's other famous patient, the Wolfman.

The "Wolfman," so called because of a dream of his discussed later here, was psychoanalyzed by Freud for four years. Previously, he was treated, to no avail, by such luminaries of those days, as Bechterev,

Kraepelin, and Ziehen. The treatment by Freud was accomplished, by good luck, a few days before the beginning of the First World War. The years of the first great massacre of this century did not allow any contact between Freud and his patient, for the Wolfman was a Russian and his country was in a state of war with Austria. After the war the Wolfman came to Vienna and Freud suggested continuing the treatment, for some problems were still left over from the earlier analysis. The Wolfman was now a penniless refugee and Freud not only received no fee, but also supported him from time to time with small sums of money.

Some years later, it was the Wolfman's turn to ask for a renewal of his treatment—he was again in bad shape. At that time, however, the physical condition of Freud did not allow him to accept the Wolfman, and he transferred him to another analyst, Ruth Mack Brunswick. With interruptions, she treated him for many years. To the end of his days (he died at ninety-two, in 1978), he was treated and cared for, financially and otherwise, by psychoanalysts and the Freud-Archive. His psychic illness became, in a manner of speaking, his profession, the only aspect of his troubled life to attract attention and payment.

It was through the case study of the Wolfman (1918) that Freud thought of demonstrating the negative Oedipus complex, that is, the homosexual love of the Wolfman to his father. The proof of this intention was a dream the Wolfman dreamed when he was less than four years old:

> I dreamt that it was night and that I was lying in my bed. . . . suddenly the window opened of its own accord and I was terrified to see that some white wolves were sitting on the big walnut tree in front of the window. There were six or seven of them. The wolves were quite white, and looked more like foxes or sheep-dogs, for they had big tails like foxes and they had their ears pricked like dogs when they pay attention to something. In great terror, evidently of being eaten up by the wolves, I screamed and woke up. (P. 29)

This dream was continuously dealt with during the years of analysis by Freud, and its final interpretation was only slowly elaborated. In short, Freud understood the dream to mean this: (1) Four-Year-old Wolfman wished to be copulated by his father. "Of the wishes concerned in the formation of the dream, the most powerful must have been the wish for the sexual satisfaction which he was at the time longing to obtain from his father" (p. 35). (2) This wish revived the memory of an experience of a very early age. When he was one-and-a-half years old, he saw his parents involved in coitus *a tergo*. Due to this form of coitus, he could see the genitals of both parents and conclude that women are "castrated." His homosexual wish was strong enough "to revive a long-forgotten trace in his memory of a scene which was able to show him what sexual satisfaction from his father was like; and the result was terror, horror, of the fulfillment of the wish . . ." (p. 36).

This is why he woke up screaming and in terror; he declined to be "castrated." "His anxiety was a repudiation of the wish for sexual satisfaction from his father—the trend which had put the dream into his head. . . . His last sexual aim, the passive attitude towards his father, succumbed to repression, and fear of his father appeared in its place in the shape of the wolf phobia" (p. 46). It was, then, his arousal with anxiety which indicated his horror of "castration." And what indicated the passive-homosexual wish of the Wolfman toward his father, the wish which led him to its counterpoint, the horror of "castration"? *"Being eaten by the wolf, was only the . . . transposition of the wish to be copulated with by his father, that is to be given sexual satisfaction in the same way as his mother"* (p. 46, emphasis added).

Many children have fantasies of being eaten, and many stories told to children inform them of the possibility of such an event. Indeed, the Wolfman knew the story of Little Red Riding Hood and could still remember, in his adult years, the wolf depicted in this book. Is this fantasy always an expression of a passive-homosexual love, for boys as well as girls, or was it a metaphor particular to the Wolfman? If so, one would like to know why the Wolfman expressed his wish, at the age of about three-and-a-half, in a disguised form; what prevented him from calling while dreaming, a spade a spade; and how do we know for certain that this rather common garden variety of spontaneous fantasy was used by him for communicating his wish to be copulated by his father? These are questions which, so to speak, arose by themselves, and one is interested to listen to Freud's explanation of his interpretation.

Apparently, Freud did not feel that there is much to explain here, for he did not go beyond his ex cathedra declaration: The fear of being eaten by wolves was a disguised expression of both his homosexual wish and his repression of it. Surprising as it may sound, in the lengthy report of the case of the Wolfman, there is no other evidence or indication which might support Freud's interpretation of this dream. Instead, the same idea is repeated with only slight changes of wording, such as: "We have been driven to assume that during the process of the dream he understood that women are castrated, that instead of a male organ they have a wound which serves for sexual intercourse, and that castration is the necessary condition of femininity; we have been driven to assume that the threat of this loss induced him to repress his feminine attitude towards men, and that he awoke from his homosexual enthusiasm in anxiety" (p. 78).

Or, elsewhere: *"But the dread was also a proof that . . . he had put himself in his mother's place and had envied her this relation with his father"* (p. 78, emphasis added). If this short comment according to which his fear of being eaten by woves was the proof of the Wolfman's negative Oedipus complex, of his homosexual wish, and if this one sentence, not supported by any evidence, is the foundation on which a conception of the highest import must rest, then the Oedipal predicament of Freud's most famous case was an interesting but never proven conjecture.

Needless to say, that was not the opinion of Freud. In his opinion, the Oedipus complex of the Wolfman, the negative constellation of this predicament, to be precise, was to all intents and purposes well proved. The following short note in his *Inhibitions, Symptoms and Anxiety* (1926) shows this quite clearly: while he admitted that, "even the most exhaustive analysis has gaps in its data and is insufficiently documented," he felt sure, "beyond a shadow of doubt," that it was from fear of being castrated that the Wolfman relinquished his homosexual love. *"The Russian boy's anxiety idea of being devoured by a wolf contained, it is true, no suggestion of castration, for the oral repression it had undergone had removed too far from the phallic stage. But the analysis of his dream rendered proof superfluous.* It was a triumph of repression that the form in which his phobia was expressed should no longer have contained any allusion to castration" (p. 108, emphasis added).

Freud was pleased by the fact that in his dream the Wolfman gave no indication of his Oedipal complex. To his understanding, it is the task of the *interpretation* of the dream nevertheless to display it. Do these interpretations lead us, can they lead us, to facts, simply and beyond reasonable doubts? Is, indeed, any further evidence superfluous?

It is rather obvious that Freud expected to be asked this question, for one reads in the case study of the Wolfman the following provocative statement:

> The whale and the polar bear, it has been said, cannot wage war on each other, for since each is confined to his element they cannot meet. It is just as impossible for me to argue with workers in the field of psychology or of the neuroses who do not recognize the postulates of psycho-analysis and who look on its results as artifacts. (P. 48)

While the message of this sentence is, by no means, ambiguous, still it is possible that Freud did not expect us to take it literally, If, however, psychoanalysis belongs to the empirical sciences, it should be willing to articulate the reasons for its interpretations and the steps leading to them. This is a demand with which Freud did not comply here. Not only Freud; reprimanding his colleagues, Stoller (1974) observed that "Despite the importance of discovering the psychodynamic sources of human behavior and the extensiveness of the literature to date, there is not a single psychoanalytic report in which conclusions are preceded by the data that led to them. . . . You and I never know when reading someone's report whether he is right because he is brilliant, imaginative, and agrees with noted authorities, or whether he is right because his conclusions follow from his data; we cannot know because we have not had access to his data" (p. 13).

Besides, if the basic assumptions of psychoanalysis are to be regarded as axioms, then we would expect that these axioms do not contradict each other. Not even this condition was met here. The self-contradiction between the two principles of Freud, the Oedipus complex as the nucleus of psychoneuroses and the principle of overdetermination of symptoms and dreams, prevails here very much as in the case of Little Hans. As quoted earlier, in the opinion of Freud (1918): "Of the wishes concerned in the formation of the dream most powerful must have been the wish for the sexual satisfaction which he was at that time longing to obtain from his father" (p. 35). Clearly, in accord with his principle of overdetermination, Freud assumed that this dream was coproduced by many wishes, that is, this dream has many meanings.

What were these other wishes and, corresponding with the nature of these other wishes, what other meanings should we assign to the arousal with fear and, last but not least, how did we know that the homosexual wish was, indeed, the strongest of all these wishes? None of these questions was ever answered or even addressed.

Salzman (1980) points out a further difficulty with the concept of the Oedipus complex. Although it is clear that the child cannot conceptualize adult sexual behavior, Freud assumed that children three years old or even younger do, in fact, comprehend the adult role of the genitals. Through some inheritance of this complex biological interaction, Freud thought, children must understand it. "To explain this knowledge," Salzman observes, "we must assume that the Lamarckian theory of acquired characteristics is a valid theory of inheritance, even though it has been roundly rejected from all quarters" (p. 5).

Freud's biographers, too, were aware of this problem, in its conceptual and personal aspects as well. Schur (1972) noted that, "Freud occasionally let his imagination run far afield as he did, for example, with the outline of a study on the application of psychoanalysis to the neo-Lamarckian theory of inheritance of acquired characteristics" (p. 312). Schur maintained that "Freud adhered stubbornly to his belief throughout his life" (p. 313). Jones (vol. 3, 1957) remarked that, "A stranger might almost suppose that Freud was ignorant of the doctrine of natural selection, which is assuredly out of the question" (p. 310) and admits that this is "a baffling problem in the study of the development of Freud's ideas and also in that of his personality" (p. 313).

The problems elaborated here: the method of inferences Freud used for establishing his basic concepts; the incompatibility between the two principles, the overdetermination of symptoms and dreams and the Oedipus complex as the fountainhead of psychoneuroses; and, finally, his belief in the inheritance of the universal Oedipus conflict lead to the question: How can we explain the meteoric "career" of the assumption of a universal Oedipus complex? While it is very likely that some individuals may suffer from the consequences of an unsolved Oedipal conflict, such individual fates do not, by any measure, justify Freud (1905b) in proclaiming:

> It has justly been said that the Oedipus complex is the nuclear complex of the neuroses, and constitutes the essential part of their content. . . . Every new arrival on this planet is faced by the task of mastering the Oedipus complex; anyone who fails to do so falls a victim to neurosis. . . . [The] recognition [of the Oedipus complex] has become the Shibboleth which distinguishes the adherents of psychoanalysis from its opponents. (P. 226n)

Recalling what we have seen in this chapter, not only adversaries of Freud or of psychoanalysis, but also nonpartisan observers will say that this shibboleth, the universal and inevitable Oedipal conflict, is in want of any adequate foundation. But, even if one maintains that the Oedipus complexes of Little Hans and the Wolfman were satisfactorily proved and, thus, that there is such a universally occurring and unavoidable intrapsychic conflict, one should feel perplexed by the lack of any indication—not to speak of evidence—supporting the assumption that, due to their makeup, Oedipal wishes emerging from the repressed unconscious may prove the strangeness of mental functioning possible there. The wish of Little Hans, very much like that of the Wolfman, and in general all of what one may define as "deep material" was treated "as though [it] were ruled by the laws of preconscious." These, as one may recall, were the words of Matte-Blanco (1975, p. 9) in complaining about contemporaneous psychoanalysis. In fact, however, this was the very way that Freud himself dealt with "deep material."

Not convincingly though, Freud related to the Oedipus complex in a manner which did not leave any doubt about the importance he attached to this topic. It is precisely because of this measure of investment that one feels baffled by his indifference about proving his assumption regarding the character of the repressed unconscious and the wishes (thoughts) belonging there. Considering, though, that Freud (1900) had no doubts whatever that "the dream-thoughts are immediately comprehensible as soon as we have learnt of them" (p. 277), one cannot be astonished if he behaved as if the repressed wishes expressed by means of neurotic symptoms, too, once made conscious are immediately comprehensible.

Such facts notwithstanding, Freud maintained that neurotic behavior disturbances are understandable and open to therapeutic influences only if one agrees with the concept of an alogical unconscious. It was in accord with this understanding that Matte-Blanco (1975) argued against the practice of treating "deep material," such as the early relationship of the child to his mother, as though it were ruled by the laws of the preconscious. By disregarding the distinction between the laws of functioning of the preconscious and the repressed unconscious, psychoanalysis, he thought, "has wandered away from itself" (p. 9). However, viewing the results of our analysis, we have to state that Matte-Blanco was wrong in his diagnosis of the situation in psychoanalysis. He reproached the innocent ones and exonerated the one whom he might have blamed. For, in fact, psychoanalysts only faithfully followed Freud in treating this "deep material" as though it were ruled by the laws of the preconscious.

Of course, Freud would have disagreed with our conclusion. His behavior, though, indicates that even if one contends that an unconscious conflict of motives is the sufficient and necessary reason for neurotic behavior disorders, there is no need to assume the existence of an alogically working unconscious mental system. One mental system functioning along the rules of logic and respecting the demands of adaptation, is sufficient to explain behavior normal and abnormal.

7.
OEDIPUS IN HISTORY

Freud's case studies do not fully reflect the measure of importance he assigned to the Oedipus complex. For Freud, the Oedipus complex was not only the nucleus of psychoneuroses, it was, in his eyes, the nidus for every aspect of culture. In his *Totem and Taboo* (1912/13), Freud stated that "the beginnings of religions, morals, society and art converge in the Oedipus complex. This is in complete agreement with the psychoanalytic findings that the same complex constitutes the nucleus of all neuroses" (p. 156).

We shall follow this disgression of Freud into prehistory and see whether his reconstruction of the beginnings of human society provides what his case studies did not: agreeable proofs of a universally existing Oedipus complex. The subject matter of his comparison between children and the childhood of mankind was the social organization of the Australian aborigines. The Australian aborigines were regarded to have the oldest prevailing culture which, due to their geographical isolation, preserved its characteristic features from remote times on. For the purposes of Freud's study, the most important of these characteristics was their system of totemism. Instead of religious ideas or social institutions, their life was regulated by the commands of their totemic system.

The totems were animals, at least originally, and were revered as the forefathers of the clan. Understandably, the members of a clan were forbidden to kill and eat their totem animal. Everyone belonged to a totemic clan, either to that of the father or mother since, and this is why "the interest of psychoanalysis turned to this institution" (p. 3), husband and wife had to belong to different totemic clans. "In almost every place where we find totems we also find *a law against persons of the same totem having sexual relations with one another and consequently against their marrying*. This, then, is 'exogamy', an institution related to totemism. . . . the bond between totemism and exogamy exists and is clearly a very firm one" (p. 4, emphasis added).

Through the analysis of the Australian system of totemism one may reconstruct, Freud thought, the original system of totemism which must have shaped the life of mankind, at the beginning of its social development everywhere. Two prohibitions, two taboos, characterize totemism from its very inception on: do not kill your totem, i.e., your forefather, and do not interact sexually with the women of your totemic clan. Given a matrilineal transfer of clanship, the mother and her children have the same totem and the father has another one. Consequently, the son will be strictly forbidden to have sexual relations with his mother and sister.

The need to conceive these taboos, Freud continues, indicates the strength of the wishes against which these taboos were directed. Significantly, psychoanalysis succeeded in displaying the existence of the selfsame wishes in our children and adult neurotics alike.

How should we understand this parallellism between the totemic system and psychoneuroses? The analysis of the phobia of Little Hans, his fear of being bitten by a horse, may give us a hint. Little Hans wished his father to be dead so that he could remain and alone enjoy his mother's love. "Thus he was situated in the typical attitude of a male child towards his parents to which we have given the name of 'Oedipus complex' and which we regard in general as the nuclear complex of the neuroses. The new fact that we have learnt from the analysis of 'Little Hans'—a fact with an important bearing upon totemism—is that in such circumstances children displace some of their feelings from their father on to an animal" (p. 129).

Applying this principle of displacement to totemism, Freud felt justified in substituting the father for the totem animal, in the case of males. If, indeed, the totem animal is the father, "then the two principal ordinances of totemism, the two taboo prohibitions which constitute its core—not to kill the totem and not to have sexual relations with a woman of the same totem—coincide in their content with the two crimes of Oedipus, who killed his father and married his mother, as well as with two primal wishes of children, the insufficient repression or the re-awakening of which forms the nucleus of perhaps every psychoneurosis" (p. 132).

Freud conjectured that, in primordial times, some sons did succeed in killing the father and taking his place with the mother, which we now wish, but never realize. Very soon, however, the sons regretted their murderous rebellion and wished to undo what was not possible to undo.

In a way, though, they succeeded in undoing at least the benefits they had gained from their rebellion: they decided that, in the future, they would not kill the father or sexually touch his women. By imposing these two taboos upon themselves, out of regret, they established the system of totems. "Totemic religion arose from the filial sense of guilt, in an attempt to allay that feeling and to appease the father by deferred obedience to him" (p. 145).

We shall now examine this construction and try to evaluate its contribution to the assumption of a universal Oedipus complex which develops inevitably in all places and all ages. Our first question will relate to the totemic system. Was it proved that all over the world human societies went through a totemic phase of organization? Freud's bold hypothesis that the totemic system of society with its two taboos is the aftermath of the primordial Oedipal drama, presumes, as a matter of fact, the ubiquitous existence of such a social organization.

Students of anthropology, on the other hand, have no doubts that the assumption of a ubiquitous totemic phase in the organization of societies is not supported by evidence, neither at the time when Freud wrote his *Totem and Taboo* nor today. In fact, there is evidence to the contrary. Studying the very society Freud relied upon, the Australian aborigines, Spencer and Gillen (1904) found that while the Arunta, a group of these aborigines, are organized into clans, with each clan having a totem, the membership in a clan (and a totem) may be determined patrilineally as well as matrilineally, and also conceptionally. People who in the opinion of their mothers have been conceived in the same place, may be grouped together in one clan. By whatever method the clans were composed, they were, invariably, *not* exogamous. Men and women who had the same totem were not prohibited from having sexual relationships. They were prohibited, however, from eating their totem animal. Each clan of the Arunta was obliged to ensure the plentiful supply of the totem animal for the benefit of the other clans, first, by not eating these special animals and, second, by performing certain ceremonies, called intichiuma, magically to ensure that its totem would easily be available to the others.

To support the theory of Freud, both taboos, i.e., not eating the totem-animal and not allowing sexual relationships between the "descendants" of the same totem, should be present. Killing a person in power or its symbol may be explained by reasons which are more simple in nature and easier to follow than the Oedipus complex. Only if the struggle for and against the incestuous wish was demonstrated would one be allowed to interpret the food taboo in relation to the Oedipus complex. As the Arunta were not exogamous, one has no reason to assume they they had to struggle against their incestuous desires. Consequently, their decision not to eat their own totem animal, but to make it available to the other clans, may have been guided by motives which have nothing in common with the Oedipal conflict.

The case of the Arunta, then, indicates that the very foundation of Freud's excursion into prehistory was misconceived. Although the Arunta had a food taboo, they were not prohibited from marrying the members of their own clan; this clearly contradicts and actually disproves Freud's totemic hypothesis. One cannot but wonder what caused Freud to believe that there is a "firm bond between totemism and exogamy."

McLennan (1870), much earlier than Freud, put forward the idea that "ancient" nations in prehistoric times went through the totem stage, conceiving of animals, plants, and the heavenly bodies as animals, as gods before the anthropomorphic gods appeared. Elaborating on this suggestion, Frazer (1887) in his *Totemism* concluded that the members of a totem clanship were prohibited from eating their own totem animal and from having sexual relationships with one another. Soon, however, Frazer felt compelled to revise his views on totemism. Under the impact of the data provided by Spencer and Gillen in 1889 and 1904, which have showed that the Arunta were not exogamous, Frazer propounded a second, revised theory of totemism. In his *Totemism and Exogamy* (1910), a work on which Freud heavily relied, Frazer did his utmost to convey the change in his outlook; "I must request the reader," he wrote, "to bear constantly in mind that the two institutions of totemism and exogamy are fundamentally distinct in origin and nature though they have accidentally crossed and blended in many tribes" (p. 20).

Freud knew of the findings of Spencer and Gillen and Frazer's change of mind, yet, for some reason he disregarded these facts. Freud also knew of Reinach (1909), whose views on totemism were even more radical than those of Frazer. In the *Code du totemism* of Reinach, Freud (1912/13) informed his readers, "one of the two principal taboos, that of exogamy, is not mentioned at all, while the belief upon which the second one is founded, namely descent from the totem animal, is only referred to in passing" (p. 107).

In the opinion of Reinach, then, there is no connection between totemism and exogamy; they are, indeed, "distinct in origin and nature," and the reasons for their existence cannot be found by means of a unitary theory which would attempt to explain them as derivatives of a common root. Thus far he agreed with Frazer. Reinach also rejected the assumption that totem animals should be seen as the forefathers of their clans. Such were the views prevailing in the literature when Freud wrote his *Totem and Taboo.* Curiously enough, Freud stuck to the first theory of Frazer, which had already been abandoned by Frazer himself.

The Arunta society, whose social system caused Frazer to revise his theory, must represent a later, decadent, phase of their totemic system, suggested Freud. Originally, they, too, regarded themselves to be descendants of a totem and were prohibited from having sexual relations with one another. If this presumption proved to be correct, one would expect Freud to explain why the later generations of Arunta were exempted from the demand of exogamy. Were they allowed to consummate their incestuous wishes?

It does not appear that Freud would have agreed with this possibility; we do not know the solution he would have agreed with, though, for surprisingly enough, he did not tackle the problem at all. But he needed to address it, for the totemic system of the Arunta either changed from the unconditional prohibition of incestuous relations to indifference to them, or it did not "deteriorate" and was never exogamous at all. If the former is true, then Freud should have offered an explanation for this change to laxity; otherwise, one must conclude that the struggle for and against incest is neither universally observable nor the root and fountainhead of human culture. If the latter is true, and Frazer was correct in abandoning his first theory, Freud doomed *Totem and Taboo* to failure by interpreting institutions which did not exist.

One has the impression that Frazer's first theory, including as it does the taboo of killing the totem animal and the demand of exogamy, fitted so well the outlines of Freud's own assumption of a universal Oedipus conflict that he succumbed to the temptation of employing it even though it was contradicted by the known facts.

The facts, as they were already known at the beginning of this century, not only have not allowed a connection between totemism and exogamy, a fact conceded by Frazer himself in his second theory, but they have also contradicted the very construction of the totemic hypothesis. While Frazer still struggled to establish totemism as a system, Goldenweiser's (1910) 110-page essay, appearing in the same year as *Totemism and Exogamy,* exerted more lasting theoretical influence, as Lévi-Strauss (1962) put it, than did the 2,200 pages of Frazer's four volumes. Goldenweiser demolished the totemic hypothesis by showing that three kinds of phenomena: (1) an organization in clans; (2) the attribution of animals and plants to the clans as names; and (3) the belief in a relation between clan and animal, were superimposed in the totemic hypothesis when, in fact, they cross and blend in only a minority of cases, and each may be present without the other. He pointed out, for example, that clan exogamy and the concept of descent from the totem are often independent of each another. Moreover, prohibitions against killing are frequently associated with animals that are not totems. "We should then have to realize," Goldenweiser (1910) concluded, "that any attempt at dealing with totemism without due realization of the essential independence of its constituent parts must result in grave misconceptions" (p. 183).

The first theory of Frazer, taken over and further elaborated by Freud, included a tightly organized construction: the totem animal is the clan's father; the members of this clan are their children, and should not kill the totem animal; neither should they have sexual relationships with one another. This whole theory of a totemic system was, in fact, a fiction. Each of these phenomena—the organization into clans, the emblems of these clans, and their relationships to their totem—while coinciding occasionally, functioned separately. No unified system of totemism ever existed, and no interpretation of this nonexisting unified system of totemism was, logically, ever possible.

What, then, is a totem? Let us begin by emphasizing that in contradiction to Freud's thesis, a totem may be an animal, but need not be one. Animals, plants, utensils, and other inanimate objects, indeed virtually everything may serve and has served as a totem. One sees immediately that a totem cannot be the transfiguration of the primordial father. It would be very difficult to see in totems such as a ship, water, a dish, a bracelet and so on, associations to fatherhood. Such inanimate totems and others even more unusual have been registered in Australia and elsewhere.

Viewing this long and often surprising list of totems, one understands that totems were not regarded as forefathers. The totems functioned as emblems, helping the clans to identify and distinguish themselves for other clans; quite obviously, any food taboo a clan may have observed was not connected with the function its members assigned to their totem. The character of a totem and a food taboo may have been overlapping, but very often they were not. Likewise, if a group did not allow sexual relationships between its members, but expected them to seek their partners exogamously, the reason for their exogamy may not be found in the assumed fatherhood of the totem. While sometimes coinciding, each of these institutions—totem, food taboo, and exogamy—had its own and separate roots, functions, and destiny. The totemic hypothesis with its two taboos was a misreading of the facts, and Freud was perhaps the last one to believe in it.

The decision of Freud to adopt an indefensible position was one of the failures of his *Totem and Taboo* and there are other reasons as well. According to the totemic hypothesis elaborated by Freud, the membership in a totem clan was determined matrilineally. This is to say, mothers and their children, but not fathers, belonged to the same totem clan. In consequence of this matrilineal transfer of clanship, a son was barred from having a sexual relationship with his mother and sisters and all other women of his totemic clan. Instead, he had to seek exogamous relationships. The necessity to erect such a barrier indicated the existence of an opposing drive, the incestuous wish of the sons. Thus had Freud proved that the Oepidal conflict was the real reason for inventing exogamy and the totemic system, in general.

Let us now turn to the daughter. A daughter was prohibited from having a sexual relationship with her brothers and other members of her totem clan. Her father, however, belonged to another totem clan. Otherwise, he could not have married her mother. By the same token, he could have married his daughter, as a second wife, for, in accordance with the principles of the totemic system on which *Totem and Taboo* was built, there is no incest barrier between a daughter and her father.

This leakage of the incest barrier notwithstanding, no totemic clanship is known to have systematically practiced and legally sanctioned father-daughter sexual relationship. Why? If we believe Freud, the incestuous wish is the strongest of wishes; what then prevented the daughter in the case of matrilineal transfer of totem clanship, and the son in the case of patrilineal, from attaining their highest desire? Not Freud but rather his contemporary, Westermarck, seems to have had the correct answer to this puzzle. In his *Short History of Human Marriage* (1926), Westermarck observed:

> *Generally speaking, there is a remarkable absence of erotic feelings between persons living very closely together from childhood. . . . This I take to be the fundamental cause of the exogamous prohibitions.* Persons who have been living closely together from childhood are as a rule near relatives. Hence their aversion to sexual relations with one another displays itself in custom and law as a prohibition of intercourse between near kin. (P. 80, emphasis added)

While Freud emphasized the pressure of an incestuous wish, Westermarck thought that, on the contrary, growing up in a family would not allow the arousal and development of erotic feelings between the members of the family. Lately, this suggestion of Westermarck received unexpected support from the studies describing the patterns of sexual behavior observed in the second kibbutz generation, and from studies on the Taiwanese practices of marriage.

In an Israeli kibbutz, children are communally reared, living together in peer groups in children's homes, where they are cared for by trained professionals. During the early evening hours, they leave their communal houses to spend a few hours in the rooms of their parents. There they will meet their brothers and sisters, who also live with their own peer groups, in other children's homes. A child, then, grows up under the emotional impact of two, separate power systems influencing his life: his family and his peer group. Usually, children who were born at about the same time will live together in the same children's home and learn in the same classroom until they reach adulthood and are accepted as members of the kibbutz.

A kibbutz is a small unit in which every family counts. Youngsters reaching adulthood and planning to marry understand that their decision will have an impact, though indirectly, on all the members of their kibbutz. If they marry someone not from the kibbutz, there is a fifty-fifty chance that the young couple will leave and settle elsewhere. As a rule, the kibbutz wants the next generation to live there and continue the pioneering work of the founders. The very ideology of the kibbutz, however, including the communal child rearing, makes it difficult for them to realize their hope, for boys and girls reared together from early childhood on do not marry one another or have sexual relationships with one another.

Following up the pattern of relationships in the second generation in three kibbutzim, Yonina Garber-Talmon (1964) found among the 125 couples studied not a single case in which two people reared in the same peer group had married. Four couples were born in the same kibbutz, but, because of a difference in age, were reared in different children's homes. Eight couples were mixed, with one partner born in the kibbutz and the other joining the educational system of the kibbutz at about the age of puberty, but not living in the same children's home.

Shepher (1971) researched the relevant details of all known second-generation marriages, 2,769 in number in the kibbutzim. He found sixteen couples who seemed to contradict Garber-Talmon's finding. It turned out, however, that none of them had been reared together between birth and six years old. "What is staggering about the Shepher evidence," as Fox (1980) says, "is the seeming lack of exceptions—of any" (p. 48).

Children reared together from early childhood on do not marry one another, and, let us emphasize, that this is not because of any obstacle created by society. Quite the contrary: the society of the kibbutz is interested in its sons and daughters remaining; marriage between two children of a kibbutz may be instrumental in achieving this purpose. Also, one might add, young people in Israel usually marry partners of their own age-group. In spite of these facilitating circumstances, the children of kibbutzim, coming of age, practice group exogamy.

This fact is a much-discussed and well-documented finding (Spiro 1958; Rabin 1965; Yonina Garber-Talmon 1964; Shepher 1971). These researchers are unanimous in their opinion that members of peer groups reared together will not marry one other and, what is more, will have no sexual relations with one another. As Spiro (1958), who was the first to point out the self-imposed group exogamy of the second generation *sabras* (native born Israeli children) put it: "In no instance have sabras from the same Kevutza had sexual intercourse with each other" (p. 347). Let us note that in a small place such as a kibbutz, under the public eye of a communal home, it would be very difficult to hide such love affairs, if indeed they existed. But there are none; as Shepher (1971) definitively stated: children who during the years 0–6 lived together in a communal children's home had no sexual relationships with each other. He investigated the premarital sexual behavior of all adults and adolescents of the second generation in one kibbutz. There were no cases of heterosexual activity between any two native adolescents of the same peer group.

As to the sexual relationships, though, Kaffman (1977) had some qualifying remarks; "[his] experience and observations," Kaffman stated, "do not bear out the widely held assumption that growing up together in the kibbutz has led to the establishment of incest barriers. The suggestion of absolute sexual abstinence within the group is less than exact. . . . There is hardly a kibbutz without its report of heterosexual relationships between adolescents brought up together from infancy" (p. 216). We may note that, in fact, he agrees with the authors quoted above. He, too, thinks that, as a rule, adolescents brought up together from infancy in the same age-group avoid in-group sexual relationships. However, this incest avoidance is not without exceptions. We may add here that neither is the incest barrier between sisters and brothers perfectly watertight. On the other hand, the avoidance of marital relationships between members of a peer group in a kibbutz is "absolute." This avoidance of in-group marriages, let us not forget, is neither enforced nor supported by society; it is spontaneous.

The ages 0–6 are, then, the critical period; children who live together during these years will not later arouse each other sexually. These years were regarded as critical by Freud, too, for establishing the Oedipal constellation. The spontaneous group exogamy of the young generation in the kibbutz and the self-imposed avoidance of sexual intimacy between the members of a communal home who lived together in their first years of life quite impressively disprove Freud and lend credibility to the contention of Westermarck. The early years of life are critical not for inciting a burning incestuous wish, but rather, for reasons not yet fully understood, for creating sexual indifference among figures who, as Westermarck noted, usually are near kin.

Incidentally, Oedipus, the son of Laius, met his father and mother as a grown-up stranger. The early years of his life, days and nights as well, he shared with his foster parents. It was his foster mother who should have aroused his incestuous desires, if he had any. The queen of Thebes who became his prize and wife, was to him a complete stranger, as was Oedipus to her. Thus, the man who became the prototype of the "Oedipal conflict" might have been chosen more properly, so it seems, for exemplifying Westermarck's thesis.

Wolf's (1968) study of the people of rural Taiwan underscores this suggestion of Westermarck. The Chinese tradition knew of two forms of marriage. Either the bride joined her husband's home as an adult, or she came to the family as a child and lived there until she was old enough to marry one of the sons. In the latter case, the couple actually grew up together as children of the same family. From the time the girl entered the family, she and her future husband were, for all practical purposes, like siblings. Until seven or eight years of age they slept together with his parents, were bathed with the other children of the family in the same tub, and played, worked, and learned together. "So far as society at large is concerned, they are free to behave as though they were siblings until they are designated husband and wife" (p. 884).

As Wolf's follow-up revealed, it is easier to adopt a daughter than to marry a sister. Wolf compared these two forms of marriage in terms of happiness, adultery, resort to prostitutes, fertility, and divorce. In every respect, the marriages of the "siblings" fared badly. Of these marriages 46.2% ended in divorce and/or adultery by the wife, as opposed to 10.5% of the form of marriage in which the bride and bridegroom meet as adults. To begin with, often the couple of "siblings" had to be forced, quite brutally, by the father to consummate their marriage. The parents' decision and wedding ceremony notwithstanding, the siblings who were turned into a married couple related to each other as sister and brother.

The only conclusion justified by his data, Wolf suggests, is that their common childhood precludes the arousal of sexual attraction between them. How can we explain this peculiar effect of a shared childhood? As a first step, let us be reminded that man belongs to the animal kingdom. It is to this common ancestry that we must look for clues. Indeed, ethology has provided us with highly relevant, some would feel provocative, information such as the following: "in the whole animal world with very few exceptions no species is known in which under natural conditions inbreeding occurs to any considerable degree" (Bischof 1975, p. 42).

This statement is trivial as long as we are dealing with animals having no attachment to conspecifics, or at best only collective-anonymous attachment, and which furthermore are not sedentary. "It is quite different with bonding-motivated animals, however, that is, animals having the ability to recognize each other *individually,* and the *inclination to affiliate with* acquainted conspecifics. This selective preference must generally hit family members, and one could expect that the maturing young would practice sexual activity inside this ready-formed game of sympathy. *This, however, is precisely what nature systematically avoids*" (p. 42, emphasis in original). It must be remembered, however, that any interference with the natural living conditions of a species may also disturb instinctive mechanisms and thus reduce their effectiveness. For this reason incest among zoo and domesticated animals is less infrequent than in the wild.

As an afterthought though, one may add that even the unnatural conditions prevailing in an animal laboratory do not abolish the incest barrier erected by nature if those conditions do allow a choice. Yanai and McClearn (1972) were able to show that female mice from some inbred strains of *Mus musculus,* in a state of induced oestrus, when allowed to choose between a male of their own strain and another of a different one, preferred to associate and mate with the males of the different strain. This information may put in the proper perspective the "incest" barrier observed between a Taiwanese adopted girl and her brother-husband, and the girls and boys of a peer group in the kibbutz.

Yanai and McClearn (1972) indicated this perspective as follows: "The 'incest taboo', or avoidance of mating with relatives, is regarded as a near cultural universal in man. Presumably behavioral mechanisms for the avoidance of inbreeding have evolved in many species" (p. 282). Overviewing the available studies, Bischof (1975) put it more strongly: "We are confronted here with a selectional force which had been operating for untold ages prior to man's emergence, and which had already led to the development of genetically determined motivational structures in the animal kingdom" (p. 58).

Saying it differently, it was nature, before man appeared on the scene, and not human culture which "invented" the incest barrier. Clearly, then, this inhibition which regulates the sexual behavior of animals and men cannot be the Oedipal conflict, but may be an inherited pattern of behavior subserving adaptation and survival.

One of the ways to prevent incest among primate species which live in groups is as simple as this: the young of one sex leave their natal troops when they reach sexual maturity and join another troop to breed. In olive baboons, observed over a six-year period, all the males that reached maturity left their natal group. On the other hand, in chimpanzee troops, the males form the permanent basis of the troops and the females transfer (Smith 1978). In one group of rhesus macaques, Sade (1968) found that, although adolescents are not expelled by dominant males, 75% left their group and joined another group. Some of them, though, returned later to the original group. Of these, only three males mounted their mothers in "single mountings," and only one copulated with his mother.

Some species have other built-in ways of preventing inbreeding, which, incidentally, are closer to the situation known by man. Lorenz (1943) and Huxley (1963) reported that in the grey-lay goose neither sexual behavior nor pair formation occurs between siblings of the same nest or between parents and young. Geese live in groups composed of separate families. Partners for pair formation are always chosen from within the group, but never from the family. Thus, geese, like so many human societies while choosing some member of their group, avoid incestuous relationships. The very occurrence of this avoidance in societies as different as that of geese, rhesus monkeys, baboons, chimpanzees, and man, leaves no ground for assuming that, geese, for example, are in love with their mother or father and only because of a "castration" threat will yield and seek sexual partners among geese from the other families.

In his last writing, Freud (1940) expressed his view that, "if psychoanalysis could boast of no other achievement than the discovery of the repressed Oedipus Complex that alone would give it a claim to be included among the precious new acquisitions of mankind" (pp. 192–93). Commenting on this statement of Freud, Lindzey (1967) felt that, "it is not an overstatement to suggest that Freud himself viewed the conceptual identification of this conflict and its psychological implications as ranking with the distinction between primary and secondary process as the most original and significant of his theoretical contributions" (p. 1057).

The facts displayed by ethology and the spontaneous "incest" avoidance of children reared in communal homes in a kibbutz do not warrant the high esteem the Oedipus complex enjoys. While sexuality is among those needs which shape the fate and outlook of mankind and, while there are individuals whose life may be characterized by the impact of an Oedipal conflict, neither has it ever been proved and, as we may now say, nor does it seem possible to prove, that human beings, in all ages and places, experience the pressure of an unrealizable incestuous wish.

8.
HYSTERIA BETWEEN NEUROSIS AND PSYCHOSIS

Viewing the results of our analysis, we may have some second thoughts in regard to definitions of hysteria and neurosis in general, such as: "[the] prime psychoanalytic discovery concerning hysteria and other neurotic disorders [is] that the neurotic conflict is not simply a conflict over sexual impulses, but a conflict over libidinal and aggressive drives directed at incestuous objects, which is the essence of infantile sexuality" (Krohn 1978, p. 157). Many, but not all psychoanalytic writers, indeed, have indicated that such an understanding of the psychoneuroses does not seem to be defendable any more. For example, in an often-quoted paper, Easser and Lesser (1965) admitted that clinical practice and psychiatric literature have increasingly challenged and modified the earlier psychoanalytic formulation of hysteria. *"Increasing stress has been placed upon oral fixations and their resultant dependency strivings with the implicit discounting of Oedipal conflict as the 'core of the neuroses'"* (p. 404, emphasis added).

Or, to take another example: relating to Freud's theory according to which hysterical symptoms arise from repressed incestuous wishes, Blacker and Tupin (1977) write: "This stereotyped formulation held sway for many years until clinical experience demonstrated its fallacies. Many analysts began to question the alleged ease with which hysterics were thought to be treated by psychoanalysis and psychotherapy, and *in 1953 Marmor brought together much of the analytic experience that raised questions concerning the Oedipal formulation of hysteria"* (p. 103, emphasis added).

Oral features have long been recognized in hysteria; globus hystericus, vomiting, anorexia, bulimia, and a history of prolonged thumb sucking in childhood are bywords in the symptomatology of hysteria. The question, therefore, wrote Marmor (1953), is not whether oral mechanisms are prominent in hysteria. That is taken for granted. The problem, rather, is whether these mechanisms may not play a more determining role in the dynamics of the hysteria than has been generally assumed. Indeed, in the opinion of Marmor, an incestuous dream of a hysteric patient may conceal behind the symbolic wish to cohabit with a father or mother a deeper, pregenital wish to be loved and protected by him or her to the exclusion of the world. The sexuality of the hysterics, Marmor thinks, is a sham, primarily because it expresses a pregenital oral-receptive wish rather than a genital one. Also, a dream or fantasy may have the manifest content of a homosexual wish or fear, while the deeper wish is to suckle at the breast as a symbol of love and protection.

One may discover here what Easser and Lesser thought to be an *implicit* discounting of the Oedipus complex as the core of the neuroses. At a closer look, however, it turns out that neither was it the intent of Marmor to challenge the assumptions of a curiously working unconscious mental system and a universally active Oedipal conflict, nor were his ideas understood as if directed against these constructions. Indeed, the authors quoted above, Blacker and Tupin (1977) summarized the prevailing views as follows: "The classical theory of genital libidinal fixation and incestuous yearnings had given way to a broader, richer, and more complex formulation emphasizing pregenital elements and ego functions. This new picture, developing from Marmor's amalgamation of classical libidinal theory with ego psychology, emphasizes oral fixations, the close relation to addiction, depression, and schizophrenia" (p. 107).

To emphasize an aspect of a complex phenomenon and amalgamate the earlier view with the present one means to acknowledge the existence of both factors. Yet, some influential psychoanalysts would reject even the modification suggested by Marmor. In a panel on "Hysteria Today," Beres (1974) argued that hysteria should be delineated as an Oedipal conflict with libidinal and aggressive components, countered by repression as the predominant mechanism, expressing in the symptom an unconscious fantasy whose expression is distorted by a compromise formation. Yet, this is the theory Blacker and Tupin characterized as the stereotyped formulation of hysteria which, "held sway for many years until clinical experience demonstrated its fallacies." It is worth emphasizing that Beres justifies his opposition to Marmor by relying, not suprisingly perhaps, on clinical experience.

Clinical experience, Beres contends, supports Freud's contention that the basic conflict in hysteria is of Oedipal origin. "That pre-Oedipal elements, mostly oral, are emphasized by some authors does not alter this conclusion, if we allow for regression and fixation which come into play secondarily when repression fails" (p. 460). Both Marmor and Beres found reasons for their opposing views in their respective clinical experiences. One is reminded here of Krohn's (1978) criticism of clinical inferences: "the higher-order processes, such as repression and Oedipal conflict, are ascertained according to each clinician's skill, theoretical bias, and personal understanding of these concepts." (p. 51).

It is, indeed, regrettable that such a vague term and such an uncontrolled process of drawing conclusions as clinical experience, may be used as a proof in a debate. At any rate, in spite of their disagreement on the question of orality in hysteria, both Mamor and Beres concurred in believing in the factuality of a universal Oedipal conflict. Indeed, while in the evaluation of some readers, Marmor implicitly discarded the Oedipal conflict as the core of neuroses, he, in fact, emphasized that his suggestions notwithstanding: "This is not in any way to deny the tremendous and unquestionable part which Oedipal fixations play in the hysteria" (p. 662). With all their criticism, psychoanalysts would not turn their back on what was their emblem.

Marmor's criticism of the Oedipus complex, indeed, seems to have been half-heartedly conceived. In contradistinction to this hesitation, in his paper Marmor directly challenged the view established by Freud according to which hysteria is to be defined as the consequences of an unresolved Oedipal conflict existing within a quite well functioning ego. In contrast, Marmor felt that hysteric patients were fixated at an oral level; they feared the loss of love and were prone to addiction, depression, and schizophrenia. "The borderline between hysterical fantasy and schizophrenic delusion, and between hysterical materialization and schizophrenic hallucination is often a narrow one; and quantitative factors may affect the qualitative transition from one to the other" (p. 658).

This paper of Marmor was, as it seems, the beginning of a now quite popular trend of distinguishing the "good," analyzable, from the "so-called good," unanalyzable hysteric patients (Zetzel 1968). In the "good" hysteric, there is a predominance of Oedipal conflicts over oral ones. In contrast, the "so-called good" hysteric suffers from infantile fixations with oral problems in the foreground. The "so-called good" hysteric defends not against sexuality but against passivity and orality. Pseudoerotic and acting-out behavior are used here as defenses against the regression to orality.

Actually, Marmor's attempt to let hysteria converge with schizophrenia is a reformulation within libido theory of an old concept: hysterical psychosis. At the end of the nineteenth century many authors, Freud included, used this term; apparently, Bleuler never let pass any opportunity to report his objection. In his *Dementia Praecox or the Group of Schizophrenias,* Bleuler (1911) was quite clear in this respect: "I have never yet had any reason for making a diagnosis of 'hysterical psychosis'. All cases so diagnosed by others differed in no ways from other schizophrenics" (p. 289). Or, again: "When a supposed hysteric becomes psychotic or deteriorates, he is, in my experience, not a hysteric at all, but a schizophrenic." In his *Textbook of Psychiatry,* Bleuler expressed the same view: A large number of women whom he considered schizophrenics passed for "hysterically insane" in other places, whereby it was implied that the insanity was somehow or other a further development of the hysteria. However, Bleuler was emphatic, he had never yet had any reasons for making a diagnosis of "hysterical psychosis."

Clearly, Bleuler objected to any attempt to put psychoneuroses and psychoses on a continuum. It looks as if Fenichel (1945) would also have defined Breuer's patient (Breuer and Freud 1895), Anna O.'s illness as a psychosis, without the adjective hysterical: "Sometimes an ego, otherwise intact, is capable of temporarily tuning away from an unpleasant reality in 'schizophrenic episodes' of short duration, which were called 'hysterical psychosis' or 'amentia' in older psychiatric terminology" (p. 442). As Fenichel's formulation indicates, following Bleuler, he did not believe that the difference between hysteria and schizophrenia is only a matter of a further step on a graded continuum.

Unlike Fenichel, Reichard (1956) explicitly stated that the five patients described by Breuer and Freud did not form a diagnostically homogeneous group. Hysteria, Reichard suggested, is to be defined as a "neurosis showing a minimal degree of ego defect and is characterized by conversion symptoms which . . . [are] expressive of unresolved Oedipal incestuous wishes" (p. 160). However, Anna O. and Emmy von N. manifested a serious defect of ego and, thus, they were suffering from schizophrenia. Also Rado (1959) had no doubt in his mind that "Joseph Breuer's famous patient suffered not as he and Freud believed from hysteria but from schizophrenia" (p. 340).

This opinion of Bleuler (and Fenichel, Reichard, or Rado) notwithstanding, the term "hysterical psychosis," as Hollender and Hirsch (1964) wrote it, is very much with us. It is their understanding that hysterical psychosis is the endpoint on a continuum beginning with hysterical character. A hysterical psychosis is temporally related to an event which has been profoundly upsetting. The manifestations may take the form of hallucinations, delusions, depersonalization, or grossly unusual behavior. Affectivity is in the direction of volatility and not flatness. Thought disorders, when they occur, are generally circumscribed and very transient. The acute episode seldom lasts more than one to three weeks, and it is sealed off so that there is practically no residue.

As mentioned above, Hollender and Hirsch believed that hysterical psychosis is the end point on a continuum beginning with hysterical character. By hysterical character they meant a personality configuration, a life-style, or type of ego function which is the product of a particular constitutional makeup and set of life experiences. This life-style is characterized by an inclination to yield to others' desires, together with often unpredictable changes in mood, relationship, and behavior. A flare for the dramatic or the histrionic is often highly developed. This life-style has some inherent weaknesses in dealing with stress. If anxiety mounts, such a person may feel overwhelmed and behave accordingly. "At this point an altered ego state (or ego feeling) and phenomena such as hallucinations or delusions are experienced. These reactions cannot be classed as defensive; they are manifestations of the disruption of ego function" (p. 1072).

For example, a patient of Hollender and Hirsch, first hospitalized twelve days after giving birth to a child, and, again three years later, declared that she had died from drowning but God had brought her back to life. She was reborn that very morning, she was invulnerable to pain and death, and she was now a form of God. Jesus took care of men; now she would take care of women. Within ten days the patient recovered from her acute psychosis.

As this short vignette indicates, Hollender and Hirsch, very much like Bleuler, did not identify hysteria with hysteric psychosis. Hysteria is the result of an intrapsychic conflict, a "defence" psychoneurosis, to use an old term of Freud; in contrast, hysterical psychosis does not evidence such a conflict but rather, an impairment of the ego functions. Indeed, they emphasized that, "In our discussion we have not ruled out the possibility that hysterical psychosis is a variant or a type of schizoprenia" (p. 1072). Yet, they contended that generally, but not with unfailing precision, one can distinguish hysterical psychosis from schizophrenia. Thus, while at first it may appear that Hollender and Hirsch agreed with Marmor in regard to the affinity between hysteria and schizophrenia, it is apparent that they differentiated between hysterical psychosis, made possible by a personality makeup, and hysteria/neurosis, caused by an intrapsychic conflict.

In complete agreement with Hollender and Hirsch, Stoller (1974) described a patient of his as follows: "Was Mrs. G. psychotic; and if so, what was her psychosis? Most diagnosticians would not hesitate to label her 'psychotic', because she suffered from hallucinations, delusions, bizarre behavior, extremely unreal appraisals of reality, and poorly controlled, dangerous impulsivity. . . . When psychotic, Mrs. G. was always diagnosed on her hospital records as schizophrenic" (p. 121). However, in the opinion of Stoller (and here Bleuler would have agreed with him), this diagnosis was unwarranted. Rather, because of the lack of deterioration in her condition over many years, the episodic nature of her psychosis which was set off by distressing events in her life, and the histrionic quality in which were mingled manipulation, dramatic visual hallucinations, and depersonalization, but no major thought disorder (and I would like to add: no blunting of affect), Mrs. G. should have been diagnosed as suffering from hysterical psychosis.

Incidentally, hysterical psychosis as described by Stoller and Hollander and Hirsch closely resembles the "schizophreniform psychosis" suggested by Langfeldt (1939). Both of these concepts, hysterical psychosis and schizophreniform psychosis, were conceived because of the necessity of differentiating between categories of psychotic behavior, and not for eliminating the borders between psychosis and neuroses. It is precisely for this reason that the terminology of Langfeldt would seem preferable. The term hysterical psychosis may tempt one to disregard these borders.

These borders, however, do exist, and the attempts of Marmor and those who have followed him in denying their reality do not seem convincing. Both common sense and expert witnesses on the meaning of schizophrenia object to such a view. Now that the interpretation of hysteria as the consequence of an unresolved Oedipal conflict is no longer tenable, and the attempt to merge hysteria with schizophrenia is not acceptable either, we need a new definition of hysteria. What is hysteria?

9. HYSTERIA IS AMNESIA

In an attempt to define concisely the Freudian view of hysteria, Beres (1974) described the case of a patient of his, a divorcé in her later thirties, who "had buried her early childhood in a profound amnesia. . . . The current symptom aetiology and recent history included varied somatic complaints, periods of dissociation and transient fugue states" (p. 462). These, then, were the observable behaviors. Regarding somatic complaints, we have seen the serious difficulties confronting anyone who would like to state that a complaint is, in fact, a conversion symptom. Aside from the necessity of comprehensive medical examinations, one must withhold one's final judgment for many years until a protracted observation gives the needed assurance concerning the nature of those complaints.

According to Krohn (1978), Freud, too, saw somatic complaints as accessories and not as a defining feature of hysteria. It is true, though, that the reading by many psychoanalysts of Freud's intentions is different. I have already quoted Laplanche (1974) who, in his effort to safeguard the original Freudian views against some new ideas wrote: "for the reporter, the hysterical symptom remains essentially a conversion symptom" (p. 468). Also Reichard (1956), as one may recall, defined hysteria by the existence of conversion symptoms (and a minimal degree of ego defect). Both of these authors were sure that by pointing out somatic complaints as *the* defining feature of hysteria, they were loyal to Freud's legacy. In any case, whether they or Krohn are the correct interpreters of Freud's understanding, somatic complaints in order to be established as conversion symptoms demand such a laborious process of proof that, for this reason alone, they cannot be relied upon for defining hysteria.

In contrast, the remaining symptoms of Beres' patient—amnesia, fugue states, and dissociation—are recognized defining features of hysteria. In spite of the statements favoring conversion symptoms as the distinguishing mark of hysteria, psychoanalytic writers, in fact, have been unanimous in pointing to repression, i.e., amnesia, as the particular characteristic of what should be labeled hysteria. For example, maintaining that in hysteria we are dealing with the involuntary eruption of unconscious Oedipal fantasies, Beres added the following specification: "Other clinical entities are, of course, also based on unconscious conflicts and unconscious fantasies. What makes hysteria distinctive is the specific role of repression" (p. 460).

Likewise, the Kleinians who reject what Laplanche (1974) called "the evident role of sexuality in the etiology of neuroses," and maintain that hysteria can only be defined as a particular method of defense against early, psychotic and nonsexual anxieties, also point to the defense mechanism, that is, repression as the defining feature of hysteria. For example, Noble (1951) suggested that schizophrenia, hysteria, and an in-between position which he called "hysterico-psychosis" are the possible results of a common conflict originating in the early relationship with the mother. While their core problem seems to have a similar origin, namely, unresolved anxieties, due to a rejection by the mother at a very early age which provoked murderous retaliatory fantasies, hysteria differs from the other disturbances in the defenses mobilized against these anxieties. Repression is the defense characteristic of hysteria.

Thus, psychoanalysts today are divided between those who, while disagreeing in regard to the contribution of the Oedipal conflict, believe in the sexual character of the conflicts responsible for hysteria and those who insist on "desexualizing" the theory of psychoneuroses. To the latter, the conflicts underlying hysteria (and not only hysteria) are related to the survival of the individual rather than to his desires. While disagreeing about the reasons they found to make sense of the phenomena, both Freudians and Kleinians agree that what is observable are phenomena of amnesia.

Sullivan (1956) defined hysteria, "the mental disorder to which the self-absorbed are peculiarly liable," as "the distortion of interpersonal relations which results from extensive amnesia" (p. 54). Last but not least, we must mention Janet. In *The Major Symptoms of Hysteria,* Janet (1907) expressed his doubts about suggestion, the idea so popular among his colleagues in France, and whether it indeed solved the riddle of hysteria. He proposed, instead, the conception of a "disposition of mind":

> Since hysteria has become a more distinctly mental malady, it is in the mind that we must seek for the stigmata. . . . the great mental stigma that modern studies have brought into evidence is the mental phenomenon of suggestion. You cause any idea whatever to penetrate into the mind of the subject. . . . In order that there may be suggestion, it is necessary that the idea should seem to develop to the extreme, without any participation of the will or of the personal consciousness of the subject.
>
> The role played by suggestion in hysteria is beginning to be known, and I shall no longer raise too many protestations by presenting to you suggestion as a hysterical stigma; but I think it is well to go farther. We should not explain the whole of this so complex disease by this single phenomenon. . . .
>
> I should like to put in the first rank of these phenomena a very singular disposition of mind, for which we have not even a very clear expression; namely, a disposition to indifference, to . . . quite exaggerated absent-mindedness. This special absent-mindedness is a stigma peculiar to hysteria.

It was the opinion of Janet that this absentmindedness allows the creation of dissociated "subconscious fixed ideas." Clearly Janet, too, saw before him phenomena of amnesia, and he understood them to be the outcome of a cognitive style, absentmindedness, rather than the result of a clash between motives. The difference between Janet and Freud, then, concern the explanation suggested for the observable phenomena but not the phenomena themselves. The term hysteria describes an impairment, or what seems to be an impairment, of memory. Whichever of the known or yet unknown reasons one may prefer for explaining it, hysteria should be understood as a synonym for phenomena of amnesia.

One hundred years ago, Charcot asked his audience to disregard the original intention expressed by the term hysteria, that is, somatic disturbances caused by the migration of the womb, and to use it, instead, for designating its very opposite, namely, somatic disturbances evoked by nonorganic causes, in women *and* men. Now, one must be asked not only to disregard any imputed connection between hysteria and hysteron, but also to disregard Charcot's revision. Not nonorganically caused somatic dysfunctions, but non-organically caused amnesias are the meaning of the term hysteria.

Agreeing with this usage of the term, one must discontinue applying the classification: hysteria, conversion type and hysteria, dissociative type. There is no other than the dissociative type, which may be accompanied by conversion symptom(s), but need not be. Regarding schizophrenia, Bleuler (1911) suggested that certain symptoms of schizophrenia are present in every case and in every period of the illness. The peculiar disturbance of thought is always present. Beside this and a few more "fundamental" symptoms, one can find a host of other, more "accessory" manifestations, which, according to Bleuler, are not specific to schizophrenia and cannot be used for diagnosing it. Similarly, amnesias are the fundamental symptom of hysteria, whereas conversion symptoms are accessory phenomena.

If so, one may ask, why use the term hysteria; would it not be more reasonable to say amnesia and avoid the confusion now prevailing? Indeed, many authors have already asked this question. Lewis (1975) gathered together a fine collection of angry prophecies from English, French, and German writers who were sure that the day of reckoning had come for "hysteria", and that no one would be able to rescue it.

Lewis himself was more skeptical: "In psychiatry there are forms of illness, with names going back two and a half millennia, which have had sentence of death passed upon more than once, yet they obstinately survive. Paranoia is one such condition and the term, hysteria is another. . . . Funeral orations upon it have often been delivered in the last 100 years" (p. 9). But the majority of psychiatrists, Lewis thinks, would be in a difficult position if they could no longer make a diagnosis of hysteria, "and in any case a tough old word like hysteria dies very hard. It tends to outlive its obituarists" (p. 12).

While such a situation is far from enviable, we may find solace in the fact that the concept of hysteria shares company with another important term, schizophrenia. Bleuler (1911) suggested that dementia praecox be relabeled schizophrenia not because he was critical of this concept, but in order to defend this category of psychopathology from the misunderstanding caused by the term dementia praecox. One of the most common objections, Bleuler observed, is strangely enough that the patients so diagnosed do not always evidence dementia praecox. "Considering Kraepelin's clear definition of the concept and his emphatic mention of cures and of the incidence in older age groups, an objection such as this must be termed a gross misunderstanding on the part of those who do not want to recognize the concept and who instead continue to cling to names" (p. 284). Therefore, Bleuler felt, one is left with no alternative but to give the disease a new name, less likely to be misunderstood. This is why he suggested the term schizophrenia.

The results of his efforts to make clear what seemed to be opaque would certainly not please Bleuler. Writing "about the impossible concept of schizophrenia," Van Praag (1976) concluded that, while the term schizophrenia has been generally accepted, the syndrome referred to by this name has remained a persistent source of controversy and uncertainty. Cancro (1970) thought it was useless to review research in schizophrenia. Of what relevance is it to review directions in an area in which there are virtually no stable coordinates? It is almost as meaningless as speaking of north and south in intergalactic space. Sarbin (1972) went so far as declaring that, "schizophrenia is a myth, born of metaphor, meaningless."

Yet, schizophrenia "may outlive its obituarists." Let us then use these terms but define them anew from time to time and, disregarding the original meaning of the term, adhere to the new definition. After all, we daily use terms such as: psychology and psychic, without even thinking of the concrete psyche the Greek philosophers thought of. Accordingly, let us again define hysteria: it designates phenomena of nonorganically caused amnesia, which may be accompanied by functional somatic dysfunctions, but need not be.

By accepting this definition, we would be in a position to clarify the meaning of the controversial concept, hysterical personality, too. Culling descriptions from various sources—textbooks, monographs, and professional journals—Chodoff and Lyons (1958) synthesized the following description of the hysterical personality: (1) vain and eccentric; (2) displays labile and excitable but shallow affectivity; (3) dramatic attention seeking and histrionic behavior which may go to the extremes of lying and even pseudologia phantastica; (4) very conscious of sex, sexually provocative yet frigid; (5) dependently demanding in interpersonal situations.

The definition of hysterical personality as "sexually provocative yet frigid" seems to be applicable to women only. All those who assume a continuity between hysterical personality and hysterical neurosis must, then, maintain—Galens', Charcot's and Freud's views notwithstanding—that hysteria is a women's disease. This, for example, was the opinion of Zetzel (1968). Suggesting the concept of the "so-called good hysteric," she wrote: "Although I have evaluated, analysed, and supervised the analysis of a number of men comparable with my sample of women, the number of whose presenting symptoms were hysterical is far smaller. My findings are thus in keeping with Easser and Lesser's (1965) conclusion that presenting hysterical symptomatology is less common in men than in women" (p. 256).

At a closer look, however, this distinction becomes blurred. The analyzable man, Zetzel thinks, who has failed adequately to resolve his Oedipal situation is likely to present, at least initially, an obsessional rather than hysterical character structure and/or symptomatology. "This same finding is, however, at least relatively true of the group I have described as the most analysable hysterical women" (p. 258). The "truly" hysterical women, then, behave like their male counterparts. If it is the consequences of an unsolved Oedipal conflict that differentiates between man and woman, then, this very finding contradicts her own statistics in regard to the distribution of hysteria among the sexes. Either her finding or her criteria for defining hysterical personality and hysterial neurosis are not valid.

Many authors, indeed, define hysteria by means of functional disturbances rather than psychodynamically. In fact, as we have seen, psychodynamic writers, too, are inclined to do this, although they label these disturbances conversion symptoms, thereby transforming the observable behavior into its suggested explanation. For the moment, however, we may disregard these subtleties and ask, instead, which sex is more afflicted by functional disturbances/conversion symptoms?

A study of Chodoff and Lyons (1958) may indicate the answer to this question. They reviewed the hospital charts of all patients in a Veterans Administration hospital who had had, during a two-year period, a discharge diagnosis of conversion reaction. They found thirty-six such charts but eliminated nineteen of them, mainly because of doubts about the presence of significant organic nervous system disease either causing or influencing the symptom. The remaining seventeen cases, as far as was known at the time of their study, were free of relevant neurological disease, and had been subjected to psychiatric investigation, in some cases, supplemented by psychological testing. The symptoms included pains, headaches, paralysis of limbs, tremors, and sensory disturbances. Of the seventeen patients, fifteen were men and two women.

Allowing for a bias "favoring" men, due to the fact that the study was conducted in a VA hospital, one may still say that functional disturbances/conversion symptoms do not seem to be the prerogative of women. Hysteria, defined either as the consequence of an unresolved Oedipal conflict or as functional disturbances, seems to offer, if one may say so, equal opportunities to both sexes. And regarding hysterical personality, as defined by the characteristics mentioned above, Chodoff and Lyons' (1958) criticism sounds rather convincing. These characteristics, they say, present a picture of women in the words of men; "it amounts to a caricature of femininity! . . . A situation analogous to the one described might be imagined if women psychiatrists spent some generations coolly and rather inimically observing the less attractive foibles of males, and then put them together as the manifestations of a kind of personality characteristic of men!" (p. 739).

It does not look as if much can be said in defense of the right of existence of the concept of hysterical personality. If, however, as suggested here, hysteria were defined as nonorganically caused amnesias, then, without the pejorative sense usually attached to it and, of course, not restricting it to women, one might continue using the concept of hysterical personality. Since we may expect that the reasons for the nonorganically caused amnesias function in a continuous rather than in a dichotomous manner, we may suggest, as did many others before us, that hysterical neurosis, i.e., nonorganic amnesia, is a further development, an exaggeration, of a central feature of the hysterical personality. These hints, as well as the possible reasons for the amnesias which define hysteria, will be elaborated in the next two chapters.

10. REPRESSION, DISSOCIATION, AND UN-INTEGRATION

There are two main trends as to how to understand those pecularities of memory which define hysteria. Freud saw in them defense mechanisms used in fending off the consequences of an intrapsychic conflict. Janet, as we have seen, suggested "to put in the first rank" of the features defining hysteria "a very singular disposition of mind . . . to quite exaggerated absent-mindedness." In fact, one should say that for the greatest part of this century, there seemed to be a consensus that motivated repression is the reason and explanation for hysteria. Lately, however, it looks as if by a dramatic shift what was in the center is now drifting to the periphery and the limelight falls against on what thus far lay in the dark background.

In a thoughtful essay, Shapiro (1965) caused us to have second thoughts about the Freudian view of hysteria. It was Shapiro's opinion that hysterical cognition, in general, is global, relatively diffuse, and lacking in precise details. In contrast to the active, intense, and sharply focused attention of the obsessive, hysterical cognition seems relatively lacking in sharp focus of attention; in contrast to the obsessive's active and prolonged searching for detail, the hysterical person tends to respond quickly and is highly susceptible to what is immediately impressive, striking, or merely obvious. This lack of factual detail and sharp definition in hysterical cognition can hardly be attributed to the operation of the defense mechanism of repression. It is not a matter of the exclusion of specific ideational or emotional contents from consciousness and does not principally have to do with the contents of thought at all.

Rather, Shapiro maintained, the style of cognition of hysterical people, comprising as it does, the same global impressionistic mode of attention and recollection is, by its nature, conducive to forgetting and repression.

In fact, we may ask ourselves whether one is allowed to speak of repression in the traditional manner. The original input, to begin with, is "not sharply, factually defined and is not likely to be logically co-ordinated with other facts but is impressionistic and highly susceptible to displacement by or fusion with other previous or subsequent impressions" (p. 166). Second, Shapiro suggests, the relative incapacity for sharply focused attention and concentration and the passive, impressionistic, distractible nature of the cognitive style may be assumed to hold for the recollection process also and to make clear, sharp, factual recollection unlikely "under the best of circumstances."

To put it briefly, given such a style of cognition, what may look like a tendentious distortion of precisely registered and preserved information turns out to be the inevitable result not of a concession to a strict censor and a compromise with it, but of a mode, a style, of mental functioning. There was no external interference and no necessity for manipulating the original information, since in any case "this mode of functioning or, specifically, of cognition decidely favors the phenomenon we describe as 'repression'. In fact, given such a mode of functioning, clear, detailed, factual recollection of contents that are highly charged emotionally is hardly imaginable" (p. 117).

Speaking of repression, we assume a process of covering up, of disguise and of substituting a fake for the true memory or thought. Nothing of the kind is true, Shapiro suggests. He who perceives precisely will recall the required details, and he who sees the world in a global, impressionistic manner will recall his experiences accordingly. These consistencies in an individual's functioning do not seem to be explainable as manifestations of specific defense mechanisms or derivatives of specific drive contents; they are too broad and extensive for that. They are, instead, formal consistencies of individual styles. "The defensive process cannot be regarded merely as an operation of specific drive-inhibiting mechanism, since it involves the whole drive-tension and stimulus organizing style" (p. 195).

Apparently, to Shapiro, the concept of repression and the impressive structure of its ramifications became, in fact, obsolete. Indeed, following up on the consequences of his approach, Shapiro pointed out that now we may be able to tackle a problem psychoanalysis was thus far unable to resolve, the problem of the "choice" of neurosis. If the neuroses are the outcome of one common, Freudian or Kleinian, conflict and the difference between them is due mainly to the principal defense applied, the question arises: what determines the "choice" of defense? This question has figured significantly in psychoanalysis without, however, receiving a satisfactory answer. To begin with, Shapiro thinks, this "choice" is better understood as a lack of choice, as a disposition. "The disposition to one or another specific form of symptom may be regarded as essentially a problem of character, and further, character may be regarded as consisting of the configuration in an individual of just such general and relatively stable forms of functioning as we have been discussing." (p. 4).

Such was the approach already suggested by Janet; it is interesting to observe how the inner development of psychoanalysis, certainly uninfluenced by the writings of this rival of the early Freud, led Shapiro to come full circle, close to some of the forgotten ideas of Janet. Unlike Shapiro, Millar (1958) explicitly urged us to reconsider favorably Janet's basic idea. He also suggested improving it by proposing a revision of the Jacksonian concept of hierarchy in the structure and function of the central nervous system. Jackson understood the organization of the CNS to follow a roughly phylogenetic principle: the evolutionally earlier and simpler structures came under the control of the later, more complex structures.

But now, Millar thinks, it is time to revise this popular view. It now seems likely that there is no such rigid hierarchy, but that a number of more or less independent systems exist, composed of both early and recent structures; there are, for instance, in the rhinencephalon old structure that have continued to develop every bit as much as the cerebral cortex, and have acquired new functions in addition to their old ones. The exact functions of these various systems are not yet definitely known, but it is apparent that they perform functions which once were assigned to the cerebral cortex only. It therefore does not seem necessary to think of mental processes as strictly hierarchical, Millar concludes. The capacity for integration and organization resides not in the cerebral cortex alone, but throughout the whole central nervous system.

Applying this principle of organization of the CNS to the question of hysteria, Millar suggests that "we now have a simple and understandable basis for the hysterical state. The basis is un-integration of autonomous systems. . . . since we know that in some manner hysteria is related to 'impressive events', we must assume that these events have a specifically evocative character for some particular independent sub-system (not related to the main personality). . . . this is therefore not dissociation but un-integration" (p. 818).

Both Shapiro and Millar, in effect, cast their votes in the old debate between dissociation and repression in favor of the former. If we assume that the mental life of any person is integrated and should be integrated, then we must explain why and how some parts of this total unity became disconnected, split off. This was the way Freud, a devoted Jacksonian, understood mental life. One may see this, for example, from the following statement in his *The Ego and the Id:*

> From the point f view of analytic practice . . . we land in endless obscurities and difficulties if we keep to our habitual forms of expression and try, for instance, to derive neuroses from a conflict between the conscious and the unconscious. We shall have to substitute for this antithesis another . . . the antithesis between the coherent ego and the repressed which is split off from it. (Freud 1923, p. 21)

We may contrast with this approach the view of some French psychologists who, impressed by the studies on double personalities so popular at the end of the century, concluded—as Hilgard (1976) put it—that "the concept of unity of the total consciousness is an attractive one, but it does not hold up under examination." Commenting on the case of a famous double personality, "Felida," Binet (1891) wrote:

> It remains, in closing, to indicate definitely the psychological problem based on Felida's history. Here are two mental lives alternating, without being confused, and each of these existences consists in a series of psychological events connected with one another. When Felida is in the first state she can remember the events of this state; on the other hand, it is impossible for her without assistance to recover the memory of events that belong to the second state, why is this?
>
> This amnesia can by no means be explained psychologically by the well-known laws of association of ideas. According to these laws all memories can be stimulated by the influence of resemblance and contiguity. But we here see these two forces of association at fault. The memories of the second condition do not reappear during the normal condition, even when they should be called forth by certain adequate associations. We need no further proof than is found in the case of the little dog that Felida loaded with caresses during her second life and did not recognise in the first. I believe that it has not been sufficiently noticed how refractory this characteristic amnesia is to current theories of association of ideas. We shall often have occasion to repeat this remark. (P. 21)

He was fully entitled to repeat this remark and would have had many occasions to do so during the greater part of this century. Lately, however, we have witnessed a kind of renaissance of the idea advocated by

Binet and Janet. Aside from Millar (1958) who suggested the concept of un-integration and Hilgard (1976) who suggested the concept of neo-dissociation, the experiments on "state-dependent learning" in man and animal helped to call attention to this feature of our mental life.

The experiments on "state-dependent learning" began with a study of Girden and Culler (1937). They noted that what an animal learned while under the influence of some drug would be available for performance only if the animal were drugged again. Conversely, what an animal learned while sober could be performed in a similar state only, but not while drugged.

The study of Girden and Culler went unnoticed, and it was Overton (1964) who drew much attention to this topic. He showed that rats trained to avoid a section of maze while drugged by sodium amytal, when tested later while they were sober behaved in a way which did not indicate that they had benefited from any earlier experience. If, however, rats trained under the influence of the drug were tested while drugged again, their behavior gave clear evidence of their previous learning. Similarly, Otis (1964) trained rats while they were under the influence of chlorpromazine or after they received an injection of saline. Animals that learned under one condition and were tested again to measure the effects of their learning under the other condition showed "greater dissociation," as he put it, that is, less evidence of learning that did animals that received only injections of saline or only injections of chlorpromazine during both training and testing sessions.

In another study, Bliss (1974) trained monkeys to select the appropriate color of two alternatives (red—correct, green—not correct) for getting their preferred food. They learned under the influence of either sodium pentobarbital or saline and were tested for remembering their learning in either the same or the alternative state. When tested under the same drug state in which they were trained, they had nearly perfect recall of the original learning. If testing, however, was conducted under the normal (saline) state and training had been under the sodium pentobarbital state, or vice versa, recall was almost nil.

It is very likely that electroconvulsive shocks may also produce dissociation of experiences. In contradiction to an earlier view according to which electroshocks wipe out, as it were, the mental events experienced immediately before and after the electroshock, it has been shown (Thompson and Nelly, 1970) that what an animal learned immediately before being shocked would be available for recall if, before it was tested, it was electroshocked again. Electroshock, then, did not destroy the mental representation of these events, but rather, dissociated them from the stream of waking consciousness. Reinstating the original confused state made the memory of learning available again for use.

There is, then, evidence in these experiments that animals store their memories in separate systems and that they are able to recollect some experience in one state of mind, but behave as if they are amnesic of this experience in another state of mind.

In experiments with human subjects alcohol has mainly been used. Goodwin (1969) was able to demonstrate experimentally that his subjects were better able to recall what they had learned while intoxicated if they were also under the influence of alcohol when retested. He offered some of his subjects a certain quantity of alcohol while leaving the others sober. Both groups had to memorize some items. Twenty-four hours later, subjects intoxicated during the first session recalled their learning better if they were intoxicated again than if they were sober. Conversely, subjects who learned while sober performed better in the same frame of mind than if they were intoxicated.

Again, it is rewarding to consult old, forgotten Binet (1891), for he knew of these facts and would have been pleased by these experiments which endorse his observations. The question arises, he wrote, whether apart from hysteria analoguous divisions of consciousness and personality are to be met with. Here is his answer:

> If the state of memory is taken as a sign of these divisions—and it is always easier to verify it exactly than changes of character—the question must be answered in the affirmative. We find in very divers conditions fragments of psychological life, each of which possesses a memory. We mean by this that these states are not remembered in the normal life, but that the return of the state recalls the memories of its previous manifestation, so that the person remembers all the facts that had been forgotten during the normal life.
>
> Occasionally, the existence of memory peculiar to these second states shows itself in a slightly different and more elementary form; the subject always recommences the same actions. Examples of similar psychological changes are known in dreams, intoxication by ether, hasheesh, alcohol, etc. in recurrent mania and epilepsy.

Fully confirming Binet's finding but, of course, uninfluenced by him and perhaps even not aware of his work, Fischer (1971) reported that a patient's thread of thought in narcoanalysis resumes, after an injection of amobarbital, exactly where it left off at the end of the previous session.

These experiments and observations, old and new, regarding the existence of separate systems of memory lend credibility to the suggestion of Millar. Hilgard's analysis (1973) of the evidence in favor of what he labels neo-dissociation is, thus far, the latest step in calling to life a theory of hysteria which was hibernating, so to speak, for so long.

"The notion of dissociation seemed so plausible, and the concept was used so widely, that it is difficult to see why it faded away as it did. . . . What happened?" Hilgard (1973) asks. Perhaps the main reason for the disappearance of the concept of dissociation was pointed out by McDougall (1926): "It is a remarkable fact that whereas Prof. Janet, Dr. Morton Prince, and other authorities regard dissociation as the most important and far-reaching explanatory principle to be applied in interpreting neurotic disorders, Freud makes no use of this conception; and the word does not, I think, appear in any of his principal writings" (p. 407).

As it seems, Freud's silence forbid, in effect, mention of the concept of dissociation, let alone debate about it. But now, perhaps because of the decline of Freud's authority, dissociation is respectable again, although with some changes in the original conception. For example, while paying due respect to Janet, Hilgard (1973) also took care to differentiate between his and Janet's definition of dissociation. "Because I do not wish to defend all that has been claimed for dissociation in the past, I prefer to state the case of a neo-dissociation concept—that is, one that has affiliations with the historical concept, but has been reformulated to account for what we know" (p. 212).

What we know, Hilgard suggests, is that there are processes carried on outside of normal ego controls, "and if, when occasionally, two systems of control appear to be operating sumultaneously, then a concept such as dissociation is inviting" (p. 212). You listen to what the other person is saying, while at the same time formulating a reply supporting or refuting it. You thus operate simultaneously a monitoring and a talking system; this means that the stream of consciousness flows in more than one channel at a time. Then, under some circumstances, conscious processes take place as in hypnosis, that in their nature and sequence are relatively independent of normal ego control. One must admit then, Hilgard thinks, that although there is some motivational pull toward consistency and toward a sense of unity of the personality, dissonance does in fact exist and persist between behavior systems of the person.

As this sketchy description of Hilgard's view may indicate, he was rather cautious in parting with the traditional Jacksonian view of hierarchy in structure and functions of the CNS. Conversely, Millar's suggestion that we consider the possibility of autonomous psychic systems which while possibly cooperative, may be dissociated or rather un-integrated, nonassociated, was straightforward in its attempt to break alternative ground for understanding mental functioning.

In a sense, Millar's term was more Janetian than Janet's was. The term "dissociation" suggests the existence of a formerly existing association. This, indeed, was Freud's understanding, as indicated in the passage quote from his *The Ego and the Id.* In contrast, Binet and Millar said simply and unequivocally what in Janet's writing remained ambiguous, namely, that we have more than one system of control. Therefore, a nonorganic amnesia does not necessarily prove the existence of a clash between motives. What we are unable to recall in one state of mind, we may be able to retrieve while under the control of another mental system. Such an amnesia, then, may indicate un-integration rather than repression.

On the other hand, Janet was more aware of the need for individual differences to be taken into consideration than Millar seemed to be. Janet, as one may recall, asked us to put in the first rank of hysterical phenomena "a very singular disposition of mind," for which he did not even have the proper word and, for want of a better term, described as a quite exaggerated absentmindedness. Let us, then, suggest that integration as well as un-integration are on a continuum, and those who are "exaggeratedly" nonintegrating persons are prone to amnesias and fugues. At this point, Shapiro and Janet could meet, for it was Shapiro who, like Janet, put in the center of his explanation of hysteria a particular personality configuration, a particular cognitive style.

By now, one would like to know what remains of the concept of repression. Is working with it still warranted? Actually, independently of Millar's and Shapiro's suggestions, some difficulties inherent in this concept make it impossible to continue working with it. This is how Freud (1915a) defined repression: "The mechanism of repression becomes accessible to us only by our deducing that mechanism from the *outcome* of the repression" (p. 154).

The idea condensed in the word "outcome" says that: (1) there are two mental systems endowed by two modes of functioning, the primary and secondary process; (2) some ideas which are incompatible with standards of the self or the society are "deflected from consciousness," that is, pushed from system ego to system id and, thereby, made not available for recall, in one word: repressed; and finally, (3) a repressed idea may become recallable again at the price of modifications or distortions only. These distortions of the original idea, referred to earlier as the outcome of the repression, are what one may observe of an otherwise hidden process.

These distortions are, to repeat what I have explicated elsewhere (Giora 1975, 1981), the pivotal point of the concept of repression, for without some distortions to which the original idea has been subjected, one could not infer that the idea was repressed.

It is implied here that one must know the original idea, for only by comparing it with its distorted expression, as in a bizarre dream, may the process of repression be demonstrated. This quite simple-sounding procedure is, unfortunately, not realizable. A repressed thought, according to Freud (1900), "has no access to conscious *except via the preconscious* in passing through which its excitatory process is obliged to submit to modifications" (p. 541, emphasis in the original); which means that the idea in its original form is never knowable. Without it, however, without comparing the unconscious but rational thought with its conscious but distorted expression, one is not allowed to speak of modification, and consequently, of repression. *Repression defined by its outcome, i.e., by modifications effected on the original and never knowable thought, is a nontestable statement.*

Interestingly enough, Freud (1939) felt so sure of his position that he even ventured to say that the true sense of a symbol escapes us unless we are informed by an analyst. Yet it is difficult to agree with this picture of exclusive knowledge, given Freud's further remark: "the archaic heritage . . . can . . . become active—that is, can advance to consciousness from its unconscious state in the id, even though in an altered and distorted shape" (p. 101). Here is the essence of the problem with which we are dealing. If these symbols appear in consciousness, that is, are knowable, only in an altered and distorted shape, how does anyone know their original form?

It goes without saying that nothing was said or implied here which should be understood as denying the possibility of motivated forgetting. There are certainly instances in which, due to some motive or a conflict between motives, we are unable to retrieve some of our memories. Not only is this statement true, it is also old knowledge. "'I did that' says my memory," wrote Nietzsche in one of his maxims, "'I could not have done that' says my pride and remains inexorable. Eventually, the memory yields"

(1886). Freud's contribution here was to postulate the existence of two psychic systems and a distortion that the repressed thought *had* to undergo before it could be admitted to consciousness again. Any attempt to deal with the nonretrievability of memories, which does not tightly connect it to the supposed distortions, eliminates the particularly Freudian from the concept of repression. It is precisely this particular contribution which makes the concept of repression unacceptable.

I would like to point to another weakness of the concept of repression, which I have labeled (Giora 1975) the continuum of defense. It was the opinion of Freud that, while one can lay down no general rule as to what degree of distortion is necessary before a repressed thought may become conscious again, one may say that the barriers erected against a repressed thought are tighter in directed wakeful thinking than while one is engaged in daydreaming.

While one is sleeping and dreaming, the ability of the system ego to resist the temptation of repressed wish is, quite logically, rather weak. The repressed thought, then, may reappear in consciousness: loosely distorted in dreams, better disguised and more distorted in daydreams, and even more so in controlled wakeful thinking. This stiffening resistance to the objected to and repressed thought from dreams through daydreams to wakeful thinking, evidenced by an increase in the rate of distortions to which the repressed idea is subjected, is the conceptual line of a continuum of defense.

I have investigated the relation between dreams and fantasy while awake with regard to the expression of hostility. My subjects first performed a Thematic Apperception Test (TAT), then were asked to write down over a period of five months every dream they were able to recall. By the end of this time, we obtained from each subject an average of 17 TAT stories and 4.5 dreams. Both the dreams and TAT stories were analyzed according to the scoring system of Hall and Van de Castle (1966). Regarding aggressive interactions, it was shown that in every subject the intensity of aggression revealed was higher in TAT stories than in dreams. Aggression was expressed more straightforwardly and more violently in TAT stories than in dreams.

In a similar study, which gave the impetus to my own experiment, Kramer, Winget, and Whitman (1971) compared the expressions of hostility in early memories and dreams. They found that while early memories contain slightly more covert hostility directed outward, in dreams covert hostility directed outward is four times as common as overt hostility directed outward. In dreams, these authors concluded, but not in early memories, the indirect expression is the preferred mode. This is not what the construct of repression would have us expect. In accord with this construct, one would predict that thoughts and feelings not endorsed by system ego enjoy more freedom of expression in dreams than in daydreams. The results of Kramer, et al., and of my experiment definitely contradict this expectation. While the reasons for this curious relationship between dreams and fantasies in waking are not quite understood, it is by no means compatible with the continuum of defense. Such a continuum, however, is a built-in demand of the construct of repression.

While the implications of these experiments are clear and do not seem to demand further elaboration, one may add here that the best way to prove the existence of the conception of defense would be to compare the dreams and fantasies of someone who is struggling with a well-defined conflict. Here we would have an opportunity to see whether or not his fantasies only faintly indicate what his dreams are able to actualize more expressly. Very few psychotherapists contributing to the literature seem to be interested in this question and it is very fortunate that Ford and Urban (1963), even though not following up the consequences of their observations, reported a pertinent case.

A young man, Ford and Urban report, was repeatedly disturbed by fearful dreams which he felt to be "inescapable indications" of homosexuality and of aggressive-sadistic impulses toward his mother. He awakened from these recurring dreams in great panic, and remained confused about the reality of the events of the dream. In addition, his waking hours were disturbed by alarming experiences in which he had the feeling that people were inserting penises into his rectum. He described his attempts to resist the sensation, to deny its existence, but the sensation persisted to such a degree that he felt forced to admit he felt it.

This patient, then, indulged in directly expressed homosexual fantasies while awake, but in his dreams the same wish was expressed rather circumstantially. This is scarcely evidence of a censorship relaxed in sleep. Further, the same experience, the homosexual wish, which during the day eventually elicited a rather positive, participating attitude, caused terror when it occurred in his dreams. Anyone following Freud would expect the opposite to be true, namely that anxiety would grow in direct relationship to the increasingly straightforward expressions of a conflict-arousing wish. Instead of demonstrating an ever-stronger control over instinctual wishes from dreams through fantasies to directed thinking, this example suggests rather that the concept of repression and its corollary, the inevitably ongoing conflict between drive and defense, do not fit the facts.

An observation of Piaget (1947) seems to further support this conclusion. One of his children, at the age of two years and nine months, awakened from her sleep with a loud scream and informed her parents: "It was all dark and I saw a lady over there (pointing to her bed). That's why I screamed" (p. 177). This lady, she explained, stood with her legs apart and played with her faeces. This lady, in fact, did only what the child pretended to make her dolls and other make-believe characters do, and yet this kind of activity, which easily becomes a joke in play, was accompanied in dreams by considerable anxiety. As play is more easily controlled than dreams, Piaget suggests, this difference between fantasies is quite natural.

Let us note that the control Piaget had in mind is not the kind of control of which Freud thought. For Freud, to be controlled meant that the instinctual wish was more disguised, better covered up in fantasies than in dreams. Piaget did not report any disguise, nor, of equal importance, any increase in disguise in fantasy. But he did point out the difference between enjoyment which turned into dread in the dream. Both what Piaget's observation did reveal (enjoyment and dread) and what it did not (disguise) contradict the prediction derived from the principle of the continuum of ego defense.

Kris (1948), who was well aware of the implications and expectations of Freud's concept of defense, was indeed puzzled by the fact that "When fantasy has taken us far enough afield, we do not, as a rule, experience shame or guilt. . . . Patients may feel ashamed or guilty when reporting such fantasies, although they did not feel so while they were engaged in them, or when they recalled them" (p. 314). Kris, though left unanswered the question of whether we can continue to work with the concept of a continuum of defenses graded from waking thought through fantasies to dreams, while at the same time pointing out that fantasies are free from censorship. However, the contradiction is too blatant to be simply overlooked.

Fantasies, whether sanctioned by society and moral or not, do not demand that disguise, condensation, or a clang association appear in place of the instinctual wish; we are alarmed, though, when we dream of the same wish. Why is that so? Why should we be shaken, as Piaget's child or Ford and Urban's patient were, by expressing a wish in dreams, but allowed to enjoy and actively elaborate the same wish in fantasy? This puzzle is even more detrimental to the concept of repression than was the stalemate created by its definition. Repression defined by its "outcome" is a never testable statement, which means that it is impossible to prove or disprove it. In contrast, the failure to substantiate the concept of the continuum of ego defense does disprove "repression."

Recalling the gallery of writers and ideas reviewed here, we may say that while Janet, Millar, and Shapiro do not see eye to eye on every aspect of the issue dealt with here, they concur in rejecting repression as the reason for amnesias. Freud put at the center the idea of a conflict between motives, whose results, the foremost being repression, are determined by the differing functions and modes of working of two interacting mental systems; Janet, Millar, and Shapiro do not mention either conflict or two mental systems at all. Rather, they emphasize stable personality configurations which, due to their constitution, may lead to dissociations or unintegration.

It is apparent that these differences in the understanding of the nonorganic amnesias imply different theories of psychoneuroses. These differences, though, were never made explicit. Unlike Freud, to whom an unresolved Oedipal conflict was the necessary and sufficient cause of the neurotic behavior disturbances, Janet, Millar, and Shapiro did not specify the pathogenic agent responsible for hysteria or obsessive states, for example. These authors, in effect, left the question in limbo. Yet, if one suggests the substitution of stable personality configurations, cognitive styles, for defense mechanisms, one can hardly evade the question: is it still true that an instinctual drive-defense conflict is at the heart of the neuroses?

11. A GENERAL THEORY OF NEUROSES

In his *Inhibitions, Symptoms, and Anxiety,* Freud (1926) observed that "a great many people remain infantile in their behavior in regard to danger and do not overcome determinants of anxiety which have grown out of date. To deny this would be to deny the existence of neurosis, for it is precisely such people whom we call neurotics" (p. 148). Again, saying it more concisely: "The neurotic will differ from the normal person in that his reactions to the dangers in question will be unduly strong" (p. 148). This definition does not really distinguish neuroses from normalcy, but rather suggests a scale of reactions to perceived dangers set more or less subjectively. Neurotics are more prone to anxiety than normal people, and it is this tendency that turns them into neurotics.

In this essay, Freud also stated that neuroses are the exclusive products of an anxious overreaction: "Why does the affect of anxiety alone seem to enjoy the advantage over all the other affects of evoking reactions which are distinguished from the rest in being abnormal and which, through their inexpediency, run counter to the movement of life? . . . After tens of years of psychoanalytic labours, we are as much in the dark about this problem as we were at the start" (p. 149).

Freud's view that only the degree of anxiety differentiates psychoneuroses from normal behavior did not go unchallenged. Taking issue with this position, Rado (1959) wrote: "In the above paragraph, Freud does not so much as mention rage, or even imply it, say, by some reference to his so-called 'death-instinct' that 'instinct of destruction and self-destruction' " (p. 339). Or, without arguing with Freud, DeNike and Tiber (1968) suggested that "psychoneuroses or neuroses . . . are characterized by anxiety and depression, and various maladaptive techniques people use to escape such feelings" (p. 345). The monopoly of anxiety for creating psychoneuroses is, then, disputed, but not the general view according to which neurotic behavior is an overmeasure of normal reactions, rather than being essentially different from them.

If not his critics, Freud himself seems to have had some doubt about his own position, for in the same essay he suggested that, after all, neuroses are qualitatively different from normal behavior: "If 'Little Hans', being in love with his mother, had shown fear of his father, we should have no right to say that he had a neurosis or a phobia. His emotional reaction would have been entirely comprehensible. What made it a neurosis was one thing alone: the replacement of his father by a horse. It is this displacement, then, which has a claim to be a symptom" (p. 103).

This view of Freud seems to contradict his other view, quoted above, according to which a neurosis is an exaggeration of a normal fear reaction. The appeal of the second definition will be stronger, I assume, for psychoanalytic readers than for the others. Unlike the first definition, the attempt to define psychoneuroses by psychodynamic means such as the assumption that while 'Little Hans' complained of menacing horses, in reality, he felt threatened by his father, is truly Freudian. This definition entails, first, the idea of an unconscious conflict between an Oedipal striving and a fear aroused by this wish and, secondly, what Meissner (1981) described as "Freud's unique contribution and the basis for all psychoanalytic understanding, [namely] the discovery that symptoms have meaning" (p. 923). As it happens, it is for these very reasons that many other readers may disagree with Freud's second definition of psychoneuroses.

To begin with, Little Hans resisted going out into the street because he was afraid of horses. Freud suggested that this fear was not reasonable, but became reasonable if we assume that, in truth, he feared his father and only transposed or displaced this fear onto horses. Such an assumption, while possible, needs proof. We have already seen the difficulties, or rather the self-contradictions, involved in proving such an assumption.

Freud (1905a), as one may recall, admitted that "the existence of an unconscious origin and the meaning attributed to the act cannot be conclusively established. We must content ourselves with recording the fact that such a meaning fits in quite extraordinarily well with the situation as a whole" (p. 77). Freud (1909a) also admitted that "during the analysis Hans had to be told many things that he could not say himself, that he had to be presented with thoughts which he had so far shown no signs of possessing, and that his attention had to be turned in the direction from which his father was expecting something to come" (p. 104). Yet, Freud regarded his conclusions to be "inevitable." But, this, precisely, is the issue: whether such conclusions are possible or inevitable.

Take, for example, the interpretation of dreams. It may be regarded as the paradigm and the best of what the psychodynamic approach may offer. I shall relate here one of the many difficulties pointed out in my study on dream styles (Giora 1981). The interpretation of a dream relies on the dreamer's associations. The associations should lead us back from the manifest content to the latent dream-thoughts. But, "we need not suppose that every association that occurs during the work of interpretation had a place in the dream-work during the night" (Freud 1900, p. 532). To begin with, fresh daytime material inserts itself into the present associations; then, "the increase in resistance that has set in since the night makes new and more devious detours necessary." Why, then, ask for these associations? "The number and nature of the collaterals that we spin in this way during the day is of no psychological importance whatever," Freud thinks, "so long as they lead us to the dream-thoughts of which we are in search" (p. 542).

Our problem now is how to identify the collaterals and to separate them from the dream-thoughts. Unfortunately, the crucial decision as to whether an association is "collateral," and therefore not worthy of being followed up, or instead, "had a place in the dream-work during the night" is left to the understanding of the interpreter. How does one know that an association was essential and not collateral? One should decide according to the result: an essential association leads to a latent dream-thought, a collateral one does not. But how does one know whether the thought an association led to actually participated in creating the dream? It is the interpreter, relying on his uncontrolled inferences and understanding, who will decide this. Since, in the precise words of Krohn (1978), "owing to the difficulty of describing the process of clinical inference, the method of inferring these dynamics has never been made explicit enough for research purposes" (p. 51), such decisions, inevitably, remain debatable.

The essence of my argument is that this is not a method of proof, and if such is the basis for all psychoanalytic understanding, in all fairness critics can be forgiven for not being convinced of the validity of these conclusions. The soul of a science is its methods of proof; the more so, if one declares, as did Freud (1916), that in his method observed phenomena must take second place to forces that are merely hypothesized. If, indeed, the observable data are unimportant, because the real facts, usually, are different from what we can see and hear, then the questions relating to the preferred and allowed ways of inferring are highly relevant and important. Yet, as the complaint of Krohn may indicate, these questions have not received the attention they deserve.

Stoller (1971), though, was aware of some difficulties with which the psychoanalytic method of proof is confronted. "One usually can see clinical data behind the jargon but is never sure just what the observations are. Granted it is impossible to reproduce any moment of a psychoanalytic hour. Still, that is our problem, and if we do not solve it, we remain outside of science, and our statements . . . can only be accepted by others as possibilities not as laws. . . . We all know this and it should make us modest" (p. 14). Important as this self-analysis is, it does not deal with the further problem dealt with here, the ways and modes of inferring. Whereas Stoller questioned the quality of data subserving psychoanalytic practice and theory, I have pointed to the danger of arbitrariness in assigning meaning to those facts.

Interestingly enough, while conceding that the psychodynamic approach, indeed, invites such a criticism, some authors suggest that, in fact, one may be proud of it. For example, Ricoeur (1970) agreed that the question of proof in psychoanalysis is as old as psychoanalysis itself. "The 1895 'Project' aims at being a project of scientific psychology. 'The Interpretation of Dreams' purports to be a science and not a fantastic construction. . . . And yet, psychoanalysis has never quite succeeded in stating how its assertions are justified, how its interpretations are authenticated, how its theory is justified" (p. 247). Likewise, Barratt (1976) consented that "Freudianism is not a positivist or empiricist doctrine; the criticisms of Nagel, Farrell, and others are unanswerable on their own grounds, and it has to be conceded that Freud's theories are not scientific statements in this particular sense" (p. 444).

But for all that, these authors suggest, there is no reason to be pessimistic. Quite on the contrary. Thus, Rycroft (1966), while not objecting much to the criticism against the psychodynamic method of proof, regretted that "the majority of Freudian analysts . . . lay themselves open to attack from critics . . . who see quite clearly that psychoanalysis cannot satisfy the canons of those sciences which are based on the experimental method" (p. 14). To his mind, the analysts are claiming that psychoanalysis is what it is not and the critics are attacking psychoanalysis for failing to be what it has no need to claim to be. Rather, Rycroft suggests, one has to acknowledge that, while owing to his training, Freud formulated his findings in the conceptual framework of the physical sciences, in fact, "the procedure he engaged in was not the scientific one of elucidating causes but the semantic one of making sense" (p. 14).

Elaborating a similar approach, Ricoeur (1974) went as far as suggesting that it does not matter if an interpretation is inconsistent with the facts, for "in analysis the real history is merely a clue to the figurative history through which the patient arrives at self-understanding; for the analyst, the important thing is this figurative history" (p. 369).

Ricoeur's preference of the figurative over the real life history reminds one of Freud's distinction between the observed phenomena which are of lesser value and the hypothetical but more important psychic forces responsible for them. Thus, we may come back to our question concerning the allowed ways of inferring from those phenomena. Are we here invited to feel free of any constraints while interpreting observational data? Indeed, while agreeing that psychoanalysis should be related to as a hermeneutic-dialectical discipline "within a continental metascientific framework", Barratt (1976) deemed it wholly unsatisfactory to assume, "as Ricoeur seems to do, that truth somehow emerges by necessity within the psychoanalytic situation" (p. 463).

What then, are the canons of such a hermeneutic exegesis? "An interpretation is valid", Barratt suggested, "if it leads to further valid interpretations, to increased self-understanding, and to the continuation of self-formative processes" (p. 463). It is quite evident, I think, that this attempt to establish the truth of an interpretation by maintaining that it led to further valid explanations, does not exactly solve the problem. By so doing, we simply transferred the burden of proof from one place to another. A is valid since B is valid; now we should be informed of how to validate B.

The same criticism applies to the concept of "self-understanding." One must have some public criteria for identifying true from false; how otherwise can one identify self-understanding A as projection or false self and self-understanding B as insight or one's true self? "The majority of Freudian analysts," Freud himself included, were correct: there is no possibility of bypassing the question of verification. Even as a hermeneutic discipline, psychoanalysis is still a discipline; that is, it instructs its disciples on how to bring order into the chaos of behavioral phenomena. By teaching the principles of a discipline, one made public one's belief in the existence of correct and false interpretations. One cannot, therefore, admit—lightheartedly as Ricoeur seems to have done—that psychoanalysis has never quite succeeded in stating how its assertions are justified, and not feel alarmed. Such confessions must have some consequences.

The consequences I am hinting at may follow from the very analysis of Rycroft, Ricoeur, or Barratt: one has to agree that the psychodynamic method of proof has yet to elaborate and submit to verification its principles of inference and interpretation. Subjectively felt truths, intuitively arrived at illuminations are important experiences, and no one intends to deny their possibility. However, their value is limited by the fact of their being a most private experience of a single individual. In order to let others, too, share a truth, one must make public the steps of reasoning which lead to this truth; one must prove it. The necessity of such a conclusion is the essence of a proof and it is, precisely, this inevitability to which the pyschodynamic method of interpretations may never come close.

Given these facts, I wonder whether one may suggest that by psychodynamically interpreting a "displacement of affects" like that of Little Hans, one has revealed and proved "the" hidden meaning of a neurotic symptom. At their best, such interpretations yield some competing possibilities enabling, in fact, obliging one to avail oneself of the possibility which may suit one's preferences. Therefore, the definition of psychoneuroses by means of "displacement" of an unconscious conflict, which invites a psychodynamic excavation of "the" true meaning of the symptom, does not seem feasible.

Instead, let us have a closer look at Freud's first definition of psychoneuroses that a neurotic person differs from the normal one in that he exaggerates his reactions to dangers. Let us also recall that Freud was puzzled and could not explain why anxiety alone "enjoys the advantage" of evoking abnormal reactions. I would like to suggest that this puzzlement was justified and that, unaware as he seemed to be, Freud (1926) himself hinted at the solution to it. We could progress further, he wrote, if we were not content to explain anxiety as a reaction to danger; rather, let us ask, what is the core, the meaning, of a danger? "Clearly, it is the evaluation of our strength relative to the greatness of the danger, the acknowledgement of our helplessness. . . . Let us call the experience of such a situation of helplessness a *traumatic* one; we have then good reasons for separating a traumatic situation from the situation of danger. . . . The situation of danger is the perceived, recalled, expected situation of helplessness" (p. 166).

Saying it differently, Freud's puzzlement, indeed, was justified: not anxiety but rather helplessness is the original factor. If so, we may continue this line of reasoning to say that the feeling of helplessness and its traumatic effects indicate that *to be in control of himself and his immediate environment is a basic need of every human being and presumably of animals, too.* A breakdown of the sense of autonomy is a traumatic experience; the knowledge of its impending occurrence arouses anxiety, and (we must expand here Freud's formula) depression. *The base for a definition of mental health is an established sense of control and autonomy and, for the definition of psychopathology, a breakdown or the felt danger of breakdown.*

While not always explicitly stated, this definition of mental health and psychopathology seems to be supported by many authors. Thus, Green (1974) suggests that the nucleus of hysteria, its essential aim, is a "violent struggle" against potential depression: "a depression in which self-value is blatantly abased." This fact emphasized at the utmost the shift between Freud's hysteria—repression erected against sexual gratification—and hysteria today, in which sexuality still holds through the desirability of the object as a label of its value, but in which the struggle is against the narcissistic injury leading to depression" (p. 465).

The abased self-value, or narcissistic injury, differently worded though, points to what, by elaborating on Freud's statement, we have suggested here as the common ground for evolving neurotic behavior disturbances: loss of autonomy and helplessness, resulting in depression. Hysteria, Green believes, is a defense against depression.

Turning now to the other main category, it is the opinion of Salzman (1980) that the purpose and adaptive function of all the traits and rituals of the obsessive personality subserve the need of achieving control of himself and the environment. "Freud called this process *displacement* and assumed that the obsessive symptom was always distracting the individual from essential concerns. However, these preoccupying thoughts and ruminations are often the very essence of the person's concerns. Ruminations about death, philosophical, and moral issues, or hypochondriacal preoccupations about one's health are attempts to control one's destiny and to guarantee one's future. It seems to me that it is the need for total control that more accurately describes the entire range of obsessive activity, rather than the simple technique of displacement" (p. 11).

Phobias often develop, Salzman suggests, around situations in which the person fears he will lose control of himself through giddiness, fainting, swaying, collapsing, or possibly dying. "Essentially in every instance the fear is that of going out of control. . . . The primary dynamism in all instances will be manifested as an attempt to gain control over oneself and one's environment in order to avoid or overcome distressful feelings of helplessness and powerlessness" (p. 24).

In addition, the obsessive behavior in children, Salzman thinks, can be readily understood as a consequence of the child's helplessness and vulnerability, and the need for order and control in dealing with his insecurities. The need to be in control and autonomous, rather than in conflict over anal-erotic impulses, is the key to an understanding of these behaviors.

In agreement with Freud's first definition of psychoneuroses, Rado (1959) saw in obsessive behavior a subdivision of the class of overreactive disorders. "Overreactive disorders arise from the organism's inability to handle danger situations effectively by its available means of emergency control" (p. 329). On the other hand, like Salzman, Rado also rejected Freud's libido theory as a possible explanation of obsessive behavior. Rather, he thought, "beyond a shadow of doubt, in the etiology of obsessive behavior the ultimate psychodynamically ascertainable factor is rage" (p. 338). The motivating system behind the obsessive behavior, in Rado's view, is a perpetuation of the infantile conflict between the child's overstrong tendency to self-assertive domination versus his still stronger clinging to the security of being loved and cared for: obedience versus defiance.

This self-assertive domination is but another name for the need to be or feel autonomous. Rado thought that there are individual differences in the strength of this basic need and this is why some people, by virtue of their extremely strong need for autonomy, are predisposed to become obsessive: "That a child is born to stubborn and tenacious self-assertion may be surmised from the inordinate strength of his rage. This provokes the parents into severe retaliatory measures which, in turn, elicit his defiant rage and even stronger fears" (p. 330). This, incidentally, was also Freud's (1909b) experience: "the obsessional neurotic starts off with a very energetic disposition, he is often extraordinarily self-willed" (p. 260). Self-will and self-assertion, to say it again, may be regarded as synonyms for a strong need for control and autonomy.

Summarizing his research on twenty obsessional patients, Mellett (1974) found that the onset of obsessive symptoms characteristically coincided with suppressed anger. By their own account of their behavior in various real situations, by the overt display of affect observed in interviews and at least one, often several, other witnesses' accounts of their behavior, the majority of these patients appeared "abnormally inclined" to suppress anger, murderous anger, as Mellett characterized it. Again, the majority felt powerless to deal with the cause of anger at the time the event occurred. Later, these events, all associated with mixed affects of pleasurable sexual excitement, guilt, and murderous anger, appeared to have been revived as ruminative symptoms, when the patient was depressed many years after their original occurrence. The anger elicited by a feeling of powerlessness in view of forces interfering with one's own strivings and mostly suppressed is the indication of a flaw or even a breakdown of the sense of control and autonomy.

Such an injury of the need for autonomy is also the ground for developing depression. This is indicated, to begin with, in dreams. Summarizing their analysis of the dreams of the depressive personality, Bonime and Bonime (1980) state that the basic depressive psychodynamics are: manipulativeness, hypersensitivity to and reaction against coercion, coupled with a tendency to interpret the intention of others as efforts to coerce, anxiety, and an emotional core of variously expressed anger. Bonime and Bonime think that depressives are unwilling to take responsibility for making a life for themselves, for all acceptance of responsibility is subjectively misperceived and experienced as submission to coercion.

Note that all these authors do not mention hostility at all. Coercion is what depressive persons are sensitized to; hypersensitivity, anger, anxiety, and manipulativeness are their reactions to it. Most attempts to describe the antecedents of depression seem to agree in emphasizing a vulnerability due to an extreme dependency on the environment for maintaining a sense of self-esteem. Bibring (1953) seems to have been the first to point out that such a blow to one's self-esteem must be felt as helplessness: "Depression can be defined as the emotional expression of a state of helplessness and powerlessness of the ego, irrespective of what may have caused the breakdown of the mechanisms which established his self-esteem" (p. 24). This helplessness and powerlessness and their counterpart, a hypersensitivity to the danger of being coerced to comply, are the two faces of one coin, of the failure to live up to one's need for autonomy.

Here is the place to be reminded of a finding of Weiss, Stone, and Harrel (1970). They were able to establish a correlation between the amount of norepinephrine in the brain and the ability to control a situation. There was consistently less norepinephrine in the brains of animals that could not control shock than in those that could. Based on the work of Schildkraut and Kety (1967), who advanced the hypothesis that a depletion of the neurotransmitter norepinephrine caused depression, one may suggest that helplessness, i.e., a breakdown of the sense of autonomy, initiates a chain of neuropsychological reactions leading to a depletion of norepinephrine and depression.

As indicated earlier, there are individual differences in the strength of the need for autonomy. Indeed, Glass (1977) found that some, the Type A individuals, exert greater efforts than Type B individuals to master stressful events which they perceive as a threat to their sense of control. Let us note, however, that these active coping attempts are eventually extinguished if the person is confronted by an extended exposure to uncontrollable situations. Failing to gain any control, despite relentless striving, the Type A individual ends up in a psychic exhaustion, which culminates in abandonment of efforts at control. "An almost ironic reversal of behavior is then observed, with Type A individuals showing greater signs of helplessness than their Type B counterparts" (p. 7).

While the initial reaction of Type A individuals is to assert control, extended experience with uncontrollability leads to more passive behavior in Type A than in Type B individuals. It seems reasonable to assume that this is the way for depression to evolve. The more passive or helpless one becomes, the more chance one has to feel thwarted, coerced, and, thus, depressed.

Considering how akin the psychodynamics of depression and obsessive behavior are and in view of findings such as the one mentioned by Rado (1959), namely, that obsessive behavior may appear during the intervals between two phases of "mood-cycling behavior" (p. 340), or that of Mellett (1974): "Depression is *always* present at the onset of obsessional symptoms when these are of pathological degree" (p. 82), or that of Lewis (1936), according to which "there were indubitable obsessional symptoms in at least a fifth of a series of casually selected depressive patients . . . ; if one takes only the patients with agitated depression the proportion is much higher" (p. 340)—the question may arise of whether we need, and are justified in presuming, the existence of neatly circumscribed categories of psychoneuroses. Indeed, Lewis (1936) pondered this question as follows:

> The question worth considering at this point is whether it is sound to regard obsessional neuroses—or Janet's psychasthenia—as a special type of morbid reaction, or as merely a manifestation of universal psychic attributes, aggravated by anxiety and depression. . . . It is still convenient to speak of obsessional neurosis, though it seems to me that the obsessional experience is so widespread over psychic activity and so commonly found with other abnor-

> mal psychic states that this neurosis is almost as insecure a category as anxiety neurosis. (P. 328)

One may add here the warning of Rado (1959): "A sprinkling of obsessive mechanisms may be found in any person" (p. 339); this may sound like a further vote for denying the right to existence of the many categories of behavior disturbances, and yet, the phenomenology of hysteria and that of obsessive states are so different that nobody would err in identifying them. We may do justice to both of these views, contradictory though they seem, if we conclude that *all forms of the neurotic behavior disturbances have a common base; their "evocative event," as Millar (1958) put it, is a disturbance of the sense of control and autonomy, and the differences between the subdivisions are due to differences in the respective personality configurations.*

Regarding personality configurations, let us be reminded of Shapiro's description of the differences in styles of cognition in hysteria and obsession. In contrast to the active, intense, and sharply focused attention of the obsessive, hysterical cognition seems relatively lacking in sharp focus of attention; in contrast to the obsessive's active and prolonged searching for details, the hysterical person tends to respond quickly and is highly susceptible to what is immediately impressive, striking, or dramatic. Assuming that the style of attention reflects the style of mental functioning, in general, one may suggest that what seemed to be a motivated forgetting, a "repression," is in fact a mode, a style of cognition. "The passive, impressionistic, distractible nature of the hysterical cognitive style, rather than the content of what seemed to be denied to consciousness, is the explanation of the selective recall in hysterical personality . . . this mode of functioning or specifically of cognition decidedly favors the phenomenon we describe as 'repression' " (Shapiro 1965, p. 117).

It is habitual modes of mental functioning, cognitive styles, which are responsible for the phenomena warranting the labels hysteria or obsessive behavior, while the basic etiology may be common to all forms of neurotic behavior disturbances. One may ask though, why should cognitive styles be defined by means of concepts which, like hysterical, themselves badly need an acceptable definition. It would seem more correct to say that it is global and impressionistic *versus* analytic and punctilious cognitive styles which, if given the conditions for evolving a neurosis, will determine the character of neurosis. But, again, one may decide to respect the traditional labels, provided one is aware of their historical and present meanings.

Concerning their present-day meaning suggested here, namely, that the differences between hysteric and obsessive neuroses, in fact, are differences in cognitive styles, we now may connect these differences in a person's preference for habitually relying on the strategies of thinking of the right or left hemisphere. Analytic persons are regarded as relying mainly on the sequential and verbal modes of functioning of the left hemisphere, whereas holistic and intuitive persons are regarded as relying on the modes of functioning of the right hemisphere. A convenient way to test the habitual preference for relying on one or the other hemisphere is to measure the direction of conjugate lateral eye movements during thought (Bakan 1971, 1973).

Upon being asked a question which requires reflection, one usually turns one's eyes to the left or right as one begins to reflect on the answer. It has been observed that the tendency for the eye to move in one direction is associated with a tendency for the contralateral brain hemisphere to be activated. Persons who usually have left conjugate eye movements, left movers, are characterized by the modes of functioning of the right hemisphere, and those who have right conjugate eye movements, right movers, by the modes of functioning of the left hemisphere.

Based on these results, Gur and Gur (1975) explored the ego defense characteristic of left movers and right movers. Using Gleser and Ihlevich's (1969) defense mechanisms inventory and their own test for determining eye-movement directionality, they found that left movers are characterized significantly more than right movers by repression and denial. We have already seen that amnesias or repressions are, in fact, an outcome of one's cognitive style; this style, in its turn, seems to be determined by the individually characteristic dominance of the left or right hemisphere. Thus, the particular form a psychoneurosis may take, very much like the conjugate lateral eye movements, is just a further indication of one's habitual mode of mental functioning.

It is apparent that such an understanding of the conditions necessary for the genesis of psychoneuroses, that is to say, an expected or experienced threat to the need for autonomy as the general factor and a personality configuration as the specific factor, may allow only a contributory role for the psychodynamic concept of a drive-defense conflict; the role of a possible but not necessary factor. I would like to emphasize that many psychoanalytic authors have indirectly come quite close to this position.

For example, explaining his concept of neurotic styles, Shapiro (1965) wrote: "Whereas some aspects of the neurotic symptom may be understood in this way, other aspects are not clearly traceable to the content of the original drive conflict . . . the moralistic attitudes, and the intensity of activity and work that are usually associated with such symptoms are not easily derived from the specific, (anal-erotic), content of the drive conflict" (p. 5).

We might add here some further features of obsessive behavior, such as the interminable nature of ruminative thinking, the difficulty in deciding, the apparent contrasts between kindness and cruelty, logicality and unreason, the predilection for self-tormenting, and we may feel that Shapiro was correct in suggesting that: "The compulsive person is interested in doubts, worries and rituals. Dynamic understanding, no matter how correct in itself, cannot explain this particular form of his interest" (p. 17).

As it stands, this statement, though, blurs rather than clarifies the issue. One does not know for sure whether, in the opinion of Shapiro, a patient is subjected to doubts, indecision, and the other features of obsessive behavior because, and only because, he has an unconscious conflict over anal-erotic impulses, or whether, irrespective of the quality of his conflict, conscious or unconscious, libidinal or otherwise, his personality makeup has predestined him to this kind of reaction. Nonetheless, reading Shapiro again, one has the feeling that he, too, could assign only a supporting role to the psychodynamic concept of conflict.

Sandler (1974) must also have left his readers wondering whether conflict still means what it meant for Freud. It is striking, Sandler wrote, that the peremptory tendency has for so long been regarded as being due entirely to an instinctual wish or its derivative. Yet, on reflection, Sandler suggested, it is evident that a large number of "peremptory," "automatic," "urgent," and "compelling" tendencies are not drive-motivated. As an example, he quotes Anna Freud's *The Ego and the Mechanisms of Defence* (1936) in which she described a boy who dealt with his castration anxiety and penis-inferiority by putting on his father's hat and walking around indoors with it. Later he was given a peaked cap, and convulsively clutched it when he was not allowed to wear it. Finally, in order to free his hands, he thrust the cap into the opening of the flap in front of his breeches.

One could safely predict, Sandler suggests, that this little boy later experienced conflict over his urge to stuff his hat into his trousers. Thus, any analysis of internal conflicts should take into consideration the role of "previous adaptations which have later in development become ego-dystonic, i.e. have come into conflict with the ego's need to maintain its self-esteem, sense of well-being, feelings of harmony and safety, and its relations to its objects, internal or external. Conflicts of this sort need to be interpreted as such and it is a major and misleading oversimplification to consider them simply as conflicts between the ego and the other major agencies of id, superego and reality" (p. 60).

Sandler, then, thinks that conflict may but does not necessarily mean an unconscious conflict over an instinctual impulse. But, then, Shapiro and Sandler seem to have adopted a position quite similar to ours. For, if what traditionally has been considered to be repression, in fact, was the inevitable result of a stable personality configuration, and if "conflict" does not necessarily mean a struggle against instinctual impulses, then the concept of drive-defense, evidently, will not be able to compete with the concepts of need autonomy and cognitive styles for the central position in explaining behavior disturbance.

12. PSYCHOTHERAPY: AIMS AND METHODS

The definition of psychotherapy follows from the definition of mental health which, in turn, is deduced from the definition of psychology. The subject matter of psychology is life phenomena which indicate reasoning. Unlike a reflex, behavior is flexible, the actualization of a possibility, not of an inevitability. This ability to do or refrain from doing, the possibility to will and choose is what distinguishes the realm of behavior from that of the reflexes. It is subjectively experienced as a sense of autonomy, as the ability to control one's fate, in accord with the well-known advice: to accept the inevitable and to choose among the existing possibilities. A damage to the sense of autonomy may result in the feeling of helplessness, followed by anxiety and depression. The task of psychotherapy is to restore one's ability to feel and behave adaptively and yet autonomously.

How may one succeed in achieving this aim? Fortunately, we are provided with plenty of ideas and methods, and anyone may avail himself of one of them. Unfortunately, however, the differences and, alas, the hostility between the many schools of psychotherapy are so great that one may feel confused and hesitant with regard to the direction to be taken. Let us, then, have a closer look at the main issues dividing psychotherapists. First and foremost is the controversy concerning the role of interpretation and transference. Not completely justifiably, perhaps, the concept of interpretation and transference became the flag and trademark of psychoanalytic therapy and, again, not completely justifiably, the watershed dividing the dynamic psychotherapies from all the others.

I share the opinion of many experts that interpretation, as understood and pursued in psychoanalysis, is not really important; often it may even be detrimental. To begin with, in spite of Freud's admonition, we use the term "interpretation" in a rather loose and even misleading manner. We all know, Freud (1937b) wrote, that patients are induced to remember something that has been experienced by them and repressed. It is the analyst's task "to make out what has been forgotten from the traces which it has left behind or, more correctly, to *construct* it" (p. 259). It is worthwhile to consider how it happened that this definition of Freud went unheeded, so much so, that one hears and reads of only interpretation and never of construction. "Interpretation," Freud suggested,

> applies to something that one does to some single element of the material, such as an association or a parapraxis. But it is a "construction" when one lays before the subject of the analysis a piece of his early history that he has forgotten, in some such way as this: ". . . Your feelings towards your mother became ambivalent, your father gained a new importance for you" . . . and so on. (P. 261)

Let us note, however, that whether one interprets or constructs, one cannot proceed without acceptable proofs. It is true though, that he who pretends to "interpret" is expected to offer more stringent evidence than he who only "constructs." For the interpreter pretends to know whereas the constructor admits that he can offer only a suggestion. Clearly, Freud asked to describe precisely the results of the psychodynamic method of inquiry. And yet, the same Freud in the same paper on "Constructions in Analysis" wrote that quite often "we do not succeed in bringing the patient to recollect what has been repressed. Instead of that, if the analysis is carried out correctly, we produce in him an assured conviction of the truth of the construction which achieves the same therapeutic result as a recaptured memory" (pp. 265–66).

If, indeed, an "assured conviction" of the truth of a construction may achieve the same therapeutic result as a faithful reconstruction of the events and feelings past, one may understand why Freud's efforts to distinguish between interpretations and constructions are disregarded by his followers. For psychotherapists, of course, are interested mainly in therapeutic results and if an "assured conviction," in fact, a suggestion, may help in achieving them, why not apply it while constructing and interpreting as well. If therapeutic results are the criterion of proof, understandably, any distinction between more stringent evidence needed for interpreting and less stringent evidence allowed for constructing became purposeless.

Not less important than the method of hermeneutics applied by Freud which, as we have seen, also includes the production of an assured conviction of the truth, is the question of why; why construct and interpret instead of accepting the patient's behavior at its face value? Constructions in a psychoanalytic treatment are used mainly to reestablish, by means of dreams, associations, and repetitions of relations, what has been repressed. Our experience has shown, Freud (1937b) stated, "that the relation of transference, which becomes established towards the analyst, is particularly calculated to favour the return of these emotional connections" (p. 258). In his "Analysis Terminable and Interminable," written in the same year, Freud (1937a) added the following qualifications: "not every good relation between an analyst and his subject during and after an analysis was to be regarded as a transference; there were also friendly relations which were based on reality" (p. 222).

This remark of Freud does not seem to have received the attention it deserves, and psychotherapists continued to identify Freud with his earlier understanding of the nature of the psychotherapeutic encounter. One may see this, for example, from Strupp's (1960) statement that "in more recent years . . . the totality of the therapist's personality and the reality aspects of the therapeutic situation have received increasing attention" (p. 288). Strupp related this change of orientation to the influence of Sullivan and Horney "some of whose views were anticipated by Rank and Ferenczi." Rank and Ferenczi, indeed, were the pioneers. Belatedly, and in contradistinction to his earlier stance, Freud followed their lead and agreed that not every good or bad relation between an analyst and his patient is to be regarded as a transference; there are also friendly and unfriendly relations which are based on reality.

This concession of Freud to Rank and Ferenczi turned the analytic situation into a complexity of relationships to which psychoanalysts were not accustomed. Quite understandably, one would expect to have been offered some guidelines, a few criteria, which should direct the analyst in his attempt to distinguish between what is real and what is transmuted in his encounters with his patients. Here, as in the previous chapter concerning the collateral and essential associations, one would like to know how to separate the signs of transference relations from those good or bad relations between analysts and patients which are based on reality. As in the case of collateral and essential associations, here too, the analyst has been granted the rights of a sovereign arbiter. He and, he alone, may decide whether this or that aspect of their relationship reflects their present, real connection, or, on the contrary, only reenacts an old tie with another person.

Considering the risks involved in this decision, many analysts decided—and who can blame them—that Freud's opposing view notwithstanding, no aspect of their encounter with their patients can be seen as related to the present reality. Nowhere have I found a more instructive description of this state of mind than in a recent paper of Basch (1983):

> I clearly remember how I and my fellow residents sat frightened and passive with our patients. We were passive because we felt we had to limit ourselves to encouraging patients to say what they were thinking and then wait for them to give us the opportunity to connect the present problem to earlier experiences in their family relationship. We were frightened because we firmly believed that everything we might say or do had an immediate and significant sexual or aggressive implication for the patient. (P. 226)

What were those sexual or aggressive implications?

> We really thought that to say or do anything other than interpret the genesis of the patient's problems would endanger our therapeutic, neutral stance, establishing an equivalence in the patient's unconscious between us and those earlier seductive and/or punitive figures who were responsible, we believed, for his or her problems. (P. 226)

In other words, the task of interpretation is to construct (or reconstruct) the Oedipus complex particular to the patient. If one expected to make the patient aware of his hidden Oedipal conflicts by interpreting his relationship to the therapist, considering what we know now, we may wonder if this approach leads us down a blind alley. Indeed, uninfluenced by such considerations, and led by his clinical experience only, Ornstein (1983), too, questioned the very reasons for the psychoanalytic practice of interpretations:

> Expectations based on classical theory have focused ultimate analytic attention exclusively on the *transference neurosis* for quite some time. Within this *transference neurosis* the repressed *infantile neurosis* was to be remobilized, containing at its core *the infantile Oedipus complex*. In spite of the fact that clear-cut, uncomplicated examples of such a transference neurosis were rare, this remained not only the theoretical ideal but also the practical-clinical standard against which analysts could judge whether an analytic process developed or not in a given clinical situation. (P. 368)

Once, however, one has freed oneself from the spell of this conception and let the facts of observation speak for themselves, one may find, instead, what Basch (1983) has also found: "I found that . . . penis envy, sibling rivalry, castration fear, the primal scene, and all the other things I had learned about seemed to play no great part in my psychotherapeutic experience. . . . What came up over and over again were the hidden wishes for love and understanding, the shame, often masquerading as anger or bravado, that was frequently associated with such desires, and the concomitant inability to voice and thereby become conscious of what it was that was really troubling them" (pp. 231–32).

One should emphasize that the conclusion of Basch is not exceptional to him or the theoretical framework he advocates. Many authors before him or Kohut understood that the "pivotal" need of many patients seeking psychotherapy was their longing for an "encounter" with an understanding and knowledgeable man or woman. For example, Snyder (1961) stated that he has "become convinced that the persons who most need psychotherapy are those who are starved for affection" (p. 2). Similarly, Strupp, Wallach, and Wogan (1967) were of the opinion that a general "warmth" factor, a solid working relationship in which the participants develop a sense of mutual trust is a *sine qua non* of all forms of psychotherapy.

Before anything else, the patient asks to be understood; to let the patient feel that he is understood is the therapist's first task. This task, however, does not require, in fact, forbids psychoanalytic interpretations. Empathy and not interpretations is what is needed here. Consequently, "we can teach even beginners to relax, become aware of their reactions to the patient's behavior in the therapeutic situation, and use their inner response to guide them in their search for appropriate therapeutic intervention. In other words, self psychology permits the therapist's empathy to be used systematically in helping the patient" (Basch 1983, p. 236).

It would be interesting to know whether Kohut or his followers, such as Basch, were acquainted with the writings or at least the ideas of Rogers. For more than forty years, Rogers promulgated some ideas which may sound quite familiar to Kohutian analysts. In a successfully directed "client-centered" therapy, as Rogers called his approach,

> the therapist has been able to enter into an intensely personal and subjective relationship with this client—relating not as a scientist to an object of study, not as a physician expecting to diagnose and cure—but as a person to a person. It would mean that the therapist feels this client to be a person of unconditional self-worth. . . . It means that the therapist is able to let himself go in understanding this client; that no inner barriers keep him from sensing what it feels like to be the client at each moment of the relationship; and that he can convey something of this empathic understanding to the client. It

> means that the therapist has been comfortable in entering the relationship fully, without knowing cognitively where it will lead, satisfied with providing a climate which will free the client to be himself. . . . He finds his behavior changing in constructive fashion in accordance with this newly experienced self. (Pp. 2–3)

Empathy, acceptance, reflecting the patient's feelings rather than interpreting them, are here the key words, accompanied by an understanding that psychotherapy has little to do with theory or ideology. Therapy, in essence, is a relationship, a genuine encounter, and not just the revival, transference of past relationships originating in the first years of life.

> In this respect I believe my views have become more rather than less extreme, I believe it is the *realness* of the therapist in the relationship which is the most important element. It is when the therapist is natural and spontaneous that he seems to be the most effective. . . . Our experience has deeply reinforced and extended my own view that the person who is able *openly* to be himself at that moment, as he is at the deepest levels he is able to be, is the effective therapist. Perhaps nothing else is of any importance. (Rogers 1962, p. 7)

It was the opinion of Rogers that consciousness of theory is not helpful in the immediate moment of the therapeutic relationship. If we think theoretically in relationships, we become spectators, not players, and it is as players that psychotherapists are effective. Of course, Rogers did not deny the necessity of a theory of personality, of psychopathology, and of the process of change in therapy. For the purpose of a therapeutic encounter, however, any theory, to his understanding, is irrelevant or detrimental. "So if theory is to be held at all, it seems to me that it should be held tentatively, lightly, flexibly, in a way which is freely open to change, and should be laid aside in the moment of encounter itself" (p. 11).

Incidentally, some psychoanalytic writers seem to agree with this understanding of Rogers. For example, discussing Kohut's theoretical contributions, Cooper (1983) observed that "Mr. Z. did better in his second analysis because Dr. Kohut had become a better analyst and more empathic, regardless of his theory, and . . . there are no detectable differences in the two analyses that are clearly attributable to theory" (p. 31).

To be empathic means that the therapist may effect changes in the patient's behavior by, paradoxically, accepting him as he is and not demanding from him efforts to distance himself from himself and strive for an inner change. Such an empathic encounter may unfreeze the inner resources necessary for the patient to regain his sense of autonomy and self-esteem, and his ability to change. Having achieved that, psychotherapy has fulfilled its function.

Many therapists (and patients), quite possibly, may feel disappointed at being offered such a definition of psychotherapy. Surely psychoanalysis promises more. Or does it? "One has the impression," Freud (1937a) observed, "that one ought not to be surprised if it should turn out in the end that the difference between a person who has not been analyzed and the behavior of a person after he has been analyzed is not so throughgoing as we aim at making it and as we expect and maintain it to be" (p. 228). In fact, the editor of the Standard Edition (vol. 23) observes that Freud's doubts extend to the prospects of preventing not merely the occurrence of a fresh and different neurosis but even a return of a neurosis that has already been treated.

Let us, then, take note of what experience taught Freud and be modest in our expectations of ourselves, our theories, and our therapeutic methods. Nature, that is, the patient will do for himself what is necessary to be done if only he feels that we are with him, that we understand and support him.

In a sense, though, it is impossible to imagine that two people continue to discuss issues, which are highly personal and vitally important for one of them and arouse keen interest in the other one, without interpreting or constructing the meaning of those life events. Let us note, however, that such interpretations, except for their name, do not have much in common with the interpretations characteristic of dynamic psychotherapies. For dynamic psychotherapies, and especially psychoanalysis, interpret in order to reveal contents and features of "the" unconscious of which, otherwise, the patient could never know. This intent, however, only makes salient one of the insoluble contradictions in psychoanalysis. It is impossible to make repressed thoughts and feelings conscious, for "the" unconscious thinks in a way which is totally different from and alien to our reasoning and commitment to the imperatives of adaptation while we are awake. Repressed ideas, on their way to being taken cognizance of, will be changed and distorted, and thus, one may never succeed in reestablishing them. It is the paradox of psychoanalysis to have suggested such a never testable statement as its foundation stone and yet to insist that its interpretations, nonetheless, reflect precisely those never knowable thoughts and feelings.

Interpretations in psychotherapy, as in life in general, help to make sense out of the individual facts by fitting them into coherent patterns.

These coherent patterns, these explanatory constructs, should keep close contact with the observable facts; as Kohut put it, they must be "experience-near." Enriched by such interpretations, the patient may feel that instead of being a helpless victim of events, he has now regained his control and sense of autonomy over his behavior and he may participate actively in shaping his own fate. This is the aim of psychotherapy and such interpretations may help to realize it.

13.
POINT AND COUNTERPOINT: CONSCIOUS AND UNCONSCIOUS

The focus of our discussion has been the concept or rather the concepts of unconscious. Its counterpoint is self-awareness. The emergence of self-awareness and with it the sense of free will and autonomy—for only a being aware of itself may perceive its motives as its own will—are more wondrous and less understood than the unconscious of whichever brand. Yet, the unconscious and dreams, mutually feeding and justifying each other's halo, have inspired an atmosphere of awe and reverence which has never been commensurate with the known facts. That field of psychoanalysis known as "ego psychology" and to an extent "self-psychology," as well, is an attempt to rectify this loss of proportion. At the other end of the spectrum, behaviorism shifting toward cognitive behaviorism accomplishes the same turning around itself. Self-awareness, long banished and despised, is slowly becoming again what it once was, the Archimedean point for understanding behavior.

Most of our psychic acts, to be sure, are performed unbeknown to ourselves, and we become aware of them only at their end point. While I am speaking, my sentences flow, as if effortlessly, and my self-awareness is able to perceive them only as the person I am talking to does. I am, as it were, only listening to what was constructed by someone else, hidden from my eyes. I, my self-awareness, am indeed listening to my outpourings, but not as a naive audience. I am the composer and the conductor; I was the one who set the direction and the sense of the words and sentences to be constructed and I have full power to check those constructs. I may be satisfied or dissatisfied and accept or reject them. I am not a passive onlooker of what goes on in my mind, nor am I pulled from here to there by hidden strings. I am autonomous, and as the literature on biofeedback demonstrates, my ability to control includes also a measure of mastery over my vegetative nervous system. This fact, incidentally, may explain why symptoms of conversion in hysteria are possible.

Self-awareness and a sense of autonomy, like the assumptions about the peculiarity of dreams and "the" unconscious, are twin concepts. Talking of dreams in the terms of Freud or Jung, one is talking of the respective concepts of Freud or Jung on the unconscious. Likewise, to suggest that the core of mental health is a sense of autonomy equilibrated by an ability for adaptation and that the core of psychoneuroses is a breakdown or a threatened shattering of the sense of autonomy means to suggest that self-awareness, and not the unconscious, is the center of our interest.

As a first step, let us pay attention to the possibility that, contrary to some prevailing views, even infants experience the world as composed of self and others or objects. This belief stems, first, from the sometimes unbelievably sounding cognitive capabilities of the infants already dealt with in chapter 4. More important, perhaps, is the direct evidence we have now for assuming that the infant perceives the world of objects and persons as separated from him or her. Bower (1971) was able to show that infants who were held in an upright or semiupright position clearly showed a defensive response to an approaching object. They widened their eyes, pulled their head back, and put their hands between their face and the object. In addition, perception of the impending collision caused distress and crying so intense that the experiment had to be terminated. If, however, the object moved away, it produced neither defensive behavior nor crying. In a similar experiment, Ball and Tronick (1971) found that infants from the age of two weeks on responded to symmetrically expanding shadows, which optically specify an approaching object, with an integrated avoidance response and symptoms of distress as detailed above. This behavior was observed in all the infants. However, this response did not occur for asymmetrically expanding shadows nor for contracting shadows that specify an object on a miss path and a receding path.

By the second week of life, as Bower puts it, an infant expects a visible object to have tactile consequences. This may be seen as an indication that the infants perceived these optical and real objects as separate from themselves. This possibility may be underscored by another experiment of Bower (1971). In this experiment, twenty-, forty-, eighty-, and one-hundred-day-old infants were placed in front of an object. A screen moved in from one side and covered the object. After various intervals

(1.5, 3, 7.5, or 15 seconds) the screen moved away. In half of the trials, the object was still there when the screen moved away. In the other trials, the object was no longer there when the screen moved away.

When the object had been occluded for 1.5 seconds, all the infants manifested greater surprise at its nonreappearance than at its reappearance. They expected the object still to be there. Bower interpreted these results as indicating that, without having had an opportunity to learn, very young infants know that an object is still there after it has been hidden; of course, if the time of occlusion is prolonged, they forget the object altogether. Now, if there is an object out there, if the nervous system has a built-in property to distinguish circumscribed external agencies, why not assume that the self, too, already exists?

The development of language acquisition, it seems to me, may substantiate this supposition. The first step in language acquisition, as Bloom (1973) put it, is "one word at a time." There is broad agreement that these single words, in fact, are holophrases. Intonation and some extraverbal cues may indicate the various meanings conveyed by the same sole word. "Holophrastic speech" refers, then, to the possibility that the single-word utterances of young children express an idea, a proposition. McNeil (1970) went one step further by suggesting that these single words do not only express a complex idea but also indicate the existence of a linguistic universal, the sentence. "Holophrastic speech is in a limited way grammatical, that is, relational speech. . . . Very young children develop a concept of a sentence as a set of grammatical relations before they develop a concept of how these relations are expressed" (p. 13).

Grammatical relations exist from the beginning; they are not to be acquired, but they may become apparent only later on, when two or three words are combined into patterned speech. Such a linguistic universal, McNeil thought, may be a reflection of a specific linguistic ability independent of any cognitive ability. McNeil found support for his provocative idea in the fact that most of the first words uttered by an infant are "nouns." One finds there a few "adjectives," too, but no "verbs." This is necessarily so, McNeil suggested, for the syntactic category of nouns is unique in that it alone appears in every grammatical relation. Because all grammatical relations are implicit, nouns can be used in every relation; verbs do not have this property. One may see this by comparing a verb such as *reach* to a noun such as *banana* for conveying the locative relation.

McNeil's suggestion met with both agreement and criticism. At any rate, the basis of his suggestion is valid: words denoting actions are conspicuous by their virtual absence in the different lists of infant's first words. For example, concluding her research, Bloom (1973) stated that children use more different object names than they use names of attributes (words for size, color, etc.) and they also use more different object names than they use names of action. Greenfield and Smith (1976) also found that children develop the ability to express the action of an object after they have expressed the object of an action. Finally, comparing the comprehension of fourteen- to twenty-six-month-old infants with their productions of nouns and verbs, Goldin-Meadow, Seligman, and Goldman (1976) found that while at a certain stage in development children understand many more nouns and verbs than they say, they increase their noun production almost to the level of their noun comprehension at the same time as they begin verb production. Nouns have the lead; verbs are only trailing them from a distance.

Naming persons and objects, then, precedes the denotation of actions; as if this priority were not enough, as the related observations of the Sterns and others indicate, nouns seem to be able to interfere with the independent existence of verbs. To put it in McNeil's term, the syntactic category of nouns is a strong universal and the category of verbs is weak.

Relating to the same problem, though from a different vantage point, Deese (1965) arrived at a similar conclusion: "Verbs which have some referential meaning, semantically, if not grammatically, are very much like nouns. Even grammatically there is, in Indo-European languages, a close relation between nouns and verbs, as is illustrated by the importance of gerundive constructions and the readiness with which nouns may be formed from verb stems" (p. 142).

How shall we understand this strength and prevalence of naming objects over denoting actions? We have already seen the reasons given by McNeil for the later appearance of verbs in the process of language acquisition. Goldin-Meadow et al. (1976) suggested that this discrepancy between a child's noun and verb rations may be explained by the relative ease in pointing to a concrete noun's referent and the difficulty in pointing to any instantaneous referent of a verb.

Rather than a difficulty, Greenfield and Smith (1976) stressed a disinterest of the infant in encoding action. Almost none of the first words used to encode action can be verbs in adult English, in which *up, down* (or similar words) refer to an action or a resultant state. It is probably most accurate to say that action and resultant state are not differentiated, that the child is basically attending to change of state rather than the action itself. "The fact that the child, jumping down, encodes the event with *down* rather than *jump* suggests that the child is focussing on the *changes* of state rather than the action itself" (p. 122).

As the following example may show, Piaget (1947) would have objected to this view of Greenfield and Smith. In one of his observations Piaget described one of his daughters, J., at one year of age using the sound "tch tch" to indicate a train passing her window, and repeating it each time a train passed. A few days later, she used it indiscriminately for denoting any vehicles she saw out of another window, including cars, carriages, and even to denote a man walking. On the same day, Piaget played peekaboo, appearing and disappearing without speaking. Again, the girl said "tch tch"; probably, Piaget thinks, "by analogy with the sudden appearance and disappearance of the train" (p. 216).

To the understanding of Piaget, this or similar expressions cannot be regarded as true concepts, for concepts are determined by the qualities of the objects composing the groups, whether or not the child himself and his own activity are also involved. On the contrary, J. applied *tch tch* to anything that appeared and disappeared. Thus, such words, "far from denoting merely singular classes . . . really represent [a] complex of actions, either related to the subject or partly objective" (p. 219).

However, if *tch tch* represented appearance and disappearance, then this observation of Piaget seems to support the contention of Greenfield and Smith rather than Piaget's own; young children indeed seem to focus on the changes of state rather than the action itself. Piaget thought that *tch tch, bowwow* (dogs and similar animals), *daddy, mummy,* are merely sensory motor schemas in process of becoming concepts. "They are still sensory-motor, in that they are modes of action capable of generalisation and of application to an increasing number of objects, but they partake of the concept in that there is already a partial dissociation from the child's own activity" (p. 220).

However, the mode of action never could have unified a noisy train and silent Piaget into one concept, though their appearance and disappearance could.

If the change of state is the attribute subserving the creation of a concept, then it is the object of the change to which the infant attends and not the mode of action of the object. One may compare the explanatory value of these two contrasting views by analyzing a further observation of Piaget. The same daughter of Piaget, at a year and two months of age was in her mother's arms and said "daddy" to a man and then a moment later "mummy" to a strange woman. For some weeks *daddy* was applied indiscriminately to all sorts of men, while the use of *mummy* was restricted, although it was applied two to three times to women who did not have children with them (observation 101a). The precise distinction between men and women is a remarkable achievement of scoring and ordering, or conceptualizing both their similarities (in contradistinction to *bow wow*) and their differences. It would be very strained and therefore not convincing to maintain that the concepts of men and women *(daddy–mummy)* were constructed by generalizing their modes of action. Piaget's daughter, let us not forget, also called women who had no children with them "mummy," while fathers who held a child in their arms and fed it were still "daddy."

Combining the findings of Greenfield and Smith with those of Goldin-Meadow et al., we may say, then, that while children at the beginning of language acquisition do understand verbs, as indicated by their verbal productions, they are more interested in objects and their change of states. Greenfield and Smith thought that the child's ability to encode changes of state before action replicated a similar process of development in perception described by Mundy-Castle and Anglin (1969). These authors set up a moving visual display in which an object appeared in a hole on a screen, then disappeared and reemerged in another hole on the screen. Infants around twelve weeks of age were "looking forward" by horizontal eye-movements from porthole to porthole. The older infants did not turn their eye in a straight line, but in an arc, as if following the path they imagined the object to be following. This new strategy of looking, Greenfield and Smith suggested, indicated an awareness not only of states change but also of a process intervening between initial and final states. Likewise, in semantic development, children represent changes of state before they represent processes.

We may, then, distinguish three stages in language acquisition. At first, the infant produces substantive words, names of persons and objects, then words for denoting their changes of state and, finally, verbs describing action. This process of acquiring classes of words reflects the importance of the "other" and the attention devoted to the nonself in the world of the infant. Putting it differently, it indicates that from the very beginning, infants are aware of an external world existing separately from the self and a self existing separately from the surroundings and are able to construct these concepts.

Stern (1983) suggested this hypothesis in its strong form; he thinks "that the infant has clearly separated experiences and schemata of the self and other by the first half-year of life, when the phrase of normal symbiosis is thought to be at its height. Also, there exists no systematic or pervasive confusion between the self and other stimuli and agents in the world, or between the other and the world at large. And finally, the experience and schemas of self and other never were symptomatically or pervasively fused or confused by the infant in the course of early development, but rather formed separately, as emergent sensorimotor-affective and cognitive constructs" (p. 51). This, then, is a strong hypothesis; but even the preference for its weak form allows one to conclude that self-awareness may be prevalent from the very beginning of our psychic life.

Stern is not alone in his daring stand. Brazelton, Koslowski, and Main (1974) observed that as early as four weeks of age, infants reacted to their mothers in a markedly different fashion from the way they reacted to a toy animal. One can look at any segment of the infant's body, they suggest, and detect whether he was watching an object or interacting with his mother—so different are his attention, vocalizing, smiling, and motor behavior with an inanimate object as opposed to the mother. According to these authors, "brief episodes" of these differential reactions were seen as early as two weeks; by four weeks, the difference "was striking."

Evaluating the impact of these findings, Klein (1981) noted that these studies by Brazelton and Stern are far removed from the standard psychoanalytic theory of development. Similarly, they are far removed from the theory of Mahler on which the autistic and symbiotic phases of development are predicated. "Concepts such as drive reduction, undifferentiation, objectlessness, and narcissism (whether absolute or conditional) can no longer theoretically support the weight of finding from infancy research. The infant is highly differentiated and begins to differentiate objects from day one. We need only to postulate a separate self that does so" (p. 102).

While Klein did not mention Piaget, perhaps because as a psychoanalyst Klein was interested in his own field, his criticism applies to Piaget, too. Like Freud, Piaget was sure that infants do not distinguish between the self and the external world. In his *Six Psychological Studies* Piaget (1964) stated, as a matter of fact, that at the outset of mental development the impressions that are experienced are not attached to a personal consciousness sensed as a "self," nor to objects conceived as external to the self. "It follows that, because of this primitive lack of dissociation, everything that is perceived is centered on the subject's own activity. The self is at the center of reality to begin with for the very reason that it is not aware of itself. . . . In other words, consciousness starts with an unconscious and integral egocentricity" (p. 12).

The infancy research, to repeat Klein's statement, can no longer support this picture of the early months of life. While some will say that the view of Freud and Piaget is refuted, the least one can say is that their conception of the beginning of mental life is not supported by the known facts. In the concise definition of Piaget (1964) sensory motoric intelligence, the first stage of mental development, is "a conquest by perception and movement of the entire practical universe that surrounds the small child" (p. 9). The cumulative evidence on cognition and especially on categorical thinking in the first months of life does not fit the expectations of a thoughtless, reflexlike "action-schema." The small child seems to think no less than to act and while acting or thinking it is well aware of the difference between the self and the world.

How is this early self-awareness mediated? This is a puzzling question and one hesitates even to determine the direction of a possible answer. The results of Lewis and Brooks' (1979) experiment made it quite clear that early self-awareness is not mediated by visual codes. These authors presented infants of various ages up to twenty-four months with a reflecting surface, a sort of mirror. After the infants became acquainted with it, an infant's mother wiped its nose and also put some red dye upon the nose. The infants then had an opportunity to look at themselves in the mirror. Below twelve months of age, almost no infant seemed to be bothered by the red dye, but beyond this age more and more of them touched their noses; from 25% of fifteen- to eighteen-month-old infants to 75% at twenty-one to twenty-four months. These findings, then, indicate that the awareness of self in a visual form develops rapidly from the end of the first year to the end of the second. We have already seen, however, that self-awareness appears to exist even earlier than that.

In passing, I would like to mention that by using the technique of exposure to mirrors, Gallup (1970) was able to show that chimpanzees, too, may have some concept of self. Gallup kept a number of wild-born, preadolescent chimpanzees in a small cage in an empty room furnished with a full-length mirror. At the beginning, the chimpanzees treated their reflection as a companion; soon, however, they began to use their reflection as a guide to receive otherwise inaccessible information about themselves and to groom parts of the body that could not be seen directly. At this phase each chimpanzee was anesthetized; the upper portion of their eyebrow bridge and the top half of the opposite ear was painted with a bright red, odorless, nonirritating, alcohol-soluble dye.

Following recovery, at first they were left without the mirror. Later on, the mirror was again facing them. Comparing the number of times the marked parts of the skin were touched, Gallup found that the number of mark-directed touches increased over twenty-five times in the presence of the mirror. In addition to these mark-directed touches, the chimpanzees smelled their fingers and visually examined them, even though the dye had long since dried and became indelible. To the extent that self-recognition implies a rudimentary concept of self, Gallup concluded that man may not have a monopoly of the self-concept. We may add here that neither is this rudimentary concept of self in man a privilege of the later, more mature years.

But we have not yet solved the question: how may early self-awareness be mediated? While it is known that the infant is sensitized to the human voice, it seems counterintuitive to assume that such vocal-verbal codes are the instruments for maintaining self-awareness. As to the favored position of the human voice relative to the other noises in an "average environment," it may suffice to mention two pieces of evidence. Wolff (1967) found that the human voice elicits smiling in two-week-old infants with greater frequency and regularity than do other stimuli. Ungerer, Brody, and Zelazo (1978) had mothers repeat to their babies sixty times per day for thirteen days, while the babies were quiet, the words tinder and beguile. The babies were from twenty-two to twenty-nine days of age. The trained infants, but not their control group, responded differentially to the words that had become familiar and new words, and this difference was clearly maintained for an average of fifteen hours following the cessation of training. Thus, by one month of age, infants are capable of delayed recognition of frequently occurring speech sounds.

And yet, it seems farfetched to assume that such verbal codes may help to maintain self-awareness for the one-month-old infant. Later on, though, this seems precisely to be the case; self-awareness seems to depend on the availability of verbal codes. As one may recall, this was the opinion of Freud (1915a): "what [repression] denies to a presentation is translation into words" (p. 202). In order to become conscious, verbal codes must be attached to any impulse or idea. For some reason, Freud did not connect this suggestion with the left, "speaking" hemisphere. Nowadays Eccles (1973, 1976), more than anyone else, has advocated this connection.

Admitting, though, that he may have made "too radical an inference" and allowing for the possibility that the minor (right) hemisphere in normals may have some linkage with the self-conscious mind, Eccles viewed conscious experience as a unique property of the left hemisphere. "The minor hemisphere is always *per se* an unconscious part of the brain and linkage through the corpus callosum is necessary for it to receive from and give information to the conscious self" (1976, p. 218). Or, quoting Sperry's investigations on commissurotomy patients which have shown that the dominant linguistic hemisphere is uniquely concerned in giving conscious experiences to the subject and in mediating his willed actions, Eccles (1973) writes: "It is not denied that some other consciousness may be associated with the intelligent and learned behavior of the minor hemisphere, but the absence of linguistic or symbolic communication at an adequate level prevents this from being discovered. It is not therefore 'self-conscious' " (p. 113).

Indeed, Sperry reported an incident which occurred while pictures were flashed and perceived by one hemisphere or the other of a commissurotomized patient. At one point in a series of geometrical forms, a picture of a naked pinup girl was shown to the left visual field (right hemisphere) of a split-brain patient. The woman patient blushed and giggled, but when asked what she saw, replied that she had seen nothing but a flash of light. When asked why she was laughing, the patient seemed confused about what to say and finally said with another laugh: "Dr. Sperry, you have some machine."

This blushing and her inability to explain the reasons for her emotional reaction may be explained as an indication that to be registered by self-awareness, the events elaborated in the right hemisphere must be first transferred to the left hemisphere. Otherwise, they remain unconscious and, let us note, it is not for psychodynamic reasons. To be repressed and made unconscious, the psychic event must already have been taken cognizance of by self-awareness. Here, due to the commissurotomy and thereby the isolation of verbal codes, the perception elaborated in the right hemisphere had no chance at all to become conscious.

Eccles' suggestion, though, to make self-awareness contingent on the availability of verbal codes has a weak point, that it depends totally on split-brain studies. Although these studies have already produced an impressive literature, they nonetheless deal with a small number of patients. At the last published count, patients in the Vogel and Bogen series who had undergone total commissurotomy numbered sixteen, to which may be added two patients from the more recent series operated upon by Wilson, and one or two surviving cases of the Akelaitis series. "The relative unpopularity of the operation outside the United States," Beaumont (1981) observes, "and the relative success of partial commissurotomy, mean that these numbers are unlikely to increase significantly within the near future" (p. 191).

Considering the small number of patients, the limits of experimentation with patients, and the evidence which sometimes is less than clear-cut, Eccles' conclusions, indeed, may seem to rest on a shaky foundation. However, there is available evidence from other sources which does support Eccles' approach. For example, correlating the level of consciousness with hemispheric side of lesion following acute cerebrovascular injury, Albert, Silverberg, Reches, and Berman (1976) found that 57% of patients with left hemisphere lesions had initial impairment of consciousness, in contrast to 25% with right-sided damage.

Albert et al. graded the level of consciousness according to a scale ranging from deep coma (no response to pain, negative corneal reflex, no spontaneous movements), through semicoma, stupor, somnolence, to consciousness (does not drift off to sleep, aware of stimuli, capable of focusing energies on a single topic). As detailed above, they found that although reduced consciousness was infrequent following right hemispheric lesions, more than 50% of patients with acute left hemispheric vascular lesions did suffer from an initial impairment of consciousness. Patients with infarction of the language-dominant hemisphere are more likely to suffer from impairment of consciousness than are those with infarction of the non-language-dominant hemisphere.

The study of Serafetinides, Walter, and Cherlow (1975) on amnestic confusional phenomena following hippocampal stimulation shows the same laterality effect. These authors implanted depth electrodes in patients for diagnostic purposes. Just before stimulation in the amygdala, hippocampus, and hippocampal gyrus, they told their patients that they would be asked a number of questions and also given a number of items to be recalled later. The findings, again, showed that with few exceptions the site of the stimulation which produced disturbances in memory and consciousness (disorientation in time, space, or person), was the left hemisphere. "Both confusion and memory, as the evidence presented here indicates, can be referred to functions of the dominant hemisphere for speech. Stimulation findings parallel those of 'consciousness' changes as seen following the intracarotic sodium amytal tests which are also referrable to the dominant hemisphere for speech" (p. 374).

The results of Serafetinides et al. may be underscored by a related finding of Moyra Williams (1973). She studied the phenomena of transitional confusion following ECT. She used four pictures of simple objects, for each of which two alternatives were available, one resembling the original in the visual modality (perceptual alternative) and one having the same name and function but being unlike it visually (nominal alternative). The original pictures were shown to groups of patients undergoing unilateral (right-sided) or bilateral ECT and to a control group, all of whom were told to look at each of these pictures and try to remember them. "I shall be coming back later on to see how many you can recognize."

After ECT was delivered, as soon as the subjects were aware enough to tell their names and occupations, even though at the time many were still disoriented as to time and place, they were presented with the pictures. When the originals were shown alongside the alternatives on the recognition test, the bilateral and unilateral ECT groups picked out the same proportion correctly. The number of correct choices was not significantly less after bilateral treatment than after unilateral treatment, but the bilateral group attributed their correct choice to a guess rather than to a recognition of a familiar item.

Williams interpreted her findings as indicating that we need verbal codes, the name of an object, subserved by the left hemisphere, to grant visual information the sense of familiarity, of "me-ness," as Claparede (1911) termed it. When verbalization is reduced (by bilateral ECT), it is only the sense of familiarity, the knowledge that it has occurred to me, that I have seen it before, which is impaired, but not the ability to recognize it correctly. While the patients said they were "only guessing," their guesses were usually correct. This sense of familiarity or "me-ness" made possible by the use of verbal codes, and its lack due to the disturbance in the left hemisphere due to ECT may be regarded as a strong support for the contention that self-awareness is contingent upon verbal codes.

This conclusion, though, could mean that self-awareness does not emerge before such verbal codes are available. How then is self-awareness possible during the first months of life? This indeed is a puzzle, a challenge to anybody who would maintain that early self-awareness *is* possible, but I do not know how to solve it. At any rate, it seems quite clear that early in the course of development verbal codes will be established as the sole agent of self-awareness.

The emergence of self-awareness brought to an end the unity of the organism. A creature which is able to follow up his own thoughts and actions is, in fact, a double and sometimes even multiple, personality. One of the early writers on the "psychic methods of cure", Reil (1803), related a dream in which the dreamer told a sad but true story to someone. At this point, a third person interrupted the dreamer to remind him of something important left out of the story. "Why did his fantasy," asked Reil, "create a third person who surprised him and made him feel ashamed, how can the ego divide itself into persons who, out of himself, produce things of which he is not aware that they were in him and surprise him as outside wisdom?" (cited in Ellenberger 1970, p. 127).

It is not our fantasy and not in dreams only. We are divided, by nature, into an acting and an observing self, into a self and one which is aware of this self. We are programmed to act and feel but also to judge whether or not to be proud of our actions; occasionally we detest ourselves. This ongoing tension between these two selves, inevitably, may lead us to question which one is our true self. Indeed, when are we truly ourselves, or, to put the same question differently, who was the wise man: the dreamer or the stranger? Paradoxically, the "stranger" is wiser, he is the "true" self. Quite appropriately, Freud called it "super-ego." The term *ego-ideal* conveys the same hierarchical order. The striving or, shall we say, the motivated self is supervised by forces more respectable than itself, forces which from time to time may be experienced as confronting the self and treating it as an alien entity.

It is important to emphasize here that feedback, reafference or whatever new cybernetic principles of which one may still learn, are not relevant to the questions posed by self-awareness. A machine and also an organism, the functions of which are controlled by means of feedback and reafference and, further, which is able to set its goals by reasoning but is lacking self-awareness, will never experience doubts, shame, guilt, or pride. If only survival and fitness subserving this survival counted, it would be difficult to justify the emergence of self-awareness. The hesitations, doubts, and pain of soul-searching generated by self-awareness hamper rather than support the struggle for survival; they add a new dimension to the burden of adapting to a mercilessly indifferent environment, namely, the quest for peace of mind.

One may ask why. While understandably, it is beyond our ability to answer such teleological questions, but we may attempt some speculations regarding the prerequisite causes. Speech and verbal memory codes, at least after infancy, seem to perform here the task of Atlas in holding the world of self-awareness on their shoulders. Speech, as Luria and Yudovich (1959) so well defined it, is a basic means of communication, but also a "higher regulator" of behavior.

For example, Lyublinskaya (1955) presented children aged twelve to thirty months with small red and green boxes, the green empty and the red containing sweets. It proved very difficult for the children to learn to select the right boxes. The situation changed completely, however, when the experimenter named the colors of the boxes. Now, choosing the correct box was nearly three times as quick as before; also, once the learning was established, it was not extinguished even after an interval of a week.

Evidently, soon after the child has gained mastery over speech and established the verbal codes, the role of speech in guiding and controlling behavior will become more salient. It may suffice to quote two experiments of Luria and Yudovich (1959) to this effect. They requested three- to four-year-old children "to press twice a small balloon when the light appears." Even children who knew the meaning of the word "twice" usually pressed the balloon three to four times and more in succession. If, however, they suggested that the child say "go" to each flash of light and simultaneously press the balloon, the child began to produce the required double pressures.

In another experiment, Luria and Yudovich (1959) asked five-year-old children to press the balloon twice in response to short signals and to do nothing in response to long signals. The correct performance of such a task often proved impossible as long as the children worked silently. If, however, the child was encouraged to verbalize his own self-instructions, he coped "easily" with such a task.

Understanding, controlling our actions, and even more so planning and foreseeing, depend to a great extent on the availability of verbal memory codes and "inner speech." And, of course, upon them depends our conscience; it is a revealing fact that nobody has yet described the figure or face of his or her conscience, but everybody is acquainted with the voice of conscience. Speech, indeed, is a higher regulator of behavior. One must admit, though, that this improvement in control of behavior was achieved at a considerable price. For ever since the emergence of self-awareness, the demand of "know thyself" became one of the moral and psychological imperatives facing mankind, and self-deception became one of the dangers of which to be aware. Thus it happened that peace of mind, peace between the striving and performing self and evaluating self-awareness became one of our most valued aims. A naive, nonreflective organism has it; we must achieve it.

In view of these considerations, we must adjust our definition of mental health as follows: a sense of autonomy equilibrated by adaptation and accompanied by peace of mind. It is this triad of autonomy, adaptation, and peace of mind psychotherapy is invoked to reestablish, if it falters. Psychotherapy, let us state it once more, does not promise to explore the secrets of an unknowable unconscious but rather is committed to encourage an appeasement between the true and false selves, both of which are governed by the same rules of functioning.

EPILOGUE

Looking through this book, it occurred to me that by now readers, whose interest in Freud's writing is less than mine, may feel tired. If you have something to say, say it, they may think, but save us the discussion of Freud's ideas.

Whatever one may think of such advice, to my understanding it only displays a shortcoming of modern psychology: its ahistorical nature. One can hardly imagine writing on dreams and the unconscious without relating to Freud's ideas. Freud's impact on the intellectual life of this century is without match and his views, especially those of dreams, the unconscious, and the Oedipus complex enchanted professionals as well as the general public. Thus one cannot, it seems to me, offer a new theory of dreams or suggest reconsideration of the concept of the unconscious or, last but not least, repudiate Oedipal conflict as a necessary condition for evolving psychoneuroses, without justifying these attempts by proving that Freud's theory falls short of its reputation.

At this point again, I find myself in a quandary. Lately, it has become quite fashionable to criticize Freud, his conception of mental energy, his libido theory, his understanding of transference in psychotherapy; yet, paradoxically, all these and many more revisions or, better, transformations of psychoanalysis have not damaged the appeal of Freud's theory of behavior. Let us imagine, however, that we agreed that Freud's concepts of the unconscious and repression are disproved; what then? What would remain, then, of Freud's endeavor?

The answer would seem quite evident were it not for the virtual impossibility of simply verifying or proving false Freud's theory. For while its fuel was a scientist's ambition, Freud's theory became an object of adoration quite alien to the tempered atmosphere of science. Fromm's (1962) story of his encounters with Marx and Freud may help me to clarify what

I have in mind. In his essay, Fromm reminds us that these two men, together with Einstein, "were the architects of the modern age." In his opinion, though, Marx and Freud are not of equal stature. "That Marx is a figure of world historical significance with whom Freud cannot even be compared in this respect hardly needs to be said. . . . I consider Marx, the thinker, as being of much greater depth and scope than Freud" (pp. 12–13). Incidentally, Fromm sees the importance of Freud "in his discovery of unconscious processes . . . which has altered the picture of man for all time to come" (p. 13).

For our purpose here, we may disregard the rank order proposed by Fromm; rather, let us assume that Marx, Freud, and Einstein are of equal stature and importance and together were the architects of our age. Then let us compare the attitude of Freudians with that of Marxists and physicists (by the way, there were never Einsteinian physicists) toward their respective spiritual guide.

I wonder whether physicists know where Einstein was born, whether or not he had children, or what his wife's name was. It would be interesting to know whether any Marxist, at all, while in London, visited the miserable apartment in which Marx lived. On the other hand, I know that many psychologists and psychiatrists, while in Vienna, would not forget to visit Berg Gasse. It does not look as if Marxists are interested in Marx's personal life, and one may wonder whether any physicist would suggest the publishing of Einstein's letters.

Unlike Marxists and physicists, to put it briefly, who are interested in the ideas of Marx and Einstein, psychoanalysts, and curiously enough a great number of people who never really studied Freud's writings, seem to be involved in a veritable hero worship. To illustrate what this hero worship means, I shall quote from Bemporad's (1978) discussion of Freud's view on depression. I would like to emphasize that it was by chance that I selected this example, and my remarks here do not, by any means, intend to detract from the value of Bemporad's excellent treatise.

> In retrospect, Freud's short essay is a master piece of clinical investigation and logical deduction. Yet it may have raised more difficulties than it resolved. The essay proposed an entirely new model of illness: the expression of affect toward an incorporated object (although Abraham, in his investigation of depression along the lines of libidinal regression, gave a similar description). (P. 23)

This formulation, Bemporad observes, has become increasingly difficult to prove or corroborate by clinical evidence.

> Therapists for decades have induced their depressed patients, with little success, to express anger so as to deflect it from the internalized effigy. Some depressives have not evidenced the crucial self-reproaches. Depressed individuals do not uniformly present a history of past or current loss. Therefore Freud's bold and imaginative formulation does not appear to have survived the test of time. (P. 23)

Then Bemporad pointed to a further difficulty. In Freud's theory of depression, the superego became the critical factor, but the superego vents its anger at the ego in all neurotic disorders, not just in depression. Indeed, "later orthodox formulations" on depression have essentially discarded the introject hypothesis in favor of one viewing depression as a result of a felt disparity (the peace of mind in our last chapter) between the ego-ideal and the actual self. "Nevertheless *Mourning and Melancholia* remains a classic in psychoanalytic literature" (p. 24).

It is difficult to understand why a proposition which has not survived the test of time, or to be more precise, has been contradicted by clinical experience, is judged a masterpiece of clinical investigation. Also, considering that the introject theory was discarded by none other than the later "orthodox" authors, one wonders what justifies labeling Freud's *Mourning and Melancholia* a classic in psychoanalytic literature. Finally, while it remained unclear whether Freud's model of depression was originally his or not, the positive statement sounded much stronger than the qualifying remark.

Bemporad calls Freud's short essay on depression a masterpiece, a classic, an entirely new model; at the same time, we know that the theory was disproved and discarded. It is a fair guess that no other authors would be treated, under similar conditions, by so many superlatives. Rather, in their case, evidence would be evidence and a failure a failure. But heroes, one can now see, are exempted from the rules scientists obey. This is why the attempt to prove that Freud's "heroic" deed, his conception of the unconscious, is a falsifiable proposition, may seem a Sisyphean task. Recalling, though, Polanyi's (1963) express advice, one may agree that precisely because of its importance, even if all my arguments will be proved correct, no decision regarding the Freudian unconscious will be close at hand. "There must be at all times," Polanyi suggested, "a predominantly accepted scientific view of the nature of things. . . . A strong presumption that any contradictory evidence has to be disregarded, even if it cannot be accounted for, in the hope it will eventually turn out to be false or irrelevant" (p. 1012).

Of course, the unaccounted for facts should be kept in mind, and eventually refuted or accepted as the beginning of a new prespective.

APPENDIX: SOME EXAMPLES OF DREAM STYLES

A. DREAMERS OF PURE LOGICAL STYLE

Subject No. 1.

1. I hurried to class. It was the last lecture of the semester. When I entered class I saw lots of new faces. I said to a friend who came in with me: "Look, everyone shows up toward the end of the year, and we don't have a place to sit." There were two vacant seats beside two guys I had never seen before, who put their bags there. I asked them to remove the bags. They said something about me, I don't remember what it was exactly, but I didn't like what I heard. I was awfully angry with them. I raised my hand, pointed a finger at them and said vigorously: "and don't you dare speak to me like that, you idiot, and move away immediately!"

2. I went on a trip abroad with a man and a woman with whom I really had traveled many years ago. We arrived at some town in the mountains and I told them I had to go and buy presents for my kids. I went out of the house and up the road and arrived at the shopping center. There was a big department store and when I approached the door I noticed that the shop was already closed. I felt very disappointed and thought to myself: "Alas, what will I bring as presents to my kids tomorrow?"

3. I came back home very tired after an exam. The questions in the exam were very difficult and my answers weren't as good as my knowledge of the material. I fell asleep and in the next room the kids were playing. They

shouted and quarreled. Angrily I ran into the room and yelled at them: "Aren't you ashamed of yourselves, grown-up children like you, disturbing your mother when she is so tired?"

4. My husband was due to arrive from abroad. I went with the kids to the airport where we then all waited impatiently. Suddenly, we saw a friend of ours going out of the airport building. We asked him: "Have you seen Z.?" and he replied: "What are you talking about, he wasn't on the plane at all."

5. I have been studying a lot for the exam. I have been sitting for hours together with a friend of mine and rehearsing the material. I arrived at the exam and we sat next to one another. I got the questionnaire and panicked: most of the questions were unfamiliar to me.

Subject No. 2

1. I visit an amusement park with a woman and her daughter. It has several playhouses; among them is an installment with balls rolling on lanes, and one must hit them with other balls. After a while we get hungry and arrive at a two-story dining room, in which one must catch a place in order to win a meal.

2. I drive my car at full speed in a wild manner on my way to work together with a woman who is working with me. I arrive at a railway barrier, which has two sets of barriers on both sides, with several railroads in between. I try to move across the double barrier in spite of the flashing light, but after I cross the first one, the other one is closing and I cannot get across. Then the first barrier closes too and I am caught between them. I move around on the railway in an attempt to avoid getting hit by the trains.

3. I am in service in the reserves, driving A.'s car together with some friends. A high-ranked officer's visit is expected, and a dress parade of the soldiers of my unit is being organized. My friends and I are sitting in a Peugeot van, in its open box and watching what is going on without taking part in it. A military truck command car causes damage to A.'s car, and I try to fix it with the help of some friends. At night we watch a helicopter circling above us. We are supposed to be in blackout; therefore we run to turn off the lights of all the vehicles in the area. In some cases

we do not succeed in finding the right switches and the officer in charge scolds us.

4. I and two of my friends serve as the security force of some rural, agricultural settlement. While patrolling I notice fire in the fields and in the gardens around the houses. We try to put out the fire with water pipes and try to call for help for more people who could help us in the fire extinguishing efforts and in removing flammable objects.

5. I visit Hatiqua suburb with a colleague. Outside a café where several people are sitting, a violent fight breaks out between two people, one of whom has bandages on his legs and wears very short shorts. During the fight some shopwindows in the vicinity are broken, and the people involved in the fight smash bottles on their legs. Meanwhile some people are engaged in breaking lanterns.

B. DREAMERS OF PURE BIZARRE STYLE

Subject No. 1

1. I was in a bus and we arrived at a crossroads. A snake-bus appeared moving toward us (two trollies attached with plastic, like an accordion). It was red. We collided with the plastic. It stretched and was torn and nothing happened. I jump and dance in this light plastic as on a trampoline. Suddenly I remember that I ought to bring home honey and a mop.

Further details which I recalled later: I was in this house. X and his father run to the bathroom wrapped in huge towels.

2. I went with L. in a white Subaru car from her house to mine, through the Beach Road. I met someone who claimed that the green bicycles still stand at a certain corner of streets in Tel Aviv. On a green pencil my name was written and that of the one who told me about the bicycles, and those of red-haired S. and other friends of my childhood.

In the University corridor I met Y. who had a haircut. His forehead was uncovered, and he was wearing rags. He had a revolutionary smile on his face. Excited I told him about the green bicycles of my childhood, and he promised to help me find them.

3. The bicycles which belonged to my brother passed to my possession. I keep looking for a lock but cannot find one. While looking at the mirror,

tossing my hair aside, I notice a huge baldness at the center of my head, surrounded with red hair.

4. Two burnt bulbs and I run with them to some corner and start cutting them with a diamond ring into small slices of thin glass. I put them in my pocket and went to Jerusalem, where I scattered the pieces of glass around —and Jerusalem glowed in a strange light. I remembered a line of Amichai's poem: "And the sun thought that Jerusalem is a sea / and in a terrible mistake set there."

5. I noticed a wound in my leg, and pulled out of it a banana. D. tasted it. S. explained that it happens because of a certain virus. Again I noticed the baldness in the center of my head. My hand was cut off—like in "Monty Python's Holy Grail"—in one blow, and blood began to pour out of my body. There was also something at my toes.

Subject No. 2

1. I dreamt that all around me ate cakes and none was left for me. One of my teachers (who knows me) passed by and asked me why didn't I have a cake. I told him that simply none was left. He took me by my hand to the cafeteria and bought a cake and a coke for me. I asked for a coke, and they gave me a half-empty bottle. He asked for coffee, and the coffee was served in a baby's bottle, but after some seconds the bottle disappeared. What I do remember is a blue color in the dream, but I don't remember what it was. Afterwards he wanted me to taste his coffee—which had been made by my aunt. I agreed, but meanwhile I spilled all the coffee. We walked a little and there I saw my aunt (another one) and my cousin (the aunt was from my father's side of the family, the cousin from my mother's), with her baby who was very thin and weak. I played with him, and when I turned around my teacher was gone.

2. I dreamt that I saw all kinds of ballet garments as if worn by a body, but I couldn't see the body itself, only the ballet dress, that kept appearing. The dress was black, and there were more dresses going around in circles, but I recall only that specific black one.

3. I dreamt of all kinds of hairpins in all sorts of colors and with various rubber bands in various colors. They were dancing. It was a sort of a very colorful dream.

4. A cave and a witch sitting in it. She cooks in a casserole a collection of bracelets and necklets. She was frightening.

5. I am in a maze, cannot find my way out. I want to cry but I am unable to. Above my head bats are flying. In order to pass through one has to jump over flames. Strange creatures around.

C. DREAMERS OF MIXED STYLE

Subject No. 1

1. A friend of mine—we served in the army together—remained in service and only recently had the guts to leave and start studying in a nursing school (a fact which is true). I call up my unit in the army and she is there. To my regret, she had despaired and returned to army service discontinuing her studies.

2. My whole family and I are at the seashore, sitting on the quay. We have blue horses and I prepare special food for them, and the family is riding them.

3. I received a car, and my neighbors, upon my visiting them, hardly wish me good luck and congratulations, and they wear "faces of envy." I don't remember what they say, but they do not congratulate me with all their hearts—while they are actually neighbors whose daughter is a good friend of mine.

4. I am at the dentist, who pulls out two of my teeth, but it doesn't hurt. I had the feeling that he pulls out two upper teeth, but at the end they were in the lower jaw, and it doesn't show so much when I am smiling. Therefore it is not urgent to put in crowns.

5. I am in school, but it is in a cave on the beach. The teacher is really my English teacher. I sit with some friends outside the cave and we listen to the lesson from the outside. Then my friends and I float huge plastic fish in the water; while the fish are in the water we are on the beach holding them by thin ropes, and thus we walk along the beach with the fish.

Subject No. 2

1. It is the middle of the night but there are lots of people at the grocery store; to all of them the owner looks familiar, but not to me. I am in a hurry because I am awaiting a phone call. I tell him that, but he wouldn't react.

2. I am in a very big department store. In it there are various stands, restaurants, and cafes. I wander around among the stores, go up staircases and down through sort of tunnels which look like slides. In one of those tunnels I fall down. I am helped up and told to be careful. I am shown how to go down these tunnels and instructed how to stop the swing. Then I meet some students with whom I study. One of them is pregnant and she intends to buy a sweater for herself. Then we are suddenly outside the store, and there is an examination.

3. I dreamt that I had gone by train to visit my sister in Haifa; I had to take a bus from there in order to get to her home. I wait and wait and it is getting dark and late and the bus does not arrive.

4. My cousin (who lives in the United States) enters [my] home and asks why I didn't come at lunchtime. I am astonished that he is here at all, and then he tells me that he arrived that morning from the States, he had opened a jewelry shop in Israel. The opening was at noon, and I should have attended that opening.

5. I ask a girl who studies in the first year for some material of a lesson I missed. She promises to bring it over. (It happens at daytime.) Suddenly it is night and I meet her and she apologizes about forgetting to bring it to me, stating that she was very busy. She promises again to bring it.

REFERENCES

Ablon, L., and J. E. Mack. 1979. Sleep disorders. In *Basic handbook of child psychiatry*, ed. J. D. Noshpitz, vol. 2, 643–660. New York: Basic Books.

Abse, D. W. 1959. Hysteria. In *American handbook of psychiatry*, ed. S. Arieti, vol. 1, 272–92. New York: Basic Books.

Albert, M., R. Silverberg, A. Reches, and M. Berman, 1976. Cerebral dominance for consciousness. *Archives of Neurology* 33: 453–54.

Antrobus, J. S. 1978. Dreaming for cognition. In *The mind in sleep*, ed. A. M. Arkin, J. S. Antrobus, and S. J. Ellman, 569–81. Hillsdale, N.J.: Erlbaum.

Arbib, M. A. 1972. *The metaphorical brain*. New York: Wiley.

Arlow, J. A., and Ch. Brenner. 1964. *Psychoanalytic concepts and the structural theory*. New York; International Universities Press.

Aronson, E., and S. Rosenbloom. 1971. Space-perception in early infancy: Perception within a common auditory-visual space. *Science* 172: 1161–63.

Bakan, P. 1971. The eyes have it. *Psychology Today* 4: 64–69.

———. 1977. Dreaming, REM sleep and the right hemisphere: A theoretical integration. *Journal of Altered States of Consciousness* 5: 21–32.

Bakan, P., and F. F. Strayes. 1973. On the reliability of conjugate lateral eye movements. *Perceptual and Motor Skills* 36: 429–30.

Ball, W., and E. Tronick, 1971. Infant responses to impending collision: Optical and real. *Science* 171: 818–20.

Barratt, B. B. 1976. Freud's psychology as interpretation. *Psychoanalysis and Contemporary Thought* 5: 443–78.

Barron, F. 1952. Personality style and perceptual choice. *Journal of Personality* 20: 358–401.

Basch, M. F. 1983. The significance of self-psychology for a theory of psychotherapy. In *Reflections on self-psychology*, ed. J. D. Lichtenberg and S. Kaplan, 223–38. Hillsdale, N.J.: Erlbaum.

Beamont, J. G. 1981. Split brain studies and the duality of consciousness. In *Aspects of consciousness*, ed. G. Underwood and R. Stevens, vol. 2, 189–214. London: Academic Press.

Bemporad, J. 1978. In *Severe and mild depressions*, ed. S. Arieti and J. Bemporad. New York: Basic Books.

Beres, D. 1974. In Panel on hysteria today, reviewed by J. Laplanche. *International Journal of Psychoanalysis* 55: 459–69.

Bergson, H. [1901] 1914. *Dreams*. London: Fisher and Unwin.

———. 1902. L'effort mental (Mental effort). *Revue Scientifique* 16.

Bibring, E. 1953. The mechanism of depression. In *Affective disorders*, ed. P. Greenacre, 13–48. New York: International Universities Press.

Binet, A. [1890] 1906. *On double consciousness*. Chicago: Open Court.

———. [1891] 1906. *Alterations of personality*. London: Chapman and Hall.

Binz, C. 1878. *Über den Traum* (On the dream). Bonn: Adolf Marcus.

Bischof, N. 1975. Comparative ethology of incest avoidance. In *Biosocial anthropology*, ed. R. Fox, 37–68. London: Malaby Press.

Blacker, K. H., and J. P. Tupin. 1977. Hysteria and hysterical structures: Developmental and social theories. In *Hysterical personality*, ed. M. J. Horowitz, 96–141. New York: Jason Aronson.

Bleuler, E. [1911] 1950. *Dementia praecox or the group of schizophrenias*. New York: International Universities Press.

———. 1924. *Textbook of psychiatry*. New York: Macmillan.

Bliss, D. K. 1974. Theoretical explanations of drug-dissociated behavior. *Federal Proceedings* 33: 1787–96.

Bloom, L. 1973. *One word at a time*. The Hague: Mouton.

Bonime, W., and F. Bonime. 1980. The dream in the depressive personality. In *The dream in clinical practice*, ed. J. M. Natterson, 107–47. New York: Jason Aronson.

Bornstein, M. H. 1975. Qualities of color vision in infancy. *Journal of Experimental Child Psychology* 19: 401–19.

Bower, T. G. R. 1971. The object in the world of the infant. *Scientific American* 225: 30–38.

Brazelton, T. B., B. Koslowski, and M. Main. 1974. The origins of reciprocity: The early mother-infant interaction. In *The effect of the infant on its caregiver*, ed. M. Lewis and L. Rosenblum, 49–76. New York: Wiley.

Breuer, J., and S. Freud. [1895] 1952. *Studies on hysteria,* Standard Edition, vol. 2. London: Hogarth Press.

Briquet, P. 1859. *Traité de l'hystérie* (A treatise on hysteria). Paris: Baillière.

Broughton, R. 1975. Biorhythmic functions. *Canadian Psychological Review* 16: 217–39.

Brown, R., and D. McNeill. 1966. The "tip of the tongue" phenomenon. *Journal of Verbal Learning and Verbal Behavior* 5: 325–37.

Bruner, J. S., J. Y. Goodnow, and G. A. Austin. 1956. *A study of thinking.* New York: Wiley.

Bryant, P. 1977. Logical inferences and development. In *Piaget and knowing: Studies in genetic epistemology,* ed. B. A. Geber, 53–64. London: Routledge & Kegan Paul.

Calkins, M. W. 1893. Statistics of dreams. *Journal of Psychology* 5: 311–43.

Cancro, R., ed. 1970. *Menninger foundation conference on the schizophrenic syndrome.* New York: Brunner/Mazel.

Charcot, J. M. [1877] 1889. *Clinical lectures on diseases of the nervous system.* London: New Syndenham Society.

Chodoff, P., and H. Lyons. 1958. Hysteria, the hysterical personality and "hysterical" conversion. *American Journal of Psychiatry* 114: 734–40.

Claparede, E. [1911] 1951. Recognition and "me-ness." In *Organization and pathology of thought,* ed. D. Rapaport, 58–75. New York: Columbia University Press.

Cooper, A. M. 1983. Psychoanalytic inquiry and new knowledge. In *Reflections on self-psychology,* ed. J. D. Lichtenberg and S. Kaplan, 19–34. Hillsdale, N.J.: Erlbaum.

Deese, J. 1965. *The structure of associations in language and thought.* Baltimore: Johns Hopkins University Press.

Delboeuf, J. 1885. *Le sommeil et les rêves* (Sleep and dreams). Paris.

Dement, W. C. 1972. *Some must sleep and some must watch.* Stanford: Alumni of Stanford.

DeNike, L. D., and N. Tiber. 1968. Neurotic behavior. In *Foundations of abnormal psychology,* ed. P. London and D. Rosenhan, 345–90. New York: Holt, Rinehart & Winston.

Dessoir, M. 1890. *Das Doppel-Ich* (The alter-ego). Leipzig: E. Gunther.

Easser, B. R., and S. R. Lesser. 1965. Hysterical personality: A reevaluation. *Psychoanalytic Quarterly* 34: 390–405.

Eccles, J. C. 1973. *The understanding of the brain.* New York: McGraw-Hill.

———. 1976. Brain and free will. In *Consciousness and the brain*, ed. G. G. Globus, G. Maxwell, and J. Savodnik, 101–12. New York: Plenum.

Ehrlichman, H., and M. S. Wiener. 1980. EEG asymmetry during covert mental activity. *Psychophysiology* 17: 228–35.

Ellenberger, H. 1970. *The discovery of the unconscious.* New York: Basic Books.

Fechner, G. T. 1889. *Elemente der Psychophysik* (Elements of psychophysics), vol. 2. Leipzig.

Fenichel, O. 1945. *The psychoanalytic theory of neurosis.* New York: Norton.

Ferenczi, S. [1913] 1950. A little chanticleer. In *Sex in psychoanalysis*, 240–52. New York: Basic Books.

Fischer, R. 1971. A cartography of the ecstatic and meditative states. *Science* 174: 897–904.

Fiss, H., G. S. Klein, and E. Bokert. 1966. Waking fantasies following interruption of two types of sleep. *Archives of General Psychiatry*, 14: 543–51.

Ford, D. H., and H. B. Urban. 1963. *Systems of psychotherapy: A comparative study.* New York: Wiley.

Foulkes, D. 1962. Dream reports from different states of sleep. *Journal of Abnormal and Social Psychology* 65: 14–25.

———. 1978. *A grammar of dreams.* Hassocks, England: Harvester Press.

Fox, R. 1980. *The red lamp of incest.* New York: E. P. Dutton.

Frazer, J. G. 1887. *Totemism.* Edinburgh.

———. 1910. *Totemism and exogamy*, 4 vols. London: Macmillan.

Freud, S. [1894] 1962. *The neuro-psychoses of defense*, vol. 3, Standard Edition, 45–68. London: Hogarth Press.

———. [1900] 1954. *The interpretation of dreams.* London: George Allen & Unwin.

———. [1901] 1953. On dreams, vol. 5, Standard Edition, 633–86. London: Hogarth Press.

———. [1905a] 1953. *Fragment of an analysis of a case of hysteria*, vol. 12, Standard Edition. London: Hogarth Press.

———. [1905b] 1953. *Three essays on sexuality*, vol. 7, Standard Edition, 125–243. London: Hogarth Press.

———. [1909a] 1955. *Analysis of a phobia in a five-year-old boy*, vol. 10, Standard Edition, 5–149. London: Hogarth Press.

———. [1909b] 1955. Notes upon a case of obsessional neurosis, vol. 10, Standard Edition, 155–318. London: Hogarth Press, 1955.

———. [1912a] 1958. *Recommendations to physicians practicing psychoanalysis,* vol. 12, Standard Edition, 109–20. London: Hogarth Press.

———. [1912b] 1958. *A note on the unconscious in psychoanalysis,* vol. 12, Standard Edition, 260–286. London: Hogarth Press.

———. [1912/13] 1955. *Totem and taboo,* vol. 13, Standard Edition, 1–161. London: Hogarth Press.

———. [1915a] 1957. Repression, vol. 14, Standard Edition, 159–215. London: Hogarth Press.

———. [1915b] 1957. The unconscious, vol. 14, Standard Edition, 166–204. London: Hogarth Press.

———. [1916] 1961–1963. *Introductory lectures on psycho-analysis,* vol. 15–16, Standard Edition. London: Hogarth Press.

———. [1918] 1963. From the history of an infantile neurosis, vol. 17, Standard Edition, 7–122. London: Hogarth Press.

———. [1922] 1955. Dreams and telepathy, vol. 18, Standard Edition, 195–220. London: Hogarth Press.

———. [1923] 1961. *The ego and the id,* vol. 21, Standard Edition, 12–68. London: Hogarth Press.

———. [1926] 1959. *Inhibitions, symptoms, and anxiety,* vol. 20, Standard Edition, 77–178. London: Hogarth Press.

———. [1933] 1964. *New introductory lectures,* vol. 22, Standard Edition, 7–184. London: Hogarth Press.

———. [1937a] 1964. Analysis terminable and interminable, vol. 23, Standard Edition, 209–54. London: Hogarth Press.

———. [1937b] 1964. Constructions in analysis, vol. 23, Standard Edition, 255–70. London: Hogarth Press.

———. [1939] 1964. *Moses and monotheism,* vol. 23, Standard Edition, 7–140. London: Hogarth Press.

———. [1940] 1964. *An outline of psychoanalysis,* vol. 20, Standard Edition, 144–208. London: Hogarth Press.

Fromm, E. 1962. *Beyond the chains of illusion.* New York: Pocket Books.

Fromm, E., F. Narvaez, and colleagues. 1968. The Oedipus complex: Comments on "The case of Little Hans." *Contemporary Psychoanalysis* 4: 178–88.

Galambos, R., T. T. Norton, and S. P. Frommer. 1967. Optic tract lesions sparing pattern vision in cats. *Experimental Neurology* 18: 8–25.

Gallup, G. G. 1970. Self-recognition in primates. *Science* 167: 86–87.

Garber-Talmon, Y. 1964. Mate selection in collective settlements. *American Sociological Review* 29: 491–508.

———. 1972. *Family and community in the kibbutz*. Cambridge: Harvard University Press.

Giora, Z. 1972. The function of the dream: A reappraisal. *American Journal of Psychiatry*. 128: 1067–73.

———. 1974. What a dream is. *British Journal of Medical Psychology* 47: 283–95.

———. 1975. *Psychopathology: A cognitive view*. New York: Gardner.

———. 1981. Dream styles and the psychology of dreaming. *Psychoanalysis and Contemporary Thought* 4: 291–379.

Girden, E., and E. A. Culler. 1937. Conditioned responses in curarized striate muscle in dogs. *Journal of Comparative and Physiological Psychology* 23: 261–74.

Glass, D. C. 1977. *Behavior pattern, stress and coronary disease*. Hillsdale, N.J.: Erlbaum.

Glass, D. C., J. E. Singer, and L. N. Friedman. 1969. Psychic cost of adaptation to an environmental stress. *Journal of Personality and Social Psychology* 12: 200–212.

Gleser, G. C., and D. Ihlevich. 1969. An objective instrument for measuring defense mechanisms. *Journal of Consulting and Clinical Psychology* 33: 52–60.

Goldenweiser, A. 1910. Totemism, an analytical study. *Journal of American Folk-Lore* 3: 179–290.

Goldin-Meadow, S., M. E. Seligman, and R. Goldman. 1976. Language in the two-year-old. *Cognition* 4: 189–202.

Goldstein, R., N. W. Stolzfuss, and J. F. Gardocki. 1972. Changes in interhemispheric amplitude relationships in the EEG during sleep. *Physiology and Behavior* 8: 811–16.

Goodwin, D. W., B. Powell, D. Bremer, H. Hasrell, and J. Stern. 1969. Alcohol and recall: State-dependent effect in man. *Science* 193: 1358–60.

Gottschalk, L. A., and G. Gleser. 1969. *The measurement of psychological states through the content analysis of verbal behavior*. Berkeley: University of California Press.

Green, A. 1974. In Panel on hysteria today, reviewed by J. Laplanche. *International Journal of Psychoanalysis* 55: 459–69.

Greenfield, P. M., and J. Smith. 1976. *The structure of communication in early language development*. New York: Academic Press.

Gur, R., and L. Gur. 1975. Correlates of conjugate lateral eye movements. In *Lateralization in the nervous system,* ed. E. Harnad, R. W. Doty, L. Goldstein, and G. Krathammer, 251–81. New York: Academic Press.

Hall, C. S., and B. V. Domhoff. 1968. The dreams of Freud and Jung. *Psychology Today* 2: 42–45, 64–65.

Hall, C. S., and R. E. Lind. 1970. *Dreams, life, and literature*. Chapel Hill: University of North Carolina Press.

Hall, C. S., and R. L. Van de Castle. 1966. *The content analysis of dreams*. New York: Appleton.

Hartmann, H. [1939] 1958. *Ego psychology and the problem of adaptation*. New York: International Universities Press.

Herbart, J. F. 1816. *Lehrbuch zur Psychologie* (A textbook of psychology). Königsberg and Leipzig: Unzer.

———. [1824] 1886. *Psychologie als Wissenschaft* (Psychology as a science). Hamburg and Leipzig: L. Voss.

Herman, J. H., S. Y. Ellman, and H. P. Roffwarg. 1978. The problem of NREM recall re-examined. In *The mind in sleep: Psychology and psychophysiology*, ed. A. M. Arkin, J. S. Antrobus, and S. J. Ellman. Hillsdale, N.J.: Erlbaum.

Hilgard, E. R. 1973. Dissociation revisited. In *Historical concepts in psychology*, ed. M. Henle, J. Jaynes and J. J. Sullivan, 205–19. New York: Springer.

———. 1976. Neo-dissociation theory of multiple cognitive control systems. In *Consciousness and self-regulation,* ed. G. E. Schwartz and D. Shapiro. London: Wiley.

Hobson, J. A., and R. W. McCarley. 1977. The brain as a dream-generator: An activation synthesis hypothesis of the dream process. *American Journal of Psychiatry* 134: 1335–48.

Hollender, M. H., and S. J. Hirsch. 1964. Hysterical psychosis. *American Journal of Psychiatry* 125: 1066–74.

Huxley, J. 1963. Lorenzian ethology. *Zeitschrift fur Tier-Psychologie* 20: 402–409.

James, W. [1890] 1950. *Principles of psychology*. Reprint, New York: Dover.

———. [1902] 1958. *The varieties of religious experience*. Reprint, New York: New American Library.

Janet, P. [1907] 1924. *The major symptoms of hysteria,* 2d ed. New York: Macmillan.

Johnson, N. F. 1970. Chunking and organization in the process of recall. In *The psychology of learning and motivation,* ed. G. H. Bower, vol. 4, 171–247. New York: Academic Press.

———. 1972. Organization and the concept of a memory code. In *Coding processes in human memory,* ed. A. W. Melton and E. Martin, 125–59. Washington, D.C.: Winston & Sons.

Jones, E. 1953–1957. *The life and work of S. Freud,* 3 vols. New York: Basic Books.

Joseph, E. D., ed. 1967. *The place of the dream in clinical psychoanalysis,* Monograph 2 of the Kris Study Group of the New York Psychoanalytical Institute. New York: International Universities Press.

Jung, C. G. [1945] 1966. *On the nature of dreams,* vol. 8, Collected Works. New York: Pantheon.

———. [1946] 1966. *On the nature of the psyche,* vol. 8, Collected Works. New York: Pantheon.

———. 1961. *Memories, dreams, reflections.* New York: Random House.

Kaffman, M. 1977. Sexual standards and behavior of the kibbutz children. *American Journal of Orthopsychiatry* 47: 207–12.

Kagan, J. 1981. *The second year.* Cambridge: Harvard University Press.

Klein, M. 1981. On Mahler's autistic and symbiotic phases: An exposition and evaluation. *Psychoanalysis and Contemporary Thought* 4: 69–105.

Koffka, K. 1925. *The growth of the mind.* Patterson, N.J.: Littlefield, Adams.

Kramer, M., C. Winget, and R. M. Whitman. 1971. A city dreams: A survey approach to normative dream content. *American Journal of Psychiatry* 127: 1350–56.

Kris, E. [1948] 1952. Aesthetic ambiguity. In *Psychoanalytic explorations in art,* Reprint, New York: International Universities Press.

Krohn, A. 1978. *Hysteria: The elusive neurosis,* Psychological Issues 45/46. New York: International Universities Press.

Kubie, L. S. 1954. The fundamental nature of the distinction between normality and neurosis. *Psychoanalytic Quarterly* 23: 167–85.

Langer, S. [1942] 1948. *Philosophy in a new key.* Reprint, New York: Mentor.

Langfeldt, G. 1939. *The schizophreniform states.* London: Humphrey Melfood.

Laplanche, J. 1974. Panel on hysteria today. *International Journal of Psychoanalysis* 55: 459–69.

Lashley, K. S. 1950. In search of the engram. Society of Experimental Biology Symposium no. 4. Cambridge: Cambridge University Press.

Leibniz, G. W. [1765] 1896. *New essays concerning human understanding.* Reprint, London: Macmillan.

Lévy-Bruhl, R. 1910. *How natives think.* London: Allen & Unwin.

———. [1949] 1975. *Les carnets de Lévy-Bruhl* (The diaries of Lévy-Bruhl). Oxford: Blackwell.

Lévi-Strauss, C. [1962] 1969. *Totemism.* London: Pelican.

———. 1963. *Structural anthropology.* New York: Basic Books.

Lewis, A. 1936. Problems of obsessional illness. *Proceedings of the Royal Society of Medicine* 29: 325–36.

———. 1975. The survival of hysteria. *Psychological Medicine* 5: 9–12.

Lewis, M., and J. Brooks. 1979. Self knowledge and emotional development. In *The development of affect,* ed. M. Lewis and L. M. Rosenblum. New York: Plenum.

Lindzey, G. 1967. Some remarks concerning incest, the incest taboo, and psychoanalytic theory. *American Psychologist* 22: 1051–59.

Lipps, Th. 1883. *Grundtatsachen des Seelenlebens* (The basic facts of mental life). Munich.

Lord, Ch. G., L. Ross, and M. R. Lepper. 1979. Biased assimilation and attitude polarization: The effects of prior theories on subsequently considered evidence. *Journal of Personality and Social Psychology* 37: 2098–2100.

Lorenz, K. C. 1943. Die angeborenen Formen möglicher Erfahrung (The inherited forms of possible ways for experiencing). *Zeitschrift für Tier-Psychologie* 5: 235–409.

Luria, A. R., and F. J. Yudovich. 1959. *Speech and the development of mental processes in the child.* London: Staples Press.

Lyublinskaya, A. A. 1955. Quoted after Luria, A. R. 1961. *The role of speech in the regulation of normal and abnormal behavior.* London: Pergamon.

McDonald, D. G., H. G. Shallenberger, and F. A. Carpenter. 1968. Spontaneous automatic responses during sleep and wakefulness. *Psychophysiology* 4: 362–63.

McDougall, W. 1926. *Outline of abnormal psychology.* New York: Scribners.

McLennan, J. F. 1870. The worship of animals and plants. *Fortnightly Review*.

McNeil, D. 1970. *The acquisition of language*. New York: Harper & Row.

Malcolmson, K. G. 1966. Radiological findings in Globus Hystericus. *British Journal of Radiology* 39: 583–86.

Marmor, J. 1953. Orality in the hysterical personality. *Journal of American Psychoanalytic Association* 1: 656–71.

Marshall, J. C., and F. Newcombe. 1966. Syntactic and semantic errors in paralexia. *Neuropsychologia* 4: 169–76.

Matte-Blanco, I. 1975. *The unconscious as infinite sets*. London: Duckworth.

Maudsley, H. 1867. *The physiology and pathology of mind*. London: Macmillan.

Maury, L. F. 1878. *Le sommeil et les rêves* (Sleep and dreams). Paris: Didier.

Meissner, S. J. 1981. Metapsychology—Who needs it? *Journal of American Psychoanalytic Association* 29: 921–38.

Mellett, G. P. 1974. The clinical problem. In *Obsessional states*, ed. H. R. Beech, 55–94. London: Methuen.

Millar, W. M. 1958. Hysteria—A re-evaluation. *Journal of Mental Science* 104: 813–21.

Miller, G. A. 1956. The magical number of seven, plus or minus two: Some limits of our capacity for processing information. *Psychological Review* 63: 81–97.

Muller, G. E. 1911. Zur Analyse der Gedächtnistätigkeit und des Vorstellungsläfes (Contributions to the analysis of remembering and ideation). *Zeitschrift für Psychologie*, Supplement, 5.

Mundy-Castle, A. C., and J. Anglin. 1969. *The development of looking in infancy*. Paper read at Society for Research in Child Development.

Myers, F. W. H. 1892. The subliminal consciousness. *Proceedings of the Society for Psychic Research* 7: 298–355.

Nietzsche, F. [1886] 1907. *Beyond Good and Evil*. Edinburgh: T. N. Foulis.

Noble, D. 1951. Hysterical manifestations in schizophrenic illness. *Psychiatry* 14: 153–160.

Ornstein, P. H. 1983. Discussion. In *Reflections on self-psychology*, ed. J. D. Lichtenberg and S. Kaplan. Hillsdale, N.J.: Erlbaum.

Oswald, J. 1962. *Sleeping and waking*. Amsterdam: Elsevier.

Otis, L. S. 1964. Dissociation and recovery of a response learned under the influence of chlorpromasine or saline. *Science* 143: 1347–48.

Overton, D. A. 1964. State-dependent or "dissociated" learning produced with pentobarbital. *Journal of Comparative and Physiological Psychology* 57: 3–12.

Palombo, S. R. 1978. *Dreaming and memory: A new information-processing model*. New York: Basic Books.

Piaget, J. 1947. *Play, dreams and imitation*. New York: Norton.

———. [1964] 1968. *Six psychological studies*. New York: Vintage.

Plato. Timaeus. Quoted after Abse, D. W. 1959. Hysteria. In *American handbook of psychiatry*, ed. S. Arieti, vol. 1, 272–92. New York: Basic Books.

Polanyi, M. 1963. The potential theory of adsorption. *Science* 141: 1010–13.

Pribram, K. 1980. Mind, brain, and consciousness: The organization of competence and conduct. In *The psychology of consciousness*, ed. J. M. Davidson and R. J. Davidson, 43–64. New York: Plenum.

Pribram, K., M. Nuwer, and R. J. Baron. 1974. The holographic hypothesis of memory structure in brain function and perception. In *Contemporary developments in mathematical psychology*, ed. D. H. Krantz, R. D. Atkinson, and P. Suppes, vol. 2. San Francisco: Freeman.

Rabin, J. A. 1965. *Growing up in the kibbutz*, New York: Springer.

Rado, S. 1959. Obsessive behavior. In *American handbook of psychiatry*, ed. S. Arieti, vol. 1, 324–44. New York: Basic Books.

Rangell, L. 1963. The scope of intrapsychic conflict. *The Psychoanalytic Study of Child* 18: 75–102.

Rapaport, D. 1951. *Organization and pathology of thought*. New York: Columbia University Press.

———. 1959. The structure of psychoanalytic theory. In *Psychology: A study of a science*, ed. S. Koch, vol. 3, 55–183. New York: McGraw-Hill.

Rass, M. 1983. Styles in dreaming and their relation to cognitive skills (in Hebrew). Unpublished M.A. thesis, Tel-Aviv University.

Reichard, S. 1956. A re-examination of "Studies on hysteria." *Psychoanalytic Quarterly* 25: 155–77.

Reil, J. C. 1803. Rhapsodien über die Anwendung der psychischen Kurmethode auf Geisteszerütterungen. Quoted after Ellenberger, H. 1970, *The discovery of the unconscious*, 47–64. New York: Basic Books.

Reinach, A. J. 1909. *Cultes, mythes et religions* (Cults, myths and religions). Paris: E. Leroux.

Reynolds, R. I. 1978. The microgenetic development of the Ponzo and Zollner illusions. *Perception and Psychophysics* 23: 231–36.

Ribot, Th. [1900] 1906. *L'imagination créatrice* (Essay on the creative imagination). Chicago: Open Court.

Ricoeur, P. 1970. *Freud and philosophy: An essay on interpretation.* New Haven: Yale University Press.

———. 1974. *The conflict of interpretations: Essays in hermeneutics.* Evanston, Ill.: Northwestern University Press.

Rivaud, A. 1950. Notice sur la vie et les travaux de Lucien Lévy-Bruhl (Notes on the life and work of Lucien Lévy-Bruhl). *Académie des Sciences morales et politiques.*

Rogers, C. R. 1957. The concept of the fully functioning person. Unpublished manuscript, quoted after Hall, C. S., and Lindzey, G. 1957. *Theories of personality.* New York: Wiley.

———. 1962. Some learning from a study of psychotherapy with schizophrenics. *Pennsylvania Psychiatric Quarterly* 2: 3–15.

Ross, A. S. C., R. F. Clarke, and N. Haddock, 1964. Edition of text from a dysphasic patient. In *Disorders of Language,* ed. A. S. DeRueck and M. O'Connor, 298–317. London: Churchill.

Ross, L., and R. E. Nisbett. 1982. *Human Inference: Strategies and Shortcomings of Social Judgment.* Englewood Cliffs, N.J.: Prentice-Hall.

Rycroft, Ch., ed. 1966. *Psychoanalysis observed.* London: Constable.

Sade, D. S. 1968. Inhibition of son-mother mating among free-ranging rhesus. *Science and Psychoanalysis* 12: 8–13.

Salzman, L. 1980. *Treatment of the obsessive personality.* New York: Jason Aronson.

Sander, F. 1928. Experimentelle Ergebnisse der Gestalt-Psychologie (Experimental results of the psychology of Gestalt). In *10. Kongress Bericht der experimentellen Psychologie,* ed. E. Becher. Jena: Fischer.

Sandler, J. 1974. Psychological conflict and the structural model: Some clinical and theoretical implications. *International Journal of Psychoanalysis* 55: 53–66.

Sarbin, S. R. 1972. Schizophrenia is a myth, born of metaphor, meaningless. *Psychology Today,* June: 18–27.

Schilder, P. [1920] 1951. On the development of thoughts. In *Organization and pathology of thought,* ed. D. Rapaport, 497–518. New York: Columbia University Press.

Schilder, P., 1939. The concept of hysteria. *American Journal of Psychiatry* 95: 1389–1415.

Schildkraut, J. J., and S. Kety, 1967. Biogenic amines and emotions. *Science* 156: 21–30.

Schur, M. 1972. *Freud living and dying*. New York: International Universities Press.

Serafetinides, E. A., R. D. Walter, and D. G. Cherlow. 1975. Amnestic confusional phenomena, hippocampal stimulation, and laterality factors. In *The hippocampus,* ed. R. L. Isaacson and K. H. Pribram, vol. 2, 363–76. New York: Plenum.

Shapiro, D. 1965. *Neurotic styles*. New York: Basic Books.

Shepher, J. 1971. Voluntary imposition of incest and exogamic restrictions in second generation kibbutz adults. Unpublished doctoral dissertation, Rutgers University.

———. [1971] 1975. Mate selection among second generation kibbutz adolescents and adults: Incest avoidance and negative imprinting. Reprint, *Archives of Sexual Behavior* 1: 293–307.

Sherwood, M. 1969. *The logic of explanation in psychoanalysis*. New York: Academic Press.

Shevrin, H., and S. Dickman. 1980. The psychological unconscious: A necessary assumption for all psychological theory? *American Psychologist* 35: 421–34.

Shouksmith, G. 1965. A sequential guessing game for studying problem solving. *Psychological Reports* 17: 127–30.

Slater, E. 1965. Diagnosis of "hysteria." *British Medical Journal* 29: 1397–99.

Smith, J. M. 1978. The evolution of behavior. *Scientific American* 239: 3.

Snyder, F. 1970. The phenomenology of dreaming. In *The psychodynamic implications of the physiological studies on dreams,* ed. L. Madow and L. Snow, 124–67. Springfield, Ill.: C. Thomas.

Snyder, W. 1961. *The psychotherapy relationship*. New York: Macmillan.

Spelke, E. 1976. Infants' intermodal perception of events. *Cognitive Psychology* 8: 553–60.

Spencer, B., and J. Gillen. 1904. *The northern tribes of Central Australia*. London: Macmillan.

Spiro, M. E. 1958. *Children of the kibbutz*. Cambridge: Harvard University Press.

Stern, D. N. 1983. The early development of schemas of self, other, and "self with other." In *Reflections on self-psychology,* ed. J. D. Lichtenberg and S. Kaplan, 49–84. Hillsdale, N.J.: Erlbaum.

Stoller, R. 1971. Introduction to *The new ego,* ed. N. Leites, 3–37. New York: Science House.

———. 1974. *Splitting: A case of female sexuality.* London: Hogarth Press.

Stone, J., H. T. Smith, and L. Murphy, eds. 1973. *The competent infant.* New York: Basic Books.

Straus, E. 1956. Some remarks about awareness. *Tijdschrift voor Philosophie* 18.

Strupp, H. 1960. *Psychotherapists in action.* New York: Grune and Stratton.

Strupp, H., M. S. Wallach, and M. Wogan. 1967. The psychotherapy experience in retrospect: A questionnaire survey of former patients and their therapists. *Psychological Monographs,* vol. 78, no. 11. Washington, D.C.: American Psychological Association.

Sullivan, H. S. 1956. *Clinical studies in psychiatry.* New York: Norton.

Sydenham, T. 1676. *Observationes medicae.* London.

Thompson, C. J., and J. E. Nelly. 1970. Dissociated learning in rats produced by electroconvulsive shock. *Physiology and Behavior* 5: 783–86.

Ullman, M., S. Krippner, and S. Feldstein. 1966. Experimentally induced telepathic dreams. *International Journal of Neuropsychiatry* 2: 420–37.

Ungerer, J. A., L. R. Brody, and P. R. Zelazo. 1978. Long-term memory for speech in 2 or 4-week-old infants. *Infant Behavior and Development* 1: 177–86.

van Praag, H. M. 1976. About the impossible concept of schizophrenia. *Comprehensive Psychiatry* 17: 481–97.

Veith, J. 1965. *Hysteria: The history of a disease.* Chicago: University of Chicago Press.

Vogel, G., B. Barrowclough, and D. Giesler. 1972. Limited discriminability of REM and sleep onset reports and its psychiatric implications. *Archives of General Psychiatry* 26: 449–55.

von Hartmann, E. [1868] 1931. Die Philosphie des Unbewussten (The philosophy of the unconscious). Reprint, London: Kegan, French & Trubner.

Wallace, E. R. 1983. *Freud and anthropology: A history and re-appraisal.* Psychological Issues, 55. New York: International Universities Press.

Warrington, E. K., and T. Shallice. 1979. Semantic access dyslexia. *Brain* 102: 43–63.

Watson, J. S. 1972. Smiling, cooing and the "game." *Merril-Palmer Quarterly Journal of Behavior and Development* 17: 319–52.

Watson, J. S., and C. I. Ramey. 1972. Reactions to response contingent stimulation in early infancy. *Merril-Palmer Quarterly Journal of Behavior and Development* 18: 219–77.

Weiss, J. J., E. Stone, and N. Harrel. 1970. Coping behavior and brain norepinephrine level in rats. *Journal of Comparative and Physiological Psychology* 72: 154–60.

Westermarck, E. 1926. *A short history of human marriage*. New York: Macmillan.

Whitlock, F. F. 1967. The aetiology of hysteria. *Acta Psychiatrica Scandinavica* 43: 144–62.

Williams, M. 1973. Errors in picture recognition after E.C.T. *Neuropsychologia* 11: 429–36.

Wolf, A. P. 1968. Adopt a daughter-in-law, marry a sister: A Chinese solution to the problem of the incest taboo. *American Anthropology* 70: 873.

———. 1970. Childhood association and sexual attraction: A further test of Westermarck's hypothesis. *American Anthropology* 72: 503–15.

Wolff, P. H. 1967. Cognitive considerations for a psychoanalytic theory of language acquisition. In *Motives and thought,* ed. R. R. Holt, New York: International Universities Press.

Yanai, J., and G. E. McClearn. 1972. Assortative mating in mice and the incest taboo. *Nature* 237: 281–82.

Yankelovich, D., and W. Barrett. 1970. *Ego and instinct: The psychoanalytic view of human nature*. New York: Random House.

Yarmey, A. D. 1973. I recognize your face but I can't remember your name: Further evidence on the tip-of-the-tongue phenomenon. *Memory and Cognition* 1: 287–90.

Zetzel, E. 1968. The so-called good hysteric. *International Journal of Psychoanalysis* 49: 256–60.

Ziegler, D. K., and V. Paul. 1954. On the natural history of hysteria in women. *Diseases of the Nervous System* 15: 301–6.

AUTHOR INDEX

SUBJECT INDEX